RAJYA SABHA
मुख्य मंत्र्यांचे सचिवालय

PRANAB
MY FATHER

PRANAB
MY FATHER
A Daughter Remembers

Sharmistha Mukherjee

RUPA

Published by
Rupa Publications India Pvt. Ltd 2023
7/16, Ansari Road, Daryaganj
New Delhi 110002

Sales centres:

Bengaluru Chennai Hyderabad
Jaipur Kathmandu Kolkata
Mumbai Prayagraj

P-ISBN: 978-93-5702-682-6
E-ISBN: 978-93-5702-643-7

Second impression 2023

10 9 8 7 6 5 4 3 2

Printed in India

For Ma…

Contents

Preface

Three women shaped the life and destiny of Pranab Mukherjee—Rajlakshmi Devi the mother, Suvra (Geeta) the wife and Indira Gandhi the leader. A fourth one, the daughter, is now chronicling his story. This is not just Pranab's story, but also the story of these women and how they influenced his life. This is my story as well—the story of how being my father's daughter influenced my life.

After deciding to write a book on my father, I faced certain problems. The first, and the most obvious one, was the fact that I am not a writer. My sole experience of writing had been limited to penning a few articles on art when I was a classical dancer, followed by a few more on political issues once I joined politics. That doesn't exactly qualify as enough experience to venture into writing a book. Some friends suggested collaborating with a professional; in other words, to employ a ghost writer. But the idea did not appeal to me. I wanted to tell my father's story in my own words. Then came the problem of how to approach the book, how to structure it. Also, what do you write about someone of whom so much has already been written? My initial idea was to write a biography. But soon, I realized that I neither have the patience nor the academic training to undertake the extensive research required to write a meaningful biography. I also did not have the emotional distance from the subject to make it an unbiased one. The answer came from a dear friend, the celebrated writer Amitav Ghosh. He advised me to make it my story and bring in my experiences with my father. That made my job simpler.

My primary source for this book is his diaries. For many years, Pranab had the habit of meticulously writing diaries. Those revealed a new world to me. Other than his diaries, there are also my conversations with him on varied issues over the years. Additionally, I also had a few conversations about Baba with some senior political figures of our time. I did not try to speak with anyone specifically in the context of the book. All the conversations happened during my short stint in politics.

Pranab had a long innings of nearly five decades in politics. It was simply not possible to write about all the momentous events that happened during the course of these years. This book is focussed on few key events that I felt impacted his life. More than events, I was personally more intrigued by his relationships with some of the leading political figures, with whom he had the opportunity to work. I got insight into that from his diaries.

Needless to say, the views expressed in the book are subjective. It's written from Pranab's point of view, or rather from what I deciphered to be his views. He was only one of the many actors in any sequence of events. Others may have a different perspective of those events. Though I have tried to consciously refrain from expounding my own opinion, I may not have always been successful. But then, even my views were shaped by my father (mostly)!

For me, writing this book was an emotional journey. Initially, I found it extremely hard to read his diaries and invariably ended up crying. But after a while, it actually became a healing process. While reading his diaries, I began to realize that he had left an enormously important part of himself with me. His joys and sorrows; his struggles and triumphs; his thoughts and his emotions over the years that he had never shared with anyone else. He had left me an invaluable gift.

I would like to thank Pavan K. Varma, Dr Pampa Mukherjee and Rajesh Jala for going through the manuscript and making valuable suggestions. My gratitude to my aunt Swagata Das Mukherjee who, after my father's passing, is now the main custodian of the family history. My thanks to my publisher Kapish Mehra and editor Yamini Chowdhury, without whose encouragement it would not have been possible to write the book. And last, but not the least, my thanks to my four furry friends—Pataka, Alpha, Haiku and Zen—who were always there to lick away my tears whenever I felt sad.

chapter 1

A Remarkable Day

My father never travelled beyond his native state of West Bengal till the age of 34. The first time he stepped outside Bengal was in 1969 to come to the capital of the nation to take oath as a newly elected member of the Rajya Sabha. As he boarded the train at the Howrah railway station, little did he realize that it was the beginning of a journey into a turbulent yet rewarding future. When he entered the magnificent, circular building—India's Parliament House[1]—the security at the gate asked for his pass. He showed his newly acquired MP (Member of Parliament) card. As he hesitantly tried to find his way to the Central Hall, he did not know that this very place would shape his destiny in the coming years and change his life forever. He could not have foreseen that exactly 48 years down the line, when he would step into Parliament for the last time, no security guard would demand to see his identity card. Rather, he would be received by the vice president, Speaker of the Lok Sabha and other dignitaries as he delivered his farewell speech as the president of India.

---

[1]Now the Old Parliament House

25 July 2012 was a hot and sultry day, quite usual for that time of year. However, it was not a usual day for the Mukherjee family. One of its members, Pranab Mukherjee, was to take oath that morning as the 13th President of India.

Pranab had a strange association with the number '13'. Generally considered unlucky, 13 turned out to be a lucky number for him. He got married on 13 July 1957; came to Delhi for the first time in his life on 13 July 1969 to take oath as a first time Rajya Sabha member; and on 13 May 2004 he won his much-cherished first Lok Sabha election. He reached the height of his political career residing at 13 Talkatora Road where he stayed for more than a decade, his room in Parliament was number 13 and, as mentioned earlier, he went on to become the 13th President of India. He passed away on 31 August 2020—'31' the reverse of '13'.

Many journalists speculated that he didn't want to change from 13 Talkatora Road, a house meant for senior MPs, to a much bigger house that he was entitled to as a senior minister in the United Progressive Alliance (UPA) government in 2004 because he considered the number '13' to be lucky. But that was not really the case. It was simply because my mother Suvra (nicknamed Geeta) refused to shift houses. Since coming to Delhi, she had changed houses innumerable times while synchronizing with the twists and turns of my father's political journey. She was utterly sick of packing, moving and settling down. By the time she started feeling settled in a place, the time came to move once more to another bigger or smaller house depending on whether Baba was in government or stayed in Opposition. For a while, she even tried staying on at our private residence at Greater Kailash in South Delhi, rather than taking a fancy official bungalow in Lutyens' Delhi when Pranab became deputy chairperson of the Planning Commission in 1991. However, given his hectic and erratic schedule, and the heavy traffic during office hours, commuting became a major problem. Ma had to reluctantly give in and shift to yet another official residence. In 2004, when the UPA came to power, she put her foot down and refused to move. Despite being quite a fighter in his political life, Pranab avoided confrontations on the domestic front. Also, it didn't matter to him whether he was staying in a big or small house. He was a man of frugal habits and the house on Talkatora Road sufficed his needs.

On the day of the swearing-in ceremony, Pranab left his house at 9.00 a.m. He first went to Rajghat to pay homage to Mahatma Gandhi. He had surrendered his official white Ambassador car, the hallmark of bureaucrats and *netas* in Lutyens' Delhi in those days, when he had resigned from the government to contest the Presidential poll. Since then, he had been using Ma's car. Much to the disappointment of her driver, who was hoping to drive the President-elect to Parliament for the swearing-in ceremony, a Mercedes S600 was sent by the Ministry of External Affairs (MEA) to take him to Rajghat and from there to Rashtrapati Bhavan to meet the outgoing President Pratibha Devisingh Patil. Under normal circumstances, my mother would have accompanied him to both locations. But, at that point, she hadn't been keeping well for many years and could not take any extra physical strain. Owing to that, Pranab went alone while Ma reached the venue directly.

For the occasion, Pranab discarded his usual *bandhgala* (close-collared) suits or *dhoti-kurta* that he wore throughout his political life, in favour of a black *achkan* and white *churidar*. Perhaps, this symbolized a transition from being an active politician to a more formal and ceremonial role of the president. However, he continued his sartorial statement (the only one) of wearing a pocket watch.

I almost missed my father's swearing-in ceremony owing to a traffic jam while commuting from my residence in GK. The plan was for the family members to gather at the official residence and leave together for Parliament from there. But by the time I reached the official residence, everyone had already left. An officer working with my father was waiting for me. He quickly sat in my car to take me to Parliament, reprimanding me all the way for getting late for such a momentous occasion. The police at the barricades outside Parliament were already informed and provided with the car number to ensure that we were not turned away. A protocol officer was waiting to usher me to the Central Hall where other personal guests of the President-elect were sitting. The privileges that we were to enjoy for the next five years had already started.

Central Hall was full of political luminaries of the time. The then Prime Minister (PM) Dr Manmohan Singh, UPA Chairperson Sonia Gandhi, union ministers, several chief ministers (CMs) from Congress-ruled states and senior leaders from allied parties were present. Leaders from opposition parties, MPs, diplomats and other dignitaries packed the spacious hall. There was palpable excitement in the air and the drone of antique floor fans with long stands added to the general buzz of conversation. The entry of West Bengal CM Mamata Banerjee created a bit of a stir, as she had reluctantly expressed her party's support for Pranab's presidential candidature after a long political drama. Nevertheless, she attended the ceremony. From the Bharatiya Janata Party (BJP), L.K. Advani, Sushma Swaraj, Arun Jaitley and some other BJP MPs were present. No BJP CM was in attendance.

Parliament was familiar ground for Pranab. For more than 40 years, he had been an active participant in momentous events; helped in creating landmark legislations; witnessed the rise and fall of governments; participated in heated debates; and brought together members across ideological divides, to generate consensus for enacting laws that could shape the destiny of our nation. For more than four decades, he had seen and participated in the twists and turns of Indian politics, not from the periphery but as one of the most important members in the treasury bench and the Opposition.

PRESIDENT OF THE REPUBLIC

The President's swearing-in ceremony is marked by conventions and traditions following similar patterns. The president-elect and the outgoing president arrive in a ceremonial procession from the Rashtrapati Bhavan to the Parliament House, escorted by the President's Bodyguard (PBG) riding on majestic horses. They are then received by the Speaker of the Lok Sabha, vice president of India (who is also the chairperson of the Rajya Sabha) and other officials. The entire group is then escorted by the presidential ADCs (aide-de-camp) to Central Hall. After the national anthem, the chief justice of India (CJI) administers the oath of office to the new president.

After the oath taking, in a symbolic gesture the newly sworn in president and the outgoing president exchange seats. The new president is then given a 21-gun salute. Thereafter, the president gives his/her speech following which another round of the national anthem concludes the ceremony. After that, the current and outgoing presidents come to the forecourt of Rashtrapati Bhavan where an inter-services guard of honour is given to welcome the new president and also as a farewell gesture to the outgoing one. The new president then escorts the old president to his/her new official residence.

On 25 July 2012, at exactly 11.20 a.m., Pranab Mukherjee, the president-elect, walked through the aisle of Central Hall—accompanied by the outgoing President Pratibha Patil, Lok Sabha Speaker Meira Kumar and Vice President Hamid Ansari—keeping time with the measured steps of the ADCs. After the national anthem and a thunderous applause, the then CJI S.H. Kapadia administered Pranab's oath of office:

> I, Pranab Mukherjee, do swear in the name of God that I will faithfully execute the office of President of the Republic of India, and will to the best of my ability preserve, protect and defend the Constitution and the law, and that I will devote myself to the service and well-being of the people of [the] Republic of India.[2]

The whole event was naturally intensely emotional for the family. Immediately after the swearing-in, all family members who were seated together—except for my mother who was seated in the front—instinctively looked at each other as if it was pre-decided! When the national anthem

---

[2]ET Bureau, 'Pranab Mukherjee Sworn in as the 13th President of India', *The Economic Times*, 26 July 2012, https://tinyurl.com/4w5v8jwf. Accessed on 18 September 2023.

played the second time, concluding the ceremony, a particular thought struck my mind. Could Rabindranath Tagore have ever imagined that this song, written by him in the colonial India of 1911, would be played after 101 years on the occasion of another Bengali taking oath to the highest constitutional office in independent India?

Pranab was first sworn in as a deputy minister in February 1973 in Indira Gandhi's Cabinet. Since then, he was sworn in several times as a union minister holding various portfolios under subsequent Congress governments by seven different presidents of India. Now, he himself was taking oath as the president. What must have been the thoughts in his mind? Was he looking back on his journey from a humble thatched roof mud house in rural Bengal to the grandest residence in India? Strangely, I never asked him this question.

As one of the most consummate politicians of his time, he must have been fully aware of the challenges ahead of him, both political and personal. He was definitely aware of the political climate threatening the stability of the government that he had served as a key member for eight years. He was conscious of the fragility of the coalition and the erratic behaviour of some of the alliance partners—particularly the tantrums of Mamata Banerjee, as he had to bear the brunt of it many times while he was in government. As the second largest coalition partner of UPA-II, the All India Trinamool Congress (or Trinamool Congress) constantly threatened to pull out of the government, which they eventually did in September 2012. He knew about the rising tension between Sharad Pawar and the government. The tensions were so high that Pawar did not attend the farewell dinner hosted by the then PM

Dr Manmohan Singh for the outgoing President Pratibha Patil. He was aware of the growing anti-government and anti-Congress mood of the people, against the backdrop of Anna Hazare's anti-corruption movement (Anna Andolan) and various allegations of scams and corruption against the government. He must have been worried about the possibility of a fractured mandate in the upcoming general election to be held in two years time. In that eventuality, he would be responsible to ensure that a stable government is formed leading to the possibility of swearing-in as president a BJP government—a party ideologically at the other end of the spectrum of the liberal, pluralistic ideology that ran through his veins.

However, the most difficult prospect for him was to psychologically distance himself from being an active politician. He firmly believed that the office of the president of India was above any party politics. For the last 43 years, he played a major and often decisive role in the Congress and in governments led by the Congress. He was not a marginal player, but one of the most influential figures both within the party and in government. To develop a degree of detachment from the party and the government led by it, and not being able to be involved in its day-to-day activities and decision-making process would have been personally the most difficult challenge for him to overcome.

While being aware of these issues, he was equally conscious of the responsibilities and limitations; and primarily, the dignity of the office that he was going to occupy for the next five years. Knowing him, he would have repeated the oath of the president of India, 'to preserve, protect and defend the Constitution of India', a thousand times in his mind and internalized the spirit of the solemn words as best as he could.

For the time being though, his mind would not have raced back and forth, to the past and future. He had a tremendous ability to focus, and he would have concentrated completely on each moment of the ceremony that marked the transition of the most significant phase of his life. It was the end of an extraordinarily active, high-voltage political career of 43 years. It was also the beginning of a new journey, with all the solemnity and dignity attached to the office, as the 13th President of the Republic of India.

chapter 2

Crossing the Stream

The most endearing image I have of my father is an imaginary one. In his childhood, he had to walk nearly 5 km every day to reach his school in our ancestral village, Mirati (currently in Birbhum district of West Bengal). There was a tiny stream on the way that would turn into a gushing torrent during heavy rains. Whenever I close my eyes trying to visualize my father then, I see this little boy standing by the roaring stream and wondering how to cross it.

However, it was not the difficulties associated with crossing the stream that prevented Pranab from going to school in his early childhood. Very soon after getting enrolled in school, he discovered the sheer joys of bunking it. By his own admission, he was an extremely naughty child.

Like all Bengalis, Pranab too had a nickname—Poltu. Soon after getting out of his home, young Poltu would dump his books under a tree and take off to play with other village boys in the paddy fields surrounding the village; climb trees to pluck the ripe and raw mangoes and *jamuns* (black plum); or jump into the ponds for a refreshing swim. It was a perfect childhood, spent growing up with nature.

Unfortunately, neither his teachers nor his mother shared his views of this idyllic childhood. After a few days, his absence would be reported to my grandmother through someone coming to the village. Then Poltu would be given a nice and proper thrashing by his mother. However, these thrashings didn't make much difference to him. Rather, it cultivated a certain strain of thought in his young mind which, perhaps, was the beginning of a budding politician. He developed the ability to evaluate pros and cons of a given situation and decide accordingly. His reasoning was that if he went to school, he would get a sound beating from the teachers for his prolonged absence or for not doing his homework. If he didn't go, he would get a sound beating from his mother. Since getting beaten was inevitable in both situations, he decided that he might as well not go and enjoy his day playing.

He was totally averse to any kind of work. Whenever my grandmother would call out his name, 'Poltu', his automatic response would be '*parbo na* (I can't do it)'. The only work he was not averse to was hoisting the Congress flag. In the 1929 Lahore session, the Indian National Congress (INC) passed the historic resolution of *Purna Swaraj* (complete independence from British rule) and urged people to observe 26 January as Independence Day. Since then, my grandfather, who was an active member of the Congress, would hoist the flag in his house. In his absence, my grandmother would do it. Sometimes, she would let the children do it as well. When his turn came, young Poltu would do it with full enthusiasm without realizing that someday, hoisting the national flag would become a part of his official duty.

I do not want to give the impression that I am boasting about my father's exceptional nature, and his unwavering patriotism as if he was destined for greatness from a young age. In fact, there was nothing unusual about his actions or enthusiasm. Rather, the time itself was unusual. He was born and raised in an atmosphere when the Indian independence movement led by Mahatma Gandhi was at its peak. When the chant of 'Vande Mataram' reverberated throughout India, it inspired millions of people across caste, class, religion and gender to forsake the security of their homes and come out on the streets to fight the British. Even children couldn't remain immune to that spirit. Young Poltu was just one of the many children emulating their elders and being swept in the strong current of nationalism that manifested in the fight for independence from colonialism.

EARLY INFLUENCES

Poltu did not have to look too far for inspiration. His father, my grandfather, Kamada Kinkar Mukherjee was a freedom fighter. In his early days, while studying in Berhampore College in West Bengal, he got associated with a certain revolutionary group which believed in armed conflict and guerilla warfare to overthrow the British. The group included Barin Ghosh, the younger brother of the early revolutionary and later spiritual leader and philosopher Sri Aurobindo. For this association, Kamada Kinkar served his first sentence in a jail in Burma (now Myanmar) in 1914. This was followed by many more in subsequent years.

When the struggle for independence became a mass movement under the leadership of Mahatma Gandhi, like millions of Indians, Kamada Kinkar too became a staunch follower of Gandhi. He was an active member of the Congress, held various offices in the Bengal Pradesh

Congress Committee and also served as the district president of Birbhum.

When he was out of prison, he actively participated in party programmes to organize local-level mass mobilization and was rarely at home. He continuously toured the district and different parts of the state. He was truly a people's person—one of the many grassroots Congress workers who would travel continuously from one village to the other. He would spend a couple of nights in each village, talk to people about the Congress and British atrocities, listen to their problems and try his level best, personally and through the party organization, to address these issues.

Congress workers in those days were not just political activists fighting the British, but were also social workers in equal measure. Congress was the original 'NGO', taking up social causes with as much enthusiasm as fighting the British. Floods, famines and epidemics were common occurrences in British India. In the absence of adequate state support, Congress workers and volunteers organized relief camps and materials, helping distressed people in need.

Kamada Kinkar was associated with Rabindranath Tagore's initiatives of Visva-Bharati Palli-Samgaṭhana for rural development and was the secretary of the Asprishwa Sevak Samiti that fought against untouchability. He also took the initiative to open the first girl's school in the area. The salary for a single woman teacher was sponsored by Sudharani Devi, wife of local businessman J.N. Bannerjee from Labhpur—a town near Mirati and home of noted Bengali writer Tarasankar Bandyopadhyay, who incidentally was Kamada Kinkar's childhood friend. Though there was a teacher and a mud house that acted as a makeshift school, there were no students. Female education was still limited to upper castes, and upper and middle-class families in large cities. Among the marginalized rural population, sending young girls to school was unheard of. To solve the problem of lack of students, Kamada Kinkar organized a sports event for young girls with prizes for participation. A door-to-door campaign announcing the event was organized and the lure of the prizes attracted some participants. Though the event itself was lacklustre, it did manage to convince some parents to send their daughters to the makeshift school. Much later, the Kirnahar Girls School (now known as Kirnahar T.P.M Girls High School) was established with generous donations from Basantalal Murarka, the first Member of Legislative Assembly (MLA) of independent India from the area, and others.

Kamada Kinkar, a soft-spoken and extremely disciplined man, was a much-respected person in his area. People would come to him for resolution of disputes. After listening to every stakeholder, he would arrive at a solution which would be accepted by most. Pranab, later known in his political life as a consensus-generator, definitely inherited this trait from his father. The ability to listen and understand, not necessarily agree, the other side of the argument and to concede to logical demands of the Opposition was one of his main political strengths. In the early years of Pranab's political life, Hirendranath (Hiren) Mukherjee—a senior MP from the Communist Party of India (CPI) and Kamada Kinkar's friend—openly chided Pranab during a heated debate saying, 'Learn politics from your father.'

Two memories of my grandfather, or Dadu as I called him, stand out in my mind. He used to call me 'Munabhai' (not Munnabhai as in the film, but Munabhai as a derivative of my nickname Munni). My first memory is from 1977 when, after Emergency, the Congress lost badly and was wiped out from every state except from the South. One day, he called me and asked, 'Munabhai, your father is no longer a minister. How do you feel about it?' I was 11 years old and least interested in politics, or in my father being a minister or not! That is exactly what I said: 'How does it matter to me.' Dadu replied, 'Good. That's exactly what I wanted to hear. Now go and play.' The other occasion was not so pleasant, and it is the only time I remember being scolded by him. I was around 15–16 years old. One of my cousins and I were cajoling a close family friend to give us some money to go and watch a movie. This involved a long drama of coaxing, sweet-talking, tantrums and lot of haggling till we arrived at a mutually agreed-upon sum. Dadu was sitting there, smilingly listening to our bargaining skills. Finally, when the money was handed over, I started counting it. Immediately, from a kind, smiling figure, Dadu transformed and roared like a lion, 'How dare you count the money? An elder has given you this out of love and you dare to count it? Don't you trust him? Apologize to him right away.' Thus, the age-old tradition of showing respect to the elders was reinforced.

From his father, Pranab learnt that politics was not a lust for power but a desire to serve the people. From his mother, my grandmother Rajlakshmi Devi (whom I called Thakuma), he learnt to live simply and the ability to carry on responsibilities with frugal resources and a smiling face. Pranab deeply loved and respected his father but he was, by the unanimous verdict of the senior members of the family, his mother's son. He even inherited her height. Barely 4.5 ft tall, Rajlakshmi was an extraordinary woman with a power-packed personality.

She was Kamada Kinkar's second wife. His first wife, Sushila Sundari Devi, died after the delivery of their son Amiya in 1922. Kamada Kinkar married Rajlakshmi in 1925. They had six children—two sons and four daughters. My father was the third child, after one elder sister Annapurna and an elder brother Pijush. He had three younger sisters—Krishna, Swagata and Jharna.

By the time they got married, Kamada Kinkar was fully involved in the freedom movement. His frequent absence from home left the entire responsibility of running the household and bringing up their seven children on Rajlakshmi. Being a full-time activist with the Congress, Kamada Kinkar did not have any regular income. His was not a rich family but they had some ancestral lands—most of which were either sold, mortgaged or confiscated owing to his refusal to pay tax to the British government. Not just land, the police would often confiscate the freedom fighters' movable properties, including grain and cattle.

Pranab recounted an amusing anecdote in the first volume of his political memoir, *The Dramatic Decade.* Having been forewarned that a police party was coming to raid the house, cattle, grain and my grandfather's papers were moved out to different houses in the village. Not finding anything substantial to confiscate, a sub-inspector in the police party asked Pranab, 'You used to have cows at home, I've seen them. Where are they?' The precocious eight-year-old boy replied, 'Cows? We ate them.' A shell-shocked sub-inspector said, 'What are you saying? You are Hindus and you ate your cows?' Young Poltu patiently explained that as his father was in jail for a long time, they had to sell the cattle for money to feed themselves.[3]

He was actually not far from truth. In the absence of any regular income, and reduced grains and crops from the ever-shrinking farm land, Rajlakshmi had to sell valuables to make ends meet. The only valuable thing she had was her jewellery. She belonged to quite a well-to-do family and, according to family lore, was gifted a large amount of jewellery for her marriage. She sold every piece of it, not only to raise her children and run the household, but also to contribute to various causes and relief measures undertaken by her husband and the Congress.

Being a political activist, Kamada Kinkar would suddenly appear with a large number of people without any notice and they were all expected to be fed. Rajlakshmi would somehow beg and borrow from neighbours to feed the unexpected but not unwelcome guests, often going hungry herself.

Kamada Kinkar never took Rajlakshmi for a holiday or a movie, never bought her any presents, not even a saree. Much later in life, when she didn't have to worry about where the next meal would come from, I asked her if she didn't mind the struggle and her husband not taking care of the family! Her answer was simple: 'Your grandfather was fighting for the country. I couldn't do that. By supporting him and not troubling him with mundane issues, I was doing my bit for the freedom movement.' We have heard and read about prominent women freedom fighters like Sarojini Naidu, Aruna Asaf Ali, Captain Lakshmi Sahgal, Matangini Hazra and so many

---

[3]Mukherjee, Pranab, *The Dramatic Decade: The Indira Gandhi Years*, Rupa Publications, 2014.

other women who actively participated in the freedom movement. But there were also innumerable 'housewives' like my grandmother who always remained in the shadows. Their silent sacrifices and contribution to the struggle for independence cannot and should not be overlooked or underestimated.

Rajlakshmi had only studied till Class IV. But she highly valued education. She insisted that all her children, including her daughters, devote their time religiously to studies. She didn't mind using her fists when they failed to match her expectations. Poltu, being the naughtiest of her children, had to face her wrath most often. He also had to report to her in detail every night all his deeds and mischiefs throughout the day. Pranab often said that his phenomenal memory was due to this practice. Later in his life, when he didn't have to report his daily activities to his mother, he kept up the practice by recalling in his own mind all the activities of the day: the people he met and the conversations he had with them, the books he read, the important news of the day, the editorials in the newspapers…in short, he revisited all the events of the day in his mind before sleeping.

Rajlakshmi was a politically-conscious woman. She was also an avid reader. Pranab once told a family friend that he had inherited his habit of reading from her, and that I had inherited it from him. Newspapers were not so common in those days in rural areas. But despite frugal resources, our household received two daily newspapers through *dak*. She insisted that all the children read them. After finishing her household tasks and lunch, she would sit with the papers to read them from top to bottom. That was her 'me' time. No one dared disturb her then. She remained abreast with all the political developments of the time till she died. She never failed to voice her opinion or disagreements over government policies with her friends and family, including her politician son. She was an ardent fan of Indira Gandhi. Her only complaint against Indira, which she often voiced to Pranab's friends and colleagues in the Congress, was: '*Aamar chhele ta ke Indira Gandhi khatiye-khatiye roga kore dilo* (Toiling away for Indira Gandhi, my boy has become all but skin and bones).'

Other than his parents, another childhood influence on Pranab was his history teacher, Shambhucharan Bandopadhyay, who was also the principal of his school—Kirnahar Shib Chandra High School. Pranab had a strong sense of history. He not only had historical facts and figures on the tip of his fingers, but also had the ability to view any event from a historical perspective and relate the causality and inter-connectedness of important historical events. He gave Bandopadhyay and his teaching methods the credit for this. While teaching history of a particular period in India, Bandopadhyay would talk about what was simultaneously happening in other parts of the world. While teaching about ancient India, he would also talk about ancient Greece and its philosophers, and the rise and fall of the Roman Empire. While talking about Mughals, he would narrate the history of the Persian Empire and medieval Europe. Often going much beyond the scope of the prescribed syllabus, Bandopadhyay instilled in his young students' minds not only an interest in history but also in the interconnectedness of the world across continents. Pranab often said that he was lucky to have a teacher with such a unique teaching methodology—whose depth of knowledge in his chosen field was most remarkable—in an insignificant school tucked away in one remote corner of rural India.

SON OF THE SOIL

In his journey from 'a flickering lamp in a remote village in West Bengal to the glittering chandeliers of India's capital'[4], his family and the historical context of the time he grew up shaped his personality, thought-process and ideology. Throughout his life, he was deeply connected to his village. The only 'holiday' he ever took was to attend the four days of Durga Puja performed in our family's *Chandi Mandap* since 1885.

My own exposure to Mirati was also through our trips to the village during Durga Puja. Since childhood, it was an annual ritual for our extended family to get together at our ancestral village during this festive occasion. The journey to the village was quite exciting for the kids. The motorable roadhead was Kirnahar. From there, we had to walk for about 5 km on narrow foot trails of rust-coloured soil, meandering through the green paddy fields. Perhaps, it is the beauty of *khoai* (rose-hued tiny mounds made of soil rich in iron-oxide) that attracted Tagore to establish his Ashram (Santiniketan) and the Visva-Bharati University in the area. He sung paeans celebrating the beauty of the red-soil: '*Gram chhada oi rangamatir path, aamar mon bhulai re* (Ah, the red, red road; the runaway road of the village; lures my mind away).'[5] Sometimes when rains continued post monsoon, and both the roads and paddy fields were

---

[4]Ibid.

[5]Roy, Kshitish, *Rabindranath Tagore: Selected Poems and Songs*, Thema, 2012, pp. 151–52.

flooded, we kids would be seated on large round vessels called *kadai.* The adults then pushed these vessels with rods or by hand through waist-deep water.

One of my earliest memories of Mirati is that of a star-studded night. I must have been around 5–6 years old. One night, I stepped outside, accompanied by my mother, and went behind the house to answer nature's call as there was no toilet in the house or in the entire village. I looked up and the stars felt so near, like I could touch them just by extending my hand. In those days, there was no pollution and no ambient light, as there was no electricity.

That was our village—with no electricity, no toilets and no paved roads. It was a little hamlet in rural Bengal characterized by modest mud houses with thatched roofs, calm, deep ponds and green paddy fields on the outskirts that turned golden in autumn. In terms of its appearance and facilities, it was not very different compared to my father's childhood. The first road to the village was built in around 1973, after Pranab became union deputy minister of industrial development, and the electricity came in the late 1970s.

Growing up in a typical rural settlement, in a generation that witnessed India getting its freedom, gave Pranab a deep-rooted, foundational understanding of the problems and issues faced by millions of Indians in rural India. He was never a mass-based leader, but he was one among the masses. These first-hand experiences of growing up in a middle class family in a rural community without any privileges, other than access to education, shaped his world view and influenced his policy decisions later in life.

After finishing his secondary school, Pranab went to attend Suri Vidyasagar College, considered to be the best college in the district. By the account of his college-mates, he was a recluse—a studious boy who preferred to spend time with his books in his small room, rather than gossiping and joining *adda*s with his friends. He never showed any interest in student politics, unlike his elder brother Pijush—a senior in the same college—who was a dynamic student leader and a great orator.

In his article, Prof. Amal Kumar Mukhopadhyay—former principal of Presidency College (now Presidency University), Kolkata, and one of Pranab's classmates—recounts how everyone thought that Pranab would pursue a career in academics, while his elder brother would become a full-time political activist. But by some strange twist of fate, Pijush became an academic and teacher, while Pranab became a politician! Mukhopadhyay explained why, in his immaturity, he thought Pranab was unsuited for politics. Back then, perhaps even more so now, politics was perceived to represent 'an area where fulfilment of political interest by any means is more important than any rational or moral thinking, and to be a successful politician one needs to be capable of making acrobatics with words in order to make his promises credible to the people and to catch their votes'. He goes on to say, 'But, as I have grown up and studied political science, I have known the politics in parliamentary democracy is essentially a highly civilized and rational affair…' He then tellingly writes that while at college, 'Pranab was perhaps unknowingly preparing himself, trying to organize his thought process in order to develop himsclf as a "thinking animal" and was really preparing himself for his role in the future, by trying to develop a mental frame suitable for the kind of politics he would later on take to'.[6]

Looking back on his younger days, the kind of politics Pranab would do became quite evident because of the interest he showed in it. Kamada Kinkar was a member of the legislative council (MLC) of West Bengal from 1952 to 1964. He would bring home volumes of proceedings and legislative debates. As per my aunts, Pranab would go through those with ardent interest and the enthusiasm of reading a bestseller. Even before joining active politics, he was keenly interested in legislative proceedings and debates—one of the strongest pillars of a healthy parliamentary democracy. This was an interest he maintained till the last day of his life.

After finishing his intermediate, graduation and post-graduation, he went on to do another masters through correspondence and finally studied law. It was while studying law in Calcutta University that he had a brush with student politics. In 1962–63, he became the chairperson of Calcutta University Law College Student's Association.

His serious involvement with politics began a few years later. In 1966, the West Bengal Congress split due to an internal power struggle between Congress stalwart Atulya Ghosh and Ajoy Mukherjee. The latter was the appointed president of the West Bengal Pradesh Congress Committee (WBPCC), but due to the overwhelming influence of Ghosh within the party, he found it difficult to work. This ultimately led to the split.

Ajoy Mukherjee launched his own party, the Bangla Congress, on 1 May 1966. The sympathy of the common people, especially the youth, was with the underdog Ajoy.

---

[6]Ray, Sukhendu Sekhar, *Pranab Mukherjee: The All Season Man*, Deep Prakashan, 2010.

Pranab met Ajoy and told him that he would like to help him if there was some 'reading–writing related' work. That was the beginning. Very soon, Pranab was writing drafts for party resolutions, preparing the manifesto for the Assembly elections in 1967 and extensively campaigning across the state. Three years down the line, he was nominated by his party and was elected as a Rajya Sabha member in 1969 from Bangla Congress. From then onwards, there was no looking back. Pranab had crossed his Rubicon.

LOVE AT FIRST SIGHT

My parents had a love marriage. Not only that, theirs was the first inter-caste marriage in our family. Love marriages were fairly uncommon those days. Given my parents' traditional, middle class, rural upbringing, it was most unusual. Moreover, given my father's nature, it seemed almost impossible!

My mother was quite a romantic person. Somehow, I could not fathom how my father proposed, what conversations they had during their courtship days and how it all unfolded! I didn't dare ask him about these matters, but I asked Ma several times. She simply said that he proposed to her one day and she accepted, and subsequently they tied the knot. She would actually blush and pretend to be irritated if I probed any further. My parents' generation had a difficult time discussing their feelings, particularly when it came to matters of love and romance. The discussion of courtship days was almost sacrilegious for them, especially in the presence of children.

My curiosity was satiated 65 years after their marriage, when both of them were no more. While going through my father's diaries after his death, I read the entry made on 13 July 2014 on their fifty-seventh marriage anniversary. He reminisced in his diary about his partner of more than five decades and wrote, 'It was love at first sight.'

Pranab was just 22 and Geeta was 18. He finished his graduation and was doing his masters from Calcutta University. She was a first-year student in college. Her family came from East Bengal (now Bangladesh). My maternal grandmother, Meera Devi, was a woman with a strong character and exemplary dignity. She was married at a very young age to Amarendranath Ghosh, son of a land owner's family from Nadail (now in Bangladesh). A few years after their marriage, Amarendranath got married again. Meera Devi refused to accept her husband's behaviour and left his home with her two children—my mother and her younger brother. She came to her brother's home in Uttarpara in West Bengal.

Meera Devi had immense self-respect and pride. She did not want to be a burden on anyone. My Dadu knew her brother's family. He helped her get a job in a hospital in Bhandarhati, West Bengal. Meera Devi raised her two children through sheer grit, determination and hard work. She wanted to ensure that her children, especially my mother, were well-educated and had a college degree. When Geeta got admission in a college in Howrah, Dadu came to her rescue again. He suggested that Geeta could stay in his daughter's (Annapurna) rented residence at Howrah. It was a common practice in those days for students from rural areas, with no base in Kolkata, to stay at a relative's or friend's house to pursue their studies. Many even did so during the early days of their working life.

Pranab's family still resided in Mirati. As he was

a student in Calcutta University, he was staying with Annapurna and her husband in Howrah. It was here, at Annapurna's place, that the two met and fell in love. It was a quick courtship. They met in November 1956, and by July 1957 they were married. Pranab probably had to take a quick decision, knowing that his mother would strongly oppose the match and would try and put a stop to it if she came to know about it. She was a headstrong person and so was Pranab. So, he decided to commit the act first before breaking the news to his family. Once the deed is done, nothing can undo it.

Annapurna was the first to know, and broke the news to my grandmother. Thereafter, all hell broke loose! The objections were manifold. First, it was an inter-caste marriage. My father's family are Kulin Brahmins, the so-called royalty among Bengali Brahmins. Whereas, my mother's family are Kayasthas. Second, my mother was dark-skinned. Though short in height, Rajlakshmi was endowed with a golden-hued complexion and a beautiful face with a sharp nose, delicate mouth and a piercing gaze. Third, my father was still a student. He engaged in part-time tutoring to cover his expenses, but that wasn't enough to support a spouse.

As soon as Pranab reached his ancestral home, he was dragged by his mother to a room. One of my aunts, Swagata, told me the story in detail. She was just a young girl at that time, but she was as curious as a cat and she eavesdropped. Rajlakshmi first asked Pranab a common question that has been made famous in many Bollywood movies, 'What did you see in her?' His response was that she had a lovely face and was a talented singer! Unfortunately, before my aunt could hear more, she was pulled away by some older family members.

Rajlakshmi was definitely not impressed with the answer and didn't talk to Pranab for quite some time. However, Dadu and Rajlakshmi's brother stepped in and argued that within a Congress family, caste and dark skin should not be considered as determining factors. So, Geeta finally came to her *sasural* (in-laws home) and was grudgingly accepted by Rajlakshmi. But Geeta knew how to win hearts. She soon became Rajlakshmi's favourite. Many years later, Pranab told journalist Suman Chattopadhyay, 'You know Geeta... very soon she became my mothers' (sic) pet and then they both would gang up against me.'[7]

My parents' marriage opened the floodgates of inter-caste marriages in our family. Of my father's three younger sisters, two had love marriages with non-Brahmins. I went a step ahead and decided to get married to a 'non-Bengali'. In the Bengali world view, the entire human race is divided into two categories—Bengalis and those who are not Bengalis or, in short, non-Bengalis. Ma tried to break the news gently to my grandmother saying, 'Ma, Munni has decided to get married to a boy who is not a Bengali. Hope you don't mind?' Grandmother's reaction was astonishing, 'Geeta, what are you saying? People have reached the moon and you are talking about Bengali or non-Bengali?' My mom retorted, 'Your reaction was very different when we got married.' Grandmother simply said that the times were different then.

The times were different indeed! There were many changes in my parents and grandparents' lives from the time my parents got married. But what did not change

---

[7]Chattopadhyay, Suman, *Prathom Nagarik*, Karigar Publishers, 2017, p. 33.

through the years was the love, mutual respect and dependence between the two love-struck people who defied society and family to be together.

As the saying goes, opposites attract! My parents had very different personalities. Baba was the serious, sober type; whereas Ma was vivacious, full of energy and had an outgoing and sociable character. Despite his erratic schedule, Baba maintained discipline in his personal life, whereas Ma was totally the opposite. She developed diabetes but never bothered to keep it under control despite constant warnings from the family doctor, or futile attempts by us to control her dietary habits.

She was the centre of our extended family. Pranab's three younger sisters, fondly recall their childhood excursions organized and led by Ma, when the family shifted to Kolkata. Pranab's salary as a college lecturer was hardly sufficient to meet the daily household needs and the education of his younger sisters. But the lack of resources never deterred a spirited and determined Geeta. She would diligently set aside every penny, and once she believed she had accumulated enough funds, she would organize an excursion for the group of children. This group included her three younger sisters-in-law, the five children of her eldest sister-in-law (Annapurna) along with a few other neighbourhood children. These outings were to the zoo, National Museum or the Botanical Garden in Kolkata. There would be just enough funds to cover the cost of the entrance fees and bus tickets. The deal was that the children would not demand any fancy treats like ice cream or *jhalmudi*.

According to my aunts, despite the lack of extra money, they never felt deprived in any way. One of their fondest memories is of Ma cutting her wedding saree to make dresses for them, as there was no money to purchase new outfits for a family wedding.

Pranab shifted to Delhi in 1970, a year after he became an MP. Soon after, a new member joined the family. Geeta adopted a street dog who showed up one day at Pranab's MP flat in North Avenue, to take shelter under the stairs from the city's severe and biting cold. Lovingly named Tumpa, she quickly became a beloved member of our family. Ever since then, we have always had dogs in our home, often more than one. Geeta was a natural with animals. According to family lore, in Kolkata, two monkeys would visit her every day and she would feed them with her own hands. In Delhi, she would feed the birds and squirrels in the sprawling gardens of the ministerial bungalows. She would sit in the garden with the feed. Birds and squirrels would come to her and literally eat out of her hand, perching and climbing on to her shoulders. She displayed a matter-of-fact attitude, shooing them off when a bird or two would start gently pecking at her neck. I tried to emulate her many times. But the birds and the squirrels kept their distance from me, unlike with my mom.

Pranab was also an avid dog lover, but he was restrained in showing his affection overtly. He was the same with us, his children. Like many in his generation, he did not wear his emotions on his sleeve. He was never a cuddly dad. I was immensely touched when I read an entry in his diary from 7 August 1974. One of our dogs, Jimbo, had died that day. As I learnt from his diary, Pranab was not only terribly depressed throughout the day, but at night he had quietly cried his heart out hiding in the bathroom.

Another dog of ours, Daku, made it to the news. Daku, true to his name, was a law unto himself, and could not be trained or restrained. We never believed in keeping our dogs in chains. Daku would often evade security guards at the gates and roam around the neighbourhood in true gangster-style. In the early 1980s, we had an illustrious neighbour—Atal Bihari Vajpayee. One morning, Vajpayee was out for a walk with his dog. Daku got into a skirmish with his dog and, in the process, bit Vajpayee's hand. On hearing about the incident from the security guards, Geeta rushed to see him. A dog bite is usually a sure-shot way to ruin neighbourly relations, especially when the neighbour in question is a tall political leader from an opposition party. But true to his nature, Vajpayee had a hearty laugh and asked my mom not to worry. She returned from his house with vegetables from his garden. Pranab was not aware of the incident, as he was out of town. He reached Parliament straight from the airport and saw Vajpayee with a bandaged hand. Upon enquiry, Vajpayee told an acutely embarrassed Pranab in Hindi, '*Ye aapke kutte ki meherbani hai* (It's thanks to your dog)!' The next day, the incident was reported in the newspapers.

To my great amazement and amusement, three decades down the line, this incident was referred to in the film *83*, which released in 2021. The film opens with a sequence showing a gentleman reading a newspaper while another gentleman walks in. The first gentleman tells the second one in Hindi that Pranab's dog has bitten Vajpayee. The second gentleman exclaims in surprise, 'Pranab Mukherjee? Our Pranab da?', before going on to add that now Vajpayee would need to take 14 injections. This proves that crimes cannot be hidden, and Daku's misdeed is now recorded for posterity.

On her arrival in Delhi, my mother quickly made friends with some Bengali families, four of which became close family friends. They were all non-political families and had children more or less my age. They would meet frequently, mostly on weekends. In the early stages of his career, Pranab was not that busy. We would often have 'cultural evenings' at home. I had already started to learn dance, along with some of the other children in our group. Ma was a very good Rabindra Sangeet singer, and Baba could recite Bengali poems beautifully. We would often have these informal cultural programmes at home, each showing off his/her artistry. Sometimes, we children would put up plays, initially directed by my mother. However, later, when we were more confident of our creativity and talent, we wrote, directed and acted in those plays. We put up these shows either in our home or in the family friends' homes. We created space by removing the furniture. Had there been an audience other than the indulgent parents of the 'performers' and their friends, we would have surely gone to a special 'hell' for torturing an unsuspecting audience!

Other than these plays, these cultural programmes also included performances by professional musicians. The famous Baul singer, Purna Das Baul, performed at our house. This performance was also attended by Sanjay Gandhi. We would also have musical evenings of Rabindra Sangeet performed by the visiting artists from Kolkata. We were fortunate to have renowned classical singers like Pt Rajan and Pt Sajan Mishra performing at our residence. However, as Pranab started getting busier with his work, these programmes slowly fizzled out.

Later, my mother started a cultural organization called 'Gitanjali Troupe' that performed Tagore's music and dance dramas. People talk about my father's legacy, but

Ma's legacy had a greater impact on me. It was her interest in music and dance that I later took up as a profession. Performing in small roles with her Gitanjali Troupe gave me the much-needed confidence and experience that helped me immensely in my later years as a professional Kathak dancer and choreographer.

With my parents, there was a perfect division of labour and sphere of influence. Like in most traditional households, Ma was the one looking after the children, running the household, taking care of the extended family and social responsibilities. This allowed Pranab to totally concentrate on his work. Pranab never interfered at home which was totally my mother's domain; and Ma never interfered in his politics. She was a warm and generous person who was totally without false pretences. She did not care for protocols, social or political.

Due to her nature, she developed an independent relationship with many political leaders, including Indira Gandhi. Indira was immensely fond of Ma and would often ask her to sing Rabindra Sangeet for her whenever she had time. Pranab would often say that he marvelled at Indira's patience, as she would sit quietly listening to my mother giving her advice on politics. Ma had an excellent relationship with Jyoti Basu and his wife Kamal as well. Whenever Jyoti babu would visit Delhi, Ma would send home-made food for him at Banga Bhawan where he used to stay. She had an equally good relationship with Vajpayee. She became very close to Sheikh Hasina, PM of Bangladesh, during her political exile in India. The relationship continued even after Sheikh Hasina left India. When Ma passed away in 2015, Sheikh Hasina came for her funeral and could not control her tears.

Ma would often say that she and her husband never fought over the many years of their marital life. It is quite true. It takes two to create a conflict. On rare occasions, if Ma would rave and rant about something, Baba would just sit there with a blank look on his face staring at the wall, reading a book or browsing through his files without uttering a single word. This lack of reaction itself was enough to infuriate a person. But hats off to my mother, she would calm down after venting for a while. Perhaps, she was too used to his ways.

However, once it developed into a serious situation when Ma had to get a minor surgery done. She was rarely demanding. But this time, she insisted that her husband accompany her to the hospital, or else she wouldn't go. The time was fixed for the evening. We kept waiting. Pranab didn't come. We tried to reach him. There were no mobile phones those days. He was in some meeting where he couldn't be disturbed. We tried our best to persuade Ma to go to the hospital. But she refused. Finally, Pranab came back home at his usual time, around 9.30–10.00 p.m. Ma was seething with anger by then. Her logic was simple and rightly so! If she wanted her husband to accompany her to the hospital and he had promised that he would, then why did he not fulfil it? Upon arrival, Pranab was immediately confronted by his furious spouse. Despite being a consummate politician, he perhaps lost his nerve and gave the most politically incorrect and undiplomatic answer. Instead of claiming that he was stuck in a meeting of great significance, one on which the destiny of the entire nation depended or something like that, he exclaimed, 'Oh my god! I totally forgot!'

All hell broke loose! With immense difficulty, I managed

to persuade my mother not to pack her bags and leave the house immediately. After nearly 30 years of marriage, she kept lamenting that her parents had thrown her in the river with her hands and feet tied (a metaphor used for a bad marriage in Bengali), very conveniently overlooking the fact that it was she who chose her husband, not her parents!

As with all couples, my parents too must have had their share of problems but they never brought it up in front of their children. Ma's major issue with Baba was that he did not spend enough time with the family. But like all wives of politicians, she learnt to cope with it. She used her time to nurture her own interests. She was a very good singer. She was a natural painter and decided to hone her skill by learning it properly under a teacher. She wrote two books in Bengali—one on her relationship with Indira Gandhi, and the other a travelogue on her visit to China.

Looking back, I feel that in her heart of hearts, she was perhaps relieved that her husband didn't breathe down her neck all the time. This gave her enough space to pursue her interests. But Baba could never forgive himself for not being able to give her enough time. This came up frequently in his conversations with us after Ma passed away.

THEIR GREATEST LEGACY

While growing up, my life centred around my mother. Pranab was becoming increasingly busy and had less time for the family. But we always met for dinner. Our dinner table conversations were rather unusual. Baba would tell us stories from Indian and world history and relate it to contemporary events. A question on Glasnost and Perestroika would lead to a discussion on the significance of the Cold War, going all the way back to the Russian Revolution and Lenin. Me talking about a visit to Jhansi for a dance performance would lead to him giving us a summary of the 1857 War of Independence. From there, depending on the mood, the conversation moved forward to the end of the Mughal rule, the rise of the East India Company, Queen Victoria, British Raj and the history of colonialism in India; or it moved backwards to the history of princely states, Doctrine of Lapse, rules of the governor-generals, permanent settlement of Bengal and so on. Typically, in the spirit of adda, the conversations followed an unstructured path meandering through different topics at a leisurely pace, often continuing over days. Baba had the ability to make history come alive by narrating it as a story. We really enjoyed these dinner time conversations.

But dinner time was also a potentially explosive situation for me and a cousin of mine who was staying with us as she was studying in Delhi. Like all teenage girls and young adults, a greater part of our time was spent chatting with friends, including boys. It was the pre-mobile days and the landline was our lifeline. Between me and my cousin, we would keep it engaged for hours much to my mother's irritation. Dinner was the only time when Ma had her husband's full attention, and she would incessantly pester him with grievances about us. I am sure many women of my generation would relate to this situation. The complaints would often revolve around how 'these girls were becoming excessively indulged, neglecting their studies, constantly engaged in phone conversations and receiving an excessive number of male visitors'. Baba would ignore it most of the time. He rarely scolded us, except maybe once in six months. Thereafter, for the next two–three days, we would be the 'good' daughters, but soon we would be back to our regular routine, and then the phone calls and visits of friends would resume.

Looking back, I think that Ma didn't really mind our chats and friends. In fact, she loved our friends, including boys, and fed them royally whenever they visited. Other than being somewhat bothersome, she never truly enforced strict rules upon us except for prohibiting late-night parties. Maybe she felt that once in a while we should be 'reined-in' a little and that should be done by the man of the house. Perhaps she was right. Ma was taken for granted, but Baba was a bit feared. In the year of my Class XII board examination, I had started performing quite frequently with my Guruji's group. I hardly studied, and Ma's nagging had no effect. A few months before the exam, Baba called me and said that it was absolutely okay if I decided not to study further, but if I didn't do well in my exams, I shouldn't expect any help from him in getting admission in a good college. It was 1983–84 and he was the finance minister then. My ego was hurt. I decided to say goodbye to the performances for a while and started preparing for my examination in earnest. A few months later, when I got admission in St Stephen's College—one of the best colleges in Delhi University—solely on the basis of my marks, Pranab was a proud father.

My father became an MP when I was four years old, and a minister when I was eight. Since then, his rise in politics was meteoric. Except for a few years in between, he was always a prominent figure in the high corridors of power in national politics, even while being in Opposition. In a way, I grew up amid 'power'. But my parents ensured that it never got to my head.

There was a certain unwritten code of conduct to be maintained, within and outside the family—the primary one being never to throw my weight around due to my father's position. His official persona was totally out of my reach. Any request for an out-of-turn promotion for a friend's father or any undue favour was refused point blank. Even I could not expect anything from my father's official position. These 'lessons' did not come through any lecture or sermons. My parents knew that with me, any lecture would fall on deaf ears. But these became a part of my growing years. As a result, I learnt neither to expect nor to get used to any 'VIP' treatment. The training held me in good stead. After five years of being the 'President's daughter', life can seem a bit unmanageable because Rashtrapati Bhavan can spoil one to the hilt. But I tried my best to not let the privileges get to my head, always reminding myself that this is temporary.

Despite Pranab's high-profile career spanning decades, my parents led a simple lifestyle and always remained grounded in their middle-class origins. They valued hard work and talent above any influential 'connections'. Their friends were mostly non-political people, and so are mine. They led by example, and tried to pass this on to their children. I think that this is my parents' greatest legacy. I am grateful to my parents for giving me a very normal childhood in a setting of an urban, middle-class family. Pranab should be thankful to his wife for this. I think he was, because commenting on their marriage in his diary after 57 years, he noted, 'Looking back, I think this was the most correct decision of my life.'

chapter 3

Temple of Democracy

Pranab was a product of Parliament. For him, it was an institution whose paramount importance in public life and deciding the fate of the nation could never be emphasized enough. He always said that his incredible journey from an obscure village in rural Bengal to the highest constitutional office in the Republic of India was possible only due to the democratic system and ethos enshrined in the institution of Parliament. He first came to the notice of the then PM Indira Gandhi through his speech in Parliament. It was there, over the years, that he developed relations with leaders of other political parties. Through debates held in its hallowed chambers, he learnt the view points from the other side of the spectrum. He learnt to argue, counter-argue, concede if necessary or held on to his point of view and convinced others when needed. He learnt to listen and disagree amicably, and incorporated the valid points made by Opposition leaders in the larger interest of the nation and its people.

Parliament taught him to respect views contrary to his own. It gave him a vast and diverse resource base of brilliant minds. He would regularly take inputs from debates to further strengthen a government bill or international negotiation. He told me how once during a debate in Parliament regarding an international treaty, he incorporated some of the points raised by Dr Subramanian Swamy (a member of the Opposition) into the agreement.

He often liked to say that Parliament is not a debating society where you score points to shine individually. It is a political institution that, through its members, represents each and every corner of this vast nation and its massive population. Decisions taken here affect more than a billion people.

While in government, he would meet Opposition leaders both formally and informally before the presentation of major bills. He would then thrash the bill out with them. Even before the bill was tabled, its key points would be discussed and efforts would be made to iron out contentious issues. This is something he learnt from Indira Gandhi. It was not that he was always able to ensure the passage of government bills. However, the idea behind this exercise was to involve the Opposition leaders in the democratic process of enacting legislations.

He did this not just when he was in the Treasury Bench. Even as an Opposition leader, he would urge his party to extend their cooperation to the government whenever it was necessary in the greater interest of the nation. In 2002, the Patents (Amendment) Bill was tabled by the Vajpayee government. It was crucial to get the Bill passed, as India was in danger of expulsion from the World Trade Organization (WTO) due to non-compliance of obligations voluntarily made by India. Hence, it was required to get the necessary amendments done in the Patents Act of 1970. Incidentally, the same amendment bill was submitted by Pranab as minister for commerce in 1994 during the P.V. Narasimha Rao government. They could not get it passed then due to stiff resistance from the Opposition parties. However, this time it had a sense of urgency, as complaints were pouring in and India's standing in the international community was in danger of being seriously compromised. In 2002, while the National Democratic Alliance (NDA) government could get the Bill passed in the Lok Sabha due to its majority, in the Rajya Sabha it needed Congress support. Prime Minister Vajpayee spoke to Pranab and Dr Manmohan Singh, seeking their support. Pranab spoke to Sonia Gandhi and explained to her the gravity of the situation, and the consequences if Parliament failed to make the necessary amendments. She agreed and the Bill was passed. In the interest of the nation, it was necessary to rise above petty party politics.

Pranab often said that in a vast and diverse country like India, politics and governance is nothing but management of conflicts and trying to create a balance between varied and contradictory interests. According to him, Parliament was the best institution to learn that.

Once during UPA-II, I was watching a debate on Rajya Sabha Television in which Arun Jaitley, the then Leader of Opposition (LoP) in Rajya Sabha was speaking. He complained about how ministers from the ruling party did not take Opposition leaders into confidence for decision-making. Pranab was about to intervene. But before he could, Jaitley corrected himself by saying that Pranab was the only one who talked to the Opposition leaders. It is ironic that just a few years down the line, when Jaitley's own party came to power and formed the government, they completely overlooked the necessity of democratic involvement of the Opposition. They indulged in bulldozing important legislations through the force of brute majority without even affording adequate time for debates.

At a personal level, Pranab was very fond of Jaitley. He was extremely upset when he passed away in August 2019.

During the course of my short stint as a political activist, I came across many senior leaders across the political spectrum, including in the BJP, who told me that Pranab was like a mentor to them in Parliament. He would not only teach them about parliamentary rules and regulations, but would also tell them which points to raise; regale them with anecdotes; boost their confidence after a good speech; help them analyse their speeches; and give suggestions on ways to improve their speech, even if that person was sitting on the other side of the fence. In his diaries, over the years, Pranab meticulously evaluated his own performance while delivering a speech. After a good speech, he would note that leaders cutting across party lines would come and congratulate him.

This practice of senior leaders encouraging bright young MPs exists even now. Sushmita Dev, who was a first-term MP from the Congress in the Lok Sabha in 2014, told me that many a time, after noisy outbreaks in the House had subsided, senior leaders from across the divide would congratulate her on delivering a good speech. She narrated an interesting anecdote to me. She had to speak on Payment and Settlement Systems (Amendment) Bill presented by the then Finance Minister Arun Jaitley. As there was little time for preparation before the speech, and the Bill was too technical, she met Jaitley 'informally' in Parliament for some clarifications. Jaitley not only explained the Bill to her but even suggested a few points that she could raise in her speech!

LESSONS FROM THE SOUL OF DEMOCRACY

Pranab learnt by himself and was also assisted throughout the initial years of his parliamentary career by his seniors, from different sides of the political spectrum. By his own admission, two stalwart parliamentarians and judicial luminaries—M.C. Chagla and M.C. Setalvad—took a liking to this shy, unsophisticated first-timer and decided to take him under their wings. Bhupesh Gupta, a member of the Communist Party of India (CPI), who was a legend in parliamentary procedures, would create tricky problems for Pranab when he became the leader of the House in Rajya Sabha, but would also offer suggestions to solve the impasse. I discovered an interesting handwritten note without any date on the Rajya Sabha notepad in Pranab's papers after his death. The yellow tinge and the fragile condition of the paper indicated that it must be quite old. It read, 'Pranab, please say no more than I have already expressed my views this morning.' It was signed as 'Piloo'. I presume it must have been a note from Piloo Mody, a veteran parliamentarian and a member of Opposition. Yet, he came to the rescue of his young friend when Pranab was probably being grilled on the floor of the House as a minister.

A different kind of lesson was imparted by a four-term Lok Sabha member, Pashupati Mandal. Elected for the first time in 1952, this gentleman perhaps created a record for not speaking in Parliament even once in the entire 20-year period of his membership. We would have a hearty laugh whenever Baba would tell us his stories. Once, during Pt Nehru's time, the Speaker threatened to announce Mandal's name for his 'maiden speech' if he would not do it voluntarily. Mandal ran and hid inside a bathroom for five hours, coming out only after much cajoling and assurances that he would not be required to deliver the speech. Baba told us that he didn't have any problem addressing a crowd, but had this morbid fear of speaking on the floor of the House. Mandal was the 'house-expert' on all the privileges and allowances an MP is entitled to, and had thorough knowledge of the most efficient mechanisms to ensure reaping the full benefits. With infinite patience and care, he would explain to each and every new member of both Houses, irrespective of their political affiliation, the allowances they were entitled to and on what grounds; which MP quarters were vacant; how to get the allocation done quickly; and which officer in Central Public Works Department (CPWD) to approach to get renovations done fast. Irked by his kind but unsolicited advice, Pranab asked him once why he didn't participate in debates. Since then, Mandal avoided Pranab like the plague. Later in life, a more mature Pranab admitted to us that it was indeed 'heartless' of him to ask that question.

Ironically, Pranab's faith in Parliament and its efficacy was reinforced during the days of Emergency. Despite many senior political leaders being jailed and the imposition of press censorship, Pranab witnessed how effectively the floor of Parliament was used by the Opposition to attack the government. For Pranab, a healthy debate in Parliament represented one of the core values of democracy. This included not just speaking, but listening as well. For him, the Constituent Assembly Debates represented the soul of Indian democracy, with all its diversity of opinions and interests that are reconciled and accommodated in the Constitution of India. When I joined politics, he made me buy the full set of the debates (12 volumes), each weighing approximately half a kilogram. He had his own copies but refused to part with those. He said that in order to be a good parliamentarian, one must read and keep on reading these debates. I checked my impulse to retort saying that his advice would be better suited for his son who was already in Parliament, rather than for me whose chances of getting into Parliament were rather bleak given the circumstances. Nevertheless, my father insisted that I read those. Needless to say, I did not.

After his death, with a sense of wistfulness, I browsed through his volumes and was not really surprised to see how thoroughly he had gone through these tomes. The 'often leafed through' feel of the pages, the underlined paragraphs and his scribbles on the margins testified how meticulously he had studied these debates.

WINDS OF CHANGE

Over the years, Pranab noted and commented over various changing practices in his diary. On the first day of the Monsoon Session in 1994, the House was adjourned after an obituary reference to a sitting member who had passed away. Pranab noted that this was a new practice, as earlier the House was adjourned only when a member passed away in Delhi so that the other members could attend his/her funeral or so that they could lay a wreath. However, he noted that it was a good practice. The same year, in the beginning of the Winter Session, he commented on the technological upgradation in both the Houses. He noted, 'A new system of microphoning, simultaneous translation [from different languages] and voting are computerized, and each seat is provided with a panel. Members fumbled with the new system for some time.'

He often expressed concerns about, what he felt was, a growing lack of seriousness of many members regarding their attendance in Parliament. During the Narasimha Rao government, as a minister he was expected to regularly answer questions raised by members. On at least two occasions, when he was present in the House to answer, the questions could not be raised as the questioners were not present. He also lamented in his diary that how one day due to lack of quorum, the sitting of the House got delayed by an hour.

His biggest concern was the tendency of opposition parties to disrupt the House. He strongly believed that disruption of the House damaged the Opposition more than the government. It deprived the Opposition of the opportunity to speak and raise pertinent issues of the day. By disrupting the House, and by not discussing issues of national importance, he felt that members were not fulfilling their obligations and duties to the people of the country. On 30 March 1995, he wrote in his diary:

> Indian Parliament today created a history by passing vote on account of central budget, railway budget, Bihar budget and J & K budget running into 70/80 thousand crores of rupees.[8] The entire exercise—passage in Lok Sabha, President's recommendation, passage in Rajya Sabha, return by Rajya Sabha and President's assent—were all done in one day and that too through voice vote. [It is] no doubt unprecedented. [For] several days,

---

[8]Due to President's Rule in Bihar and J&K, the state budgets were passed by the Centre.

> a section of members paralyzed the House, Speaker allowed them to do so and suddenly everyone woke up and completed the formalities. How fast the system is losing credibility.

As president, he raised this issue multiple times through his speeches on different occasions. He observed that while it is primarily the responsibility of the government to ensure smooth functioning of Parliament, the Opposition should also cooperate and not disrupt. In his book, *Thoughts and Reflections*, he wrote, 'Disruption of proceedings cannot and should not be tolerated under any circumstance. Dissent should be expressed with decency and within the contours and parameters of parliamentary devices. Democracy should comprise the three "D"s—"Debate", "Dissent", and "Decision", not "Disruption".'[9] As president, he advised the government to take into consideration the concerns and interests of not just those who voted for them, but also of those who did not. The people who didn't vote for the ruling party are represented by the Opposition members. The Opposition has a legitimate space in a democracy. As per him, it is the duty of the government to carry along the Opposition. He wrote, 'The cardinal principle of the parliamentary system is that the majority will rule, and the minority will oppose, expose, and if possible, depose. However, the minority has to accept the decisions of majority while the majority has to respect the views of the minority.'[10]

Pranab wrote in *The Presidential Years* how he disagreed with Sonia Gandhi after the 1999 elections, when she

---

[9]Mukherjee, Pranab, *Thoughts and Reflections*, Rupa Publications, 2014.
[10]Ibid.

became the LoP in Lok Sabha, on how to function as an opposition party in both the houses:

> As a member of the Upper House, I, along with Dr. Manmohan Singh, opposed the tendency of the party's leadership to support disruptions in the Lower House. I made it amply clear that this practice of disruptions may have become the norm in the Lok Sabha, but it would not be implemented under my leadership in the Rajya Sabha. Dr. Singh agreed with me. I further reiterated to the party leadership that it would be better off finding a replacement for me in case it wished to carry forward such tactics. Owing to my stand, we were faced with the happy situation where it was business as usual in the Rajya Sabha, even as the lower House remained disturbed.[11]

In 2014, I once had a 'heated exchange of words' (to use Pranab's often-used phrase, mentioned several times in his diaries) with him on this issue. The BJP was at the Centre. He was lamenting about continuous disruption of Parliament by the Congress and other opposition parties. I got irritated and snapped at him, reminding him that the BJP did it too during UPA-I and -II governments. They were getting paid back in their own coin, I said. Pranab retorted sharply saying two wrongs do not make a right. He said that the BJP was utterly irresponsible. Even though it was not justified, still they could be somewhat effective because they had 100 plus members. 'By trying to do a poor imitation of the BJP with your 44 MPs, you are just cutting a sorry figure,' he added.

---

[11]Mukherjee, Pranab, *The Presidential Years: 2012–2017*, Rupa Publications, 2021.

He said that he had advised Sonia to not disrupt the House when she came to meet him before the commencement of the 16th Lok Sabha after the 2014 elections.

In his diary, Pranab wrote that he had suggested a speech that he thought Sonia should deliver during the motion of thanks to the President:

> I am grateful to the people of India that they gave my party (the opportunity) to govern this country for fifty-five years since independence... My party brought parliamentary democracy in this country and strengthened it during past fifty-five years and showed how to rule. Now, though much reduced in number, we will show you how an opposition party should oppose the government in the floor of the House. Your party disrupted all sessions of parliament both in 14th and 15th Lok Sabha. But I assure you, Mr Prime Minister, that my party will not oppose your government through disruptions but through debates and discussions.

But the advice was 'summarily dismissed' and Sonia said that nobody would listen. As late as 2018, while recollecting this meeting, Pranab wrote in his diary:

> I still do not understand even today how a person who made an amazing sacrifice by refusing to accept the prime-ministership, did precise little to stop disruption of Parliament. How could she not understand the implications and dangers of disruption? In the party's constitution in Article I, the objective of Congress party is to strengthen parliamentary democracy. The longest serving president of that organisation is indulging in disruption of parliament. It is truly tragic.

One of Pranab's greatest fears was that a dysfunctional Parliament would lose credibility and eventually erode people's faith in the system, further lowering the image of politicians (especially the image of the elected representatives) in people's minds. In the long run, it could be irreversibly detrimental to the cause of democracy. I wonder how Pranab would have responded to the current scenario if he was in Parliament today. Would he have been able to convince the party leadership to not take an obstructionist approach? More importantly, how would he have reacted to the allegations of the Opposition members' microphones being muted during a speech; some Opposition members being suspended for entire sessions; or the PM making statements on issues of national importance outside Parliament during session, rather than addressing the House? I am sure he would have been deeply worried. He feared that a dysfunctional Parliament would eventually impact every other institution in the country. In this context, he noted in his diary with a sense of dejection, 'We are in twilight of democracy but unfortunately unaware of the impending dangers.'

FIRST LOVE

Parliament was Pranab's first love. In 2002, Pranab was keen to contest for the office of the vice president. Narasimha Rao advised against it, telling Pranab that it was not yet time for him to retire from active politics. Pranab replied to him saying that if elected as vice president, he would still be associated with Parliament as chairperson of the Rajya Sabha. He told Rao that Parliament mattered more to him than being in government. After being in the Rajya

Sabha for so many years, it would be nice to be its presiding officer, he had added. But Sonia was not keen to nominate him as the vice-presidential candidate and Left parties objected to it as well.

Looking back, it's clear that Rao was right. It was indeed too early for Pranab to quit active politics. But he was not happy. On 17 July 2002, a disheartened Pranab vented in his diary: 'Communists vetoed my candidature… I'm feeling bad. She [Sonia Gandhi] will understand the real character of Communists when they will drop her like hot potato.'

Strangely, five years later, the same Communists proposed his name as the UPA presidential candidate to Sonia, though he had to wait another five years for that. He told me several times that if he was not a minister, he would have been quite happy to devote more time to his parliamentary work which he thoroughly enjoyed.

In 2004, then PM Dr Manmohan Singh, with concurrence of the Congress President nominated Pranab as the leader of the House in Lok Sabha. Pranab had the distinction of being the longest serving leader of the Lok Sabha (for eight years), who was not a PM. He was also the only parliamentarian in India who was not PM, yet had the unique privilege of being the leader of the House in both Rajya Sabha and Lok Sabha at different points in his life. In Rajya Sabha, he was the leader of the House from 1980 to 1984, and in Lok Sabha from May 2004 till June 2012. Lal Bahadur Shastri was the only other parliamentarian to have that distinction.[12] But then, he was a prime minister.

---

[12]'Leader of the House', Lok Sabha, https://tinyurl.com/dbhatnac. Accessed on 5 October 2023; *Role of the Leader of the House, Leader of the Opposition and Whips,* Parliament of India, Rajya Sabha, Rajya Sabha Secretariat, p. 11.

Of the many awards that Pranab received in his life, it was the 'Award for Outstanding Parliamentarian' for the year 1997 that remained one of his most cherished ones. He was the first member from the Rajya Sabha to receive the award. He noted in his diary that when this was announced in the House in 1999, members from both sides of the aisle shouted 'we are proud of him' in unison amid loud thumping of the tables. Another proud moment came in December 2003, when Rajya Sabha celebrated its 200th session. Pranab was 'honoured by the President for being the only sitting member completing 108 sessions of Rajya Sabha out of its 200 sessions'.[13]

In addition to these rare distinctions and awards, Parliament also gave Pranab some lifelong friends across party lines. He would always say that in politics, there are opponents, not enemies. Despite being bitter critics ideologically, it is possible to have genuine regard and affection for your staunchest critics. Though it's hard to believe in the context of today's vitiated atmosphere, I witnessed it myself growing up in a political family. That's why, when Pranab became depressed after Jaitley passed away, or when Advani broke down while talking to me over the phone after Pranab's demise, I believed that the emotions expressed were genuine and went beyond mere courtesy.

In his presidential years, Pranab missed being in Parliament much more than being in government. Famous Bengali writer Syed Mujtaba Ali, in one of his books, humorously described how retired captains of ships behaved on stormy nights. They would get restless

---

[13]As per Pranab's diary on 11 December 2003

and climb on to the roof of their houses shouting out instructions to invisible, non-existent sailors to navigate the ship right.[14] Pranab would behave almost like that during Parliament sessions in his presidential years. The television would always be on, and in between visitors, his eyes and ears would be glued to the screen. He would religiously listen to all the important debates. Once, I walked into his office while he was raptly listening to a debate. One of the Opposition members was speaking. Pranab was truly agitated. He turned towards me and barked, 'Stupid! Why isn't he raising these points?' He rattled off a few. I suppressed my smile and nodded gravely in sympathy.

Pranab walked into Parliament for the last time on 23 July 2017 on the occasion of his farewell function as president, hosted by the then Lok Sabha Speaker Sumitra Mahajan. As he recounted his long journey, a visibly emotional Pranab said: 'As I retire from the Office of the President of the Republic, my association with the Parliament also comes to an end. I will no longer be a part of the Parliament of India. It will be with a tinge of sadness and a rainbow of memories that I will be leaving this magnificent building today.'[15]

It was exactly 48 years after Pranab first entered Parliament. Strangely, the date on which he stepped into the Parliament building for the first time was 22 July 1969, the first day of the Rajya Sabha session after his election. Life had indeed come to a full circle for Pranab

---

[14] Syed Mujtaba Ali, *Rachanabali, Vol. 7*, Mitra & Ghosh publishers, 2015.
[15] 'With a Tinge of Sadness and a Rainbow of Memories, Pranab Leaves Parliament', *Deccan Herald*, 24 July 2017, https://tinyurl.com/ea3h5znd. Accessed on 25 September 2023.

Mukherjee. But before he could make his farewell speech in Parliament, Pranab had to traverse a long distance, face many challenges and cross multiple hurdles.

chapter 4

Can't Square the Circle

Pranab's thick Bengali-accented English was the butt of jokes in Lutyens' Delhi. The city's public-school-educated elites found the accent hilarious. Perhaps, they were also perplexed at the rapid rise of a short, quintessential Bengali 'bhadralok' in the power corridors of the capital. Even his mentor, Indira Gandhi, mentioned it to him a few times during the early days of their interaction. 'Pranab, why don't you keep a tutor? That will do you a world of good,' she would say. After hearing this a few times, Pranab got a bit irritated and said, 'Madam, you can't square the circle. I am who I am. You have to tolerate it.'

As the future unfolded, it was obvious that Indira not only tolerated but came to value the man whose political acumen, administrative skills, quick grasp of difficult issues, aptitude for solving tricky problems and strong sense of loyalty to her far outweighed any deficiency in his English. Perhaps, she even appreciated his stodgy determination to hold on to his roots despite his meteoric rise in the high-voltage power circuit of national politics.

Pranab came to Indira's notice during his second speech in Parliament regarding the nationalization of banks. He was one of the junior-most members of the Rajya Sabha. As per House rules, the total time allotted to a party for speaking is as per the strength of members of the party within the House. As there were only two members from the Bangla Congress in the Rajya Sabha, Pranab was given only three minutes to speak, and that too pretty late in the evening. However, he managed to speak for nearly 20 minutes without interruption, and the chairperson did not object. As luck would have it, Indira walked into the House just before his speech, followed by a large number of Congress MPs. So, Pranab not only had a full house but also the PM listening to his speech.

After the speech, Indira asked Om Mehta, the then chief whip of the Congress in the Rajya Sabha, about the 'boy'. After the House was adjourned, Bhupesh Gupta, Indira's close friend, introduced Pranab to her. In her speech in Parliament the following day, Indira mentioned Pranab's speech.

A few days later, Pranab received a call from the Prime Minister's Office (PMO) to meet the PM. At that time, another landmark bill, the Privy Purse Bill to abolish the constitutional provision guaranteeing privy purses and princely privileges, was about to be introduced in the Lok Sabha. In the meeting, Indira asked Pranab about the Bangla Congress' stand on the Bill. Pranab assured her that his party would support the Bill. Indira then asked him to find out about the Lok Sabha MP from Bangla Congress, Sardar Amjad Ali. She said that she had received information about Amjad Ali hobnobbing with the representatives of the erstwhile princely states, who were naturally against the Bill and were regular visitors to Amjad's house. Indira requested Pranab to speak to him to ascertain his position and ensure his support. Pranab assured her that he would do the needful.

Amjad Ali was Pranab's close friend. When Pranab asked him about these royal visits, Amjad's response was quite candid. He said, 'Brother, we belong to an ordinary middle-class family. Never in my life I thought that I would get a chance to fraternize with royalty whose ancestors I read about in history books. They come to my humble house in their big limousines to try to enlist my support. Let me feel important, though temporarily, but don't worry, I will support the Bill.' And he did!

Incidentally, when the Bill was presented for the first time in 1970, it was passed in the Lok Sabha but failed to get the required two-thirds majority (a requirement for any Constitutional Amendment) in the Rajya Sabha by just one vote. It was finally passed in both the houses in 1971 and Privy Purse was abolished through the 26th Constitutional Amendment. That same year, Bangla Congress merged with the Indian National Congress. In 1972, Pranab was made a member of the Congress Parliamentary Party (CPP).

Since then, Indira kept an eye on the 'boy' who was longing to participate in every debate, whenever given a chance. He would attend Parliament every day during the sessions, with the utter devotion and discipline of a studious school boy. By Pranab's own admission, he never missed Parliament for a single day except when he had to travel outside Delhi for some official errand. Indira once joked that perhaps Pranab was given the duty of cleaning the House literally, not metaphorically, as he was always the first to arrive and last to leave.

Indira was a true mentor to Pranab. She had the keen eye to see the potential in a simple, unsophisticated first-time MP. She not only taught him the intricacies of politics and diplomacy but guided him to become one of the most astute politicians of his generation, with a razor-sharp mind and instinct.

On numerous occasions, her guidance proved invaluable. In 1973, shortly after Pranab was inducted in the Cabinet for the first time as deputy minister for industrial development, the PM called him to her office for a discussion. In those days, Pranab usually wore a half-sleeved shirt (called bush shirt) and trousers, or dhoti-kurta. He walked into her office wearing his usual bush shirt. He received a strong dressing-down from Indira for not dressing up properly. 'Pranab, now you are a minister. You have to meet people from the industry, foreign ambassadors and others from various fields. You have to dress more formally,' she said. Not only that, she personally called up my mother and asked her to ensure that he was 'dressed properly'. Unlike her suggestion for keeping a tutor to improve his English, this advice was taken seriously. A few bandhgala suits were stitched immediately and the bush shirts were discarded permanently. Since then, the bandhgala suits for office, and dhoti-kurta for party functions became Pranab's official dress code.

The lessons in parliamentary etiquette came the hard way. Once during a heated debate, when Pranab was speaking on behalf of the government, Bhupesh Gupta tried to intervene. A five-term member of the Rajya Sabha, Gupta was known for the outstanding quality of his speeches, sharp repartee and quick humour. Once, after the speech of a member, Gupta quipped, 'Thank God delivering bad speeches is not a ground for divorce. Else, our esteemed friend would have been in serious trouble.' The entire House, including the targeted member, burst out laughing. Pranab had great regard for Gupta and the latter was also equally fond of Pranab.

However, on the day of that intense debate, in the heat of the moment, Pranab snapped at Gupta. He later admitted that he had spoken quite rudely. Indira Gandhi was present in the House. She sent a slip to Pranab that said 'Apologize right now'. Pranab stopped his speech and apologized to Gupta for speaking rudely. After the House got adjourned, Gupta asked Pranab with a beaming smile, 'Got a scolding from Didimoni?' In those days, in West Bengal, a female teacher in a school used to be addressed as 'didimoni'.

Two days after Pranab was inducted in the Union Cabinet in 1973, he wrote in his diary that on 7 February he went to see off the PM at the airport, with a large bouquet of flowers. Seeing him, the PM joked, 'Pranab, the size of the bouquet is almost your size.' This good-humoured dig at his short height continued later as well. After the presentation of his first budget as the finance minister in 1982, Indira famously quipped, 'India's shortest finance minister has delivered the longest budget speech.'[16] Once while travelling abroad with the prime ministerial delegation, Pranab couldn't resist the temptation of having an ice cream. He was caught red-handed at the hotel lobby by Indira. She then, very seriously, asked someone to call Piloo Mody who was accompanying the delegation. Piloo was well-known for his quick wit in Parliament and also for his ever-expanding girth. While he was approaching them, Indira said to Pranab, 'Do you see how Piloo's tummy is

[16]Barman, Abheek, 'Pranab Mukherjee: The Ultimate Insider', *The Economic Times,* 19 March 2012, https://tinyurl.com/yc2cehu3. Accessed on 5 October 2023.

coming ahead than the rest of his body? If you don't control yourself, you will also become like that. You can't grow vertically any more. Please ensure that you don't spread horizontally.'

Those days, between serious debates in Parliament, there would be light-hearted banter between members. Once, Piloo Mody remarked that there were only two permanent PMs in the House (Rajya Sabha)—Piloo Mody and Pranab Mukherjee. Indira, who was present in the House at the time quipped, 'Pranab is not PM, he is PKM, Pranab Kumar Mukherjee.' Perhaps there was something providential in that statement, as Pranab never did become the PM.

I once asked Baba how he became such a close confidante of Indira Gandhi. His reply was simple—by doing the small tasks assigned to him. It's not that he became part of Indira's inner circle from day one. It happened over time. On 1 September 1975, he wrote in his diary, 'PM called. Spoke to PM on phone for the first time.' He became a minister in February 1973. It took two-and-a-half years before the PM considered him important enough to call and discuss some matter over the phone. Among other things, Indira involved Pranab extensively to deal with the Northeast. Thus, almost from the very beginning of his political career, Pranab formed his connections with the leaders and Congress workers in that part of the country. Over the years, he built upon his knowledge and understanding of the complexities of politics based on the complicated socio-ethnic web of connections in the area. He often pushed their interests both within the Congress and in government. As they are relatively small states (other than Assam), tucked away in one corner of this vast country, even their CMs were neglected in the power corridors of Delhi both within Congress and in government. Many years later, when I joined politics, one veteran CM from a Northeastern state remarked that no one in the Congress understood the region better than Pranab da and no one in the All India Congress Committee (AICC) looked after their interests more.

POWER AND ACCOUNTABILITY

During that time, Pranab's daily routine involved reading parliamentary papers in the morning. Once he became a minister, he started bringing files home. He would clear those before going to bed. I remember doing something mischievous when he was still new to his ministerial role. I was fascinated by his 'files', those important-looking documents that were placed on the table in his home office and were off-limits to everyone else in the house. However, as any parent knows, if you tell a child not to do something, they will most likely do it. So, one day, when he wasn't in the room, I sat down on his chair and took one file from the top of the stack. I signed my name in big, bold letters—'SHARMISTHA MUKHERJEE'—on the first page. I was only eight years old at the time. Unfortunately, what followed was not pleasant. No one listened to my argument that if my father could sign so many files, what was the harm in me signing just one? As a result, I was prohibited from entering his office again. I never found out what happened to that file or if there was a government protocol for such situations. I never had the courage to ask my father about the fate of that file.

A year after his inclusion in the Union Cabinet, Pranab

was shifted to the Shipping and Transport Ministry under the veteran Congress leader Kamalapati Tripathi. In his diary, Pranab wondered whether it was a promotion or a demotion. He shared his confusion with Dev Kant Barooah, a senior Congress leader who went on to become the Congress president in 1975. Barooah assured him that it was a promotion, though technically the status remained the same, as he was still a deputy minister. He also reassured the young politician that the PM held a very good opinion of him, which was later confirmed by Tripathi as well.

Soon after taking charge of the new office, Tripathi revealed to Pranab the inside story of this new assignment. It seems that Tripathi was not very happy about his ministry as he found it too 'technical' and had complained to Indira about it. He had also made a faux pas regarding some numbers while replying to a question in Parliament. Indira had reassured him by saying that she would assign him a bright and efficient deputy who would help him perform his duties as a minister.

Tripathi was happy, and passed on more and more of his work to his deputy. Pranab was happy that he had more work to do. His earlier boss C. Subramaniam, the minister for industrial development, was not very generous about deputing work and didn't entrust his junior ministers with many responsibilities. Pranab grumbled in his diary that very few files were coming to him, and whatever work he was given was finished in two hours. Under Tripathi, he happily took on more responsibilities.

In his diaries from that period, Pranab also wrote about the rigid structure of the bureaucracy and complained about how they obstructed work by citing different rules and regulations. He mentioned that senior ministers may not encounter any challenges, but as a junior minister, he was experiencing difficulties. Interestingly, it was a bureaucrat who offered a solution to Pranab's problem. A senior Indian Civil Service (ICS) officer—perhaps from the last batch of ICS officers recruited by the British to administer this vast 'empire' on behalf of their colonial masters—advised Pranab to study the files carefully, especially the 'notings' by various department officers and other ministers. That made him aware of the movement of the file from the bottom to the top, and also revealed the arguments, interests and discrepancies (if any), at various stages. He suggested that the key to effectively dealing with bureaucrats and avoiding any conflict was to extensively study and improve one's own understanding of the subject matter. Additionally, he advised Pranab to thoroughly study the rules and regulations, which served as the bureaucracy's ammunition, and disarming them with superior knowledge.

Pranab followed his advice quite seriously. I have personally met many senior bureaucrats who worked with him, all of them unanimously applauding his comprehensive understanding and knowledge of a particular subject and his ability to grasp complicated briefs very quickly. Additionally, they were impressed by his thorough familiarity with government rules and regulations. One of them categorically said: 'No bureaucrat could take Pranab Mukherjee for a ride!'

Indira too was impressed by Pranab's meticulous preparation for any topic he tackled. During Cabinet meetings, despite his junior position, he would push the agendas of his ministry (if any) in his usual figure-crunching method. Typically, these proposals were approved without any objection.

From the same ICS officer, Pranab learnt something even more important than how to negotiate bureaucracy. Though he was much older in age, and a very senior member of the civil service, the officer insisted on addressing Pranab as 'sir' much to the latter's embarrassment. He was perhaps a bit overawed as well by the officer who represented the last vestige of an imperial system. For a common man born in colonial India, ICS officers represented the visible face of the power of the Empire. When asked why he insisted on calling such a junior minister 'sir', the officer bluntly replied that he was not addressing the person, but the 'chair' that the person occupied. The 'chair' represented the collective will of the people of India. He reminded young Pranab that it was owing to the mandate of the people that he occupied the chair, and that he should never forget his duties towards those people. The 'chair' represented responsibilities, not power.

Early on in his political journey, Pranab acquired a few valuable life lessons. He learnt that there is no shortcut to success and no alternative for hard work. Also, a ministerial office is not just 'power' but duty as well. Remembering these lessons paid him dividends throughout his life as a politician and an administrator.

A few months later, he was given additional charge of Steel and Industry. In October 1974, he was elevated to the position of minister of state (MoS) in the Ministry of Finance. In December 1975, he was given independent charge of the Ministry of Revenue and Banking that he continued till the crushing defeat of the Congress in the general elections of March 1977.

EMERGENCY AND THE AFTERMATH: NEMESIS OF GREEK TRAGEDY

Even as Pranab was honing his governance skills, major political developments were taking place in India that later had a profound impact on his political future, and also on the history of post-Independence India. Volumes have been written about Emergency. It is often referred to as the darkest era in Indian politics. Anyone with a cursory interest in politics would be aware of the details of Emergency. Large numbers of political arrests were made, civil rights were suspended, press censorship was imposed and national elections as well as elections in states were postponed indefinitely.

The background for the imposition of Emergency was perhaps as turbulent as Emergency itself. Saddled with the responsibility of 10 million refugees after Bangladesh's war for independence; sky-rocketing international crude oil price; adverse balance of payment situation; and successive droughts in previous years, the country was going through a serious economic crisis resulting in high inflation and economic hardship for people. Political unrest was brewing in the country. In 1974, the country was rocked by a nationwide railway strike consisting of 1.7 million railway workers led by the firebrand socialist leader George Fernandes. The strike brought the nation to the verge of collapse, as the power plants and steel factories were left with just two days of coal supply.[17]

In 1973–74, there were large-scale agitations in Gujarat and Bihar initiated by students, later joined by political

[17]'12 June 1975: The Day That Changed India, Shook Indira', *Open*, 13 June 2022, https://tinyurl.com/3fzb63by. Accessed on 16 October 2023.

leaders. Jayaprakash Narayan (JP), the veteran leader and perhaps the most-respected public personality of the time, put his weight behind the protesting students and became increasingly critical of Indira. He launched Sampoorna Kranti (Total Revolution Movement) in March 1974 in Bihar. These protests were not peaceful and often turned violent leading to arson, destruction of public properties, strikes and unrests disrupting public life. The rampant violence in Gujarat made news internationally. In an article by *The New York Times*, dated 3 March 1974, bomb blasts in government buildings in Ahmedabad and burning down of government offices housed in a former palace in Bhaunagar, a town apporximately 160 km from Ahmedabad, were reported.[18] The situation turned so bad that the army had to be called in, the Congress state government led by Chimanbhai Patel was dismissed with imposition of President's Rule.

In Bihar, on 18 March, protestors first picketed the Bihar Assembly in Patna, then torched government buildings, one public warehouse and two newspaper offices.[19] Ten months down the line and six months before the declaration of Emergency, L.N. Mishra, the union railway minister was assassinated by a bomb blast in Bihar in January 1975. JP did little to contain the violence. While inaugurating an All-India Youth Conference at Allahabad in June 1974, he reportedly said that 'though he himself

[18]'Mrs. Gandhi Ousts Party Chief in a State Racked by Violence', *The New York Times*, 3 March 1974, https://tinyurl.com/bp8vj9e2. Accessed on 16 October 2023.

[19]Karnad, Raghu, 'How Extreme Student Protests Launched Narendra Modi's Career', *The Wire*, 16 December 2019, https://tinyurl.com/mpmpczmf. Accessed on 16 October 2023.

would not take part in any armed insurrection or rebellion, he would not restrain revolutionaries from taking to the gun'.[20]

Against this backdrop, came the Allahabad High Court judgment on the petition of Raj Narain, challenging the validity of Indira's election victory in 1971. On 12 June 1975, the Allahabad High Court gave a verdict that declared the election void and barred Indira from contesting elections for six years. Indira was found 'guilty' of using government resources to construct rostrums and supply of power for loudspeakers at two election rallies and taking assistance of one government officer—Yashpal Kapur. The judgment sent shock waves throughout the country. A western newspaper commented that the judgment was 'too severe, akin to giving out a death sentence to someone for violating traffic rules'.[21] Pranab wrote in his diary on that night that he was 'shaken'.

The Opposition leaders led by JP intensified their agitation and asked for immediate resignation of the PM. JP questioned, '...whether there is a rule of law in the country and whether it applies to everyone, high or low...'[22] It was ironic that those agitating against Indira Gandhi in the name of protecting democracy and the 'rule-of-law' were trying to deprive an elected PM of the largest democracy in the world her basic right under the law of the land—to appeal against a judgment that had an impact not only on her personally; but on millions of Indians who by voting for

---

[20]Dhar, P.N., *Indira Gandhi, the 'Emergency' and Indian Democracy*, Oxford University Press, 2000, p. 251.

[21]Mukherjee, Pranab, *The Dramatic Decade: The Indira Gandhi Years*, Rupa Publications, 2014, p. 71.

[22]Ibid. 73.

the Congress under the leadership of Indira reiterated their faith in her to lead the nation.

On 25 June 1975, JP addressed a mammoth rally at Ramlila Maidan in Delhi and called for total civil disobedience. He asked the police and army not to obey 'illegal' or 'immoral' orders of the government. That night, President Fakhruddin Ali Ahmed declared a state of Emergency on the advice of the PM.

At that time, Pranab was in Kolkata for his Rajya Sabha election scheduled for 26 June, the day after Emergency was declared. He came to know about it on the day of the election and got a call from the PMO asking him to return to Delhi after his election. As he went to the Legislative Assembly for the election, it was abuzz with rumours like 'the Constitution was abrogated', 'Indira Gandhi usurped power with the help of the army' and 'democracy was over'. Pranab's response was that the state of Emergency was declared as per the provision in the Constitution. He also mentioned that if democracy was over, what was the point of holding this election?

While writing this book, Sudhindra Bhadoria, senior political leader and spokesperson of the Bahujan Samaj Party (BSP)—who was actively involved with the students' movement during the pre-Emergency period and was close to Chandra Shekhar—asked me about my father's opinion on Emergency and JP. The questions were answered by Pranab himself in his book. He wrote:

> [...] many of us who were part of the Union Cabinet at that time (I was a junior minister) did not then understand its deep and far-reaching impact. While there is no doubt that it brought with it some major

> positive changes—discipline in public life, a growing economy, controlled inflation, a reversed trade deficit for the first time, enhanced development expenditures, and a crackdown on tax evasion and smuggling [...] it was perhaps an avoidable event. Suspension of fundamental rights and political activity (including trade union activity), large-scale arrests of political leaders and activists, press censorship, and extending the life of legislatures by not conducting elections were some instances of the Emergency adversely affecting the interests of the people. The Congress and Indira Gandhi had to pay a heavy price for this misadventure.[23]

He has echoed similar sentiments in his diaries from that period. I sensed that he, as well as others in the government, considered the imposition of Emergency the right decision given the unruly situation at that time. However, that came at the huge cost of suppressing civil liberties and political opponents along with the excesses of Emergency, including the infamous *'Nasbandi'* (sterilization) programme.

In the same book, he has given a point-by-point rebuttal of JP's accusations against Indira, in his letters to Indira from jail.[24] While he had great regard for JP as an upholder of moral principles in politics and a public figure of impeccable integrity, he felt that JP was allowing persons and organizations to use his name to further their own agenda, rather than fighting to uphold democratic and moral values in politics. Pranab's diary entries from the time of the agitation show that he often wondered how a person

[23]Ibid. 77–78.

[24]Ibid.

like JP could not see through this political opportunism. One of the entries mention that by allowing divisive and fanatical organizations like Ananda Margis and Naxals to work under his umbrella, JP was legitimizing them. He further noted that JP was capable of doing irreversible damage to the Congress, perhaps even destroy it forever but also questioned whether JP had the ability to build a viable alternative.

As subsequent events unfolded, the answer was clear. The Janata Party that came into being with JP's blessings collapsed within a couple of years due to its inherent contradictions. The Bharatiya Jana Sangh (BJS), a Right-wing political party that became a major component of the Janata Party, metamorphosed later into the BJP. The Rashtriya Swayamsevak Sangh (RSS), which till then was a marginal organization, got moral legitimacy and authority after JP included it in his anti-Congress fight. In the Janata government, BJS members held key ministerial positions and their party organization was strengthening in different states. JP, who truly abhorred religious fanaticism of any kind, ended up giving the RSS political legitimacy in his zeal to fight Indira. As the future unfolded, most of the student leaders who emerged from the JP movement and became major players in Indian politics, could hardly be applauded for furthering 'moral values' in politics. This is perhaps the greatest tragedy of JP.

In his later years, well after his presidency and political career had ended, I asked my father why he hadn't opposed the imposition of Emergency. He turned thoughtful and responded that while one is within the system, it's difficult to have an objective view. He candidly admitted that he was not politically mature enough then to understand the far-reaching impact of Emergency for the Congress or the country. He categorically stated that the party had accepted Emergency totally, no matter what many of its leaders might have said during the Janata government regime. Pranab felt that had Indira personally met JP before 1975, perhaps things would have been very different. In an article published in the 35th anniversary issue of *India Today* in December 2011, he wrote, 'Everyone makes mistake, the best of those in power. This is the nemesis of Greek tragedy. If Mrs. Gandhi had even once approached JP before 1975, things would have been different. A useless ego takes people to strange situations… It was her nemesis.'[25] Strangely, Bhadoria, who was sitting on the other side of the fence, held the same opinion that if this 'clash of egos' between two strong individuals could have been averted, things perhaps would have been different.

Pranab felt that Emergency, in a way, perhaps, strengthened Indian democracy (albeit in a twisted manner) by making it go through an acid test. He said that it showed that the Indian electorate and the institution of parliamentary democracy had matured enough to do a course correction. I countered his observation, saying that the period of Emergency also served as a reminder of how a democracy can effortlessly transition into a dictatorship by exploiting a constitutional loophole. Worse still, it provided future generations of leaders with a blueprint for subverting democracy by systematically eroding the independence of institutions without formally declaring a state of emergency. It was one of the rare moments in my life when my father

---

[25]Mukherjee, Pranab, 'India Today 35 Anniv Issue: Pranab Mukherjee on Indira Gandhi', *India Today*, 26 December 2011, https://tinyurl.com/2kp7ycua. Accessed on 26 September 2023.

did not demolish my arguments immediately. He remained silent.

When Indira declared elections in March 1977, it came as a surprise to many, including the Opposition leaders. Of the countless theories circulating, there were some outlandish ones suggesting that both the US and USSR were pressuring India to lift Emergency. Many people, particularly her detractors, preferred to believe that intelligence reports had given Indira the impression of a resounding victory for the Congress in the upcoming elections. However, people close to her maintained that she had her ear very close to the ground and knew very well that in all probability, she would lose badly.

Baba told me that after the elections were announced, Indira enquired about his thoughts on the potential election results. Pranab, with the arrogance and confidence of youth, answered that the Congress would emerge victorious. Indira said, 'We are going to get wiped out.' A bit shaken, Pranab asked her why she had decided to hold elections in that case? Indira Gandhi kept quiet for a while, then answered, 'Else history will never forgive me.' Perhaps, she realized that further continuation of Emergency would do irreversible damage to democracy in India and it might become a point of no return. She made a mistake and it was time to rectify it, even at the cost of a devastating defeat. She had a sense of history. After all, she was the daughter of Pt Jawaharlal Nehru.

In the general elections of 1977, the Janata Party triumphed with a landslide victory, taking 295 of the 405 seats it contested. Congress won only 154 seats. It was wiped out completely from North India, and failed to win even a single seat in the states of Uttar Pradesh (UP), Bihar,

Haryana and Himachal Pradesh. In Rajasthan and Madhya Pradesh, it got one seat each. In Maharashtra, it secured victory in 20 constituencies. To everyone's surprise, in Gujarat—where the students' movement and Navnirman Andolan originated and spread to Bihar, paving the way for JP's involvement and ultimately resulting in the declaration of Emergency—the Congress party was able to secure 10 seats. In the South, the Congress won handsomely getting 92 seats out of the total 154 it won. Incidentally, the Dravida Munnetra Kazhagam (DMK) which allied with the Janata party, managed to win only two seats. It lost the 22 seats that it had won in the previous elections.

The North–South divide in the election results was surprising. Emergency was declared in the whole of India. The South also experienced press censorship, the suppression of civil liberties, the imprisonment of Opposition leaders and 'raid-raj'. Then why was there such a difference in the results? Perhaps, the answer lies in the fact that JP's influence was limited to the North, and the newly emergent leadership that fought so vehemently against Emergency developed mostly in the region. They did not have much influence in the South. It is telling that just three years down the line, in 1980, the Congress came back with a thumping majority where it was earlier wiped out.

The first non-Congress government at the Centre was formed in post-Independent India under the leadership of PM Morarji Desai. Soon after, the government instituted the Shah Commission to investigate the 'excesses' committed during Emergency. Additionally, a number of tribunals and investigations by the Central Bureau of Investigation (CBI) and other agencies were set up.

The media, dominated by journalists who were

put behind bars during Emergency, clamoured for punishment for Indira and Sanjay Gandhi. It did not spare anyone perceived to be close to Indira, including Pranab. Incidentally, the Ministry for Information and Broadcasting was held by L.K. Advani (then a senior member of BJS). The whole atmosphere was chaotic. Nasty rumours floated around, and nobody bothered to question their veracity. *Blitz*, a news magazine, ran a story that my mother supposedly visited Copenhagen at the expense of the State Bank of India (SBI) during Pranab's tenure as minister for revenue and banking. This was extremely strange, considering the fact that my mother visited Europe for the first time in 1978 along with my father. He was accompanying Indira during her visit to London, which was after the Congress defeat in 1977.

The same magazine reported that the then chairman of SBI, T.R. Varadachary, had personally carried ₹9 crore in 'tin boxes' to Malda (in West Bengal) for distribution in election. This was where Pranab was contesting from in 1977. The report also stated that the 'Marxist' quietly put signs on these boxes containing the money and witnessed Varadachary personally carrying them. The utter absurdity of the allegation comes to light when one pauses to think about the sheer number of 'tin-boxes' that would be required to carry ₹9 crore, all presumably in ₹100 currency notes as higher notes of ₹1,000 could not be used for normal transaction, hence were useless for distribution. How could any individual carry so many boxes? Why didn't anyone attempt to locate these 'signed tin-boxes' and press charges against the perpetrators? As Pranab wrote in his book, describing the mood of that time, 'Anger and venom had replaced cold logic and the need for proof. The general mood of the people was frenzied. They had not approved of the Emergency and thought that everything, and every individual, associated with it should be discarded ruthlessly. Sanity and rationality were replaced by strong emotional resentment.'[26]

Despite my parents' best efforts to shield me from the events of that time, and despite my young age (I was just 11 years old) and lack of interest in politics, I couldn't help but sense the tension in the air. In school, some of my classmates stopped talking to me suddenly. On one occasion, during a quarrel in a game, one of them shouted, 'Your father is a murderer!' Refusing to remain silent, I retorted with the same accusation towards her father. Nevertheless, I was quite shaken by this most astounding allegation, and after coming home I reported it to my mother. She just held me and said that we were going through a rough time. 'You just have to ignore what people say and not react,' she said. Looking back, I don't blame my classmate. Children overhear elders' discussions and are not really immune to the happenings of the day. Her reaction to me was, perhaps, triggered by what she had heard from her elders.

There were other indications that clearly showed that not all was well. The house that used to be full of visitors when my father was a minister (although a junior one) now wore a deserted look. As mentioned earlier, when we came to Delhi, our family got very close to four other Bengali families who would often meet on weekends. Out of them, there was one family with a Bengali journalist. While the behaviour of the other three families remained unchanged,

---

[26]Mukherjee, Pranab, *The Dramatic Decade: The Indira Gandhi Years,* Rupa Publications, 2014, p. 114.

this particular gentleman and his family suddenly stopped visiting us after the election defeat. As they were frequent visitors during Emergency days, he couldn't have developed some 'moral' qualms suddenly. My mother reached out to them a few times, inviting them for meals as usual, but stopped when she felt the lack of response. She obviously understood the reason behind it. The journalist's daughter, along with the children of the other family friends, had become a close friend of mine and we spent a lot of time together. As the father stopped visiting, we children naturally missed our friend and speculated about the possible reasons for their absence. I asked my mother about the same. She gave some vague reply. That night I overheard my parents' conversation. Ma informed my father that even the children had started noticing the journalist's absence. Baba replied (in Bengali), 'These people are *basanter kokil.* What can be done?' 'Basanter kokil' is a euphemism in Bengali, equivalent to the English phrase 'fair weather friends'. The Bengali phrase developed from the observation that kokil (the koel bird) could be seen only during spring (basant).

Anyway, as soon as our gang met up during our next gathering, I reported my parents' conversation and the reason of the journalist family's absence to my other friends. We were all justifiably indignant. We were not angry with our friend, as we understood her inability to come without her parents, but the anger was fully directed towards the father. We decided to nickname the father 'Kuhu', after the beautiful melodious song of the koel bird. It is beyond comprehension as to why we opted for such a beautiful name to depict a 'villain'. In our young minds, we thought that we were heaping a great insult on him. In all our further conversations, he was referred to as 'Kuhu'.

In 1980, following Indira's successful return to power and Pranab's appointment as a minister, I saw 'Kuhu' walking through the gate of our house one day. I ran and excitedly reported to my mother that Kuhu had arrived. Ma was surprised and asked who Kuhu was. I said, the 'journalist uncle'. Ma was even more surprised, 'Why are you calling him Kuhu?' I replied, 'Because he is basanter kokil.' Ma responded with a puzzled expression, but chose not to pursue the topic further. Kuhu was welcomed with courtesy, but was never invited to any family gatherings thereafter. I mention this incident just to indicate how growing up in a political family could be a bane for children—one can never be sure of one's friends. Nevertheless, we feel blessed for the few friends acquired over the years, the ones who stood the test of time and have been there through thick and thin irrespective of the political fortunes of the family.

In the world outside our narrow family circle, a bigger game of desertion and betrayal was taking place. One after another, senior ministers of the Congress government led by Indira distanced themselves and pinned all the blame for Emergency on Indira and Sanjay. Leaders who proclaimed 'Indira is India' just a few months ago, deserted and decried her. Siddhartha Shankar Ray—the then CM of West Bengal, one of Indira's main lieutenants and the one who had pointed out the constitutional provisions that allowed Emergency to be declared on the grounds of internal disturbance—deposed against her before the Shah Commission. Ray was a personal friend of Indira's and was close enough to address her by name. Being a barrister, he was in-charge of the case against Indira filed by Raj Narain at the Allahabad High Court. It was generally felt within the Congress that he didn't handle the case properly. Despite Sanjay Gandhi's reservations against him, he continued to enjoy Indira's confidence. It must have come as a shock to Indira when Ray shrugged off his responsibility, and pinned the blame of happenings during Emergency entirely on her. As the story goes, he ran into Indira at the lobby of the Shah Commission office and tossed her a compliment, 'You look pretty today.' Indira Gandhi retorted, 'Despite your efforts.'

Pranab wrote about those turbulent times in *The Dramatic Decade*: 'Interestingly, though not surprisingly, once it [Emergency] was declared, there were a whole host of people claiming authorship of the idea of declaring the Emergency. And again, not surprisingly, these very people took a sharp about-turn when the Shah Commission was set up to look into "excesses".'[27]

From the very beginning, Pranab was clear that he would neither leave the Congress, nor Indira. On 24 April 1977, just about a month after his and his party's devastating defeat, he wrote in his diary:

> The anti-Indira camp is increasingly becoming stronger [within the party] and is in majority. We need to wait and watch... My belief is that there is no alternative to Congress, Janata [party] cannot become an alternative. No question of my leaving Congress or deserting Indira ji. She picked me from outside [Bangla Congress] and reposed faith in me. Not only politically, she has helped me personally whenever I sought her help. If I leave

[27]Ibid. 47.

> her in bad days, not only I would (sic) be considered guilty by the public, but I'll never be able to face myself.

Pranab did not deviate from his stand. Throughout his long political career (and even later) he remained openly, unabashedly and unashamedly an Indira Gandhi loyalist. It was not that he was unaware of her flaws and weaknesses. He wrote in his diary, 'It was not that all her actions were right, but I thought [that] as a soldier I have to accept both good and bad, and I cannot pick and choose.'

However, towards the fag end of his life, just a month before his death, while introspecting about his long political journey, along with the journey of the nation and that of the party he served, he questioned the wisdom of his own blind loyalty to Indira.

After the defeat of Congress in 1977, I recollect a small incident that happened in Kolkata. After relocating from our village to Kolkata, my parents, grandparents and aunts rented a place in Howrah. When Baba became an MP, we moved to Delhi with him but the rest of the family continued to live in the same house. Our landlords lived on the top floor of that building. During one visit, while I was playing, I overheard a conversation among the adults. They were clearly dismayed by a particular Congress leader, who had appeared before the Shah Commission and placed all the blame for Emergency and its excesses on Indira. They viewed it as a betrayal and a display of political opportunism. One of them remarked, 'God knows what Pranab da will do, perhaps he will follow suit like the others.' The lady of the house (whom I lovingly called Annoma) firmly said that Pranab would never stoop to such actions. He would never betray Indira.

I narrate this incident to suggest that perhaps for some people, who were not politically inclined, Indira getting betrayed by her own leaders had sowed the seeds of sympathy. This sympathy further grew due to the harassment she endured under the Janata government.

As it happened, Annoma's faith in Pranab was justified. He was called by the Shah Commission for the first time on 1 October 1977. He appeared but did not depose on the grounds that as a central minister he was bound by the oath of secrecy. To divulge any information that he had received while serving as minister would be violating that oath. Justice Shah responded by stating that since he was no longer a minister, he was not obligated by his oath. Pranab then asked him to give his observation in writing. The idea was that if it was given in writing, he could challenge it in court on the grounds of being forced to violate his oath. Justice Shah declined to give it in writing.

Pranab was summoned again on 19 November 1977. This time he inquired as to why they were being denied their right to obtain legal assistance. Justice Shah responded that at this point in the inquiry, he was just trying to find out Pranab's involvement in certain cases, and as of now he was not prima facie guilty. In case he was found guilty, he could avail legal protection. As of now, Justice Shah just expected him to 'cooperate'. Pranab then asked Justice Shah whether this 'cooperation' was compulsory or optional, to which Justice Shah replied, 'You are free to cooperate or not. You are free to come and go.'[28] Pranab chose not to cooperate. For this refusal to cooperate, he was prosecuted under Sections 178–179 of the Indian

[28]Ibid. 156–57.

Penal Code (IPC). Similarly, Indira was prosecuted under the same sections of the IPC. When summoned, rather than submitting to questions, she read out a full statement challenging the functioning of the Commission and blamed the Janata government for political persecution.

On 3 October 1977, Indira Gandhi was arrested. Four central ministers and five others were arrested too. Pranab was at home when he received news from a journalist of the possibility of his imminent arrest. I remember being at one of our family friend's place. The daughter was a friend of mine. Both our mothers had gone to watch a movie together. Pranab sent someone to contact them. As Ma rushed back home, Pranab packed a small suitcase and awaited the arrival of the police. I was asked to stay put at my friend's place and spend the night there. This was an unusual occurrence. Pranab continued to wait at home for the police. When they did not arrive, he left a note for them stating that he was going to 12 Willingdon Crescent—Indira's residence post her defeat—and could be contacted there. He and my mother went there. A large number of Congress workers had gathered there shouting anti-government slogans. There were a large number of police personnel as well. Sanjay arrived later and was surprised to find Pranab there, as he had been informed of Pranab's arrest.

Before her arrest, Indira made a statement about the arrest being politically motivated. Thereafter, she was taken to an undisclosed location. As she had a meeting with her lawyer Frank Anthony at her residence, he followed her along with Rajiv, Sanjay, Sonia, Maneka and some journalists and supporters. They were taken towards Faridabad. The original idea was to take her to Badkhal Lake in Haryana. As the convoy stopped at a crossing, Indira quickly stepped out of the car and sat down on a culvert. While her lawyers argued with the police that it was illegal to take her out of the territorial jurisdiction of Delhi, she gave interviews to journalists. Eventually, the police brought her to Police Lines in Delhi. The charges against her were that she had connived to 'illegally' get some Jeeps for election purposes, and that her government had given oil drilling contracts to a French company for unethical considerations.

Indira was acquitted after she reported in court the next day. Pranab wrote in his book many years later that a joke was going around those days, 'Look at the competence of this government. A woman who had put a few hundred leaders in jail for nineteen months could not be put behind bars by them even for nineteen hours.'[29]

Jokes aside, the arrest was a disaster that had major repercussions for the government and only led to further blame game. While the then Home Minister Chaudhary Charan Singh complained of 'sabotage' against him, many of his colleagues blamed him for this fiasco. It is surprising that though the party and the government was new, many of its senior ministers (including Morarji Desai and Jagjivan Ram) had solid experience of governance as ministers in previous Congress governments. But despite that, the 'fool proof' case against Indira Gandhi turned out to be a damp squib. As Pranab wrote, 'It not only reflected the vindictiveness of the Janata Party government but also proved its utter inefficiency and casual attitude towards administration.'[30]

Pranab maintained that the arrest was made due

---

[29]Ibid. 138.

[30]Ibid. 138.

to the increasing nervousness of the Janata government. Indira Gandhi, after a short-lived inertia, was back with renewed vigour. She travelled across the country and her appeal as a crowd-puller had not diminished despite all the mud-slinging by the press and the government. The government was already facing a crisis due to an internal power struggle. The personal ambition of its leaders and the ideological conflicts between various component groups of the party—Right-wing Jana Sangh on one hand and Left-leaning socialist groups on the other—exposed the internal and inherent contradictions of the party and the government. Their inability to govern properly led to soaring inflation and price rise, thus hurting the common man. There were numerous labour strikes by various trade unions across the country. After being released from jail post-Emergency, the trade union leaders hoped that all their demands would be met by the new government. This did not happen. The government also faced growing criticism due to its inability to take critical decisions.

Amid this came the turning point in the post-Emergency innings of Indira's political journey, the 'Belchi moment'. Strangely and symbolically, her political revival started in Bihar, the state that led the agitation against her under JP. On 27 May 1977, Belchi, a remote village in Bihar, witnessed a horrific incident of caste atrocity in which 11 Dalit men were shot point-blank and thrown into a burning pyre by some people belonging to the rich Kurmi clan. The government's handling of the issue was far from satisfactory. The Congress, dominated by anti-Indira elements by then, did not show much enthusiasm in taking up the issue. Finally, Indira decided to go to Belchi herself. She set off for this remote part of

Bihar, travelling first by train, then by Jeep, then through the incessant rain on a tractor and finally, on elephant back.

Pratibha Singh, the Congress leader and MP who accompanied Indira Gandhi on elephant back, happened to be our family friend. She described the harrowing journey to my mother and narrated the story to us several times, as it seemed to be one of her favourites. She could speak Bengali fluently. Every time her account would begin with: *'Ore baba'* (something similar to 'Oh my God'). By her own admission, she was terrified and clung to Indira for dear life. Despite being swayed wildly in every direction by the movement of the elephant and while trying to keep her balance, Indira kept reassuring her. It was that indominable spirit of Indira's at the age of 60, which inspired Pranab and thousands of other Congress workers who never left her despite many senior Congress leaders deserting her. It was that spirit which faced the challenges from the Janata government and within her own party, and led the Congress to a glorious victory within a short span of three years after the major setback.

Meanwhile, the Janata government at the Centre dissolved the Congress-led state assemblies (where the Congress had lost in the Lok Sabha elections) on the grounds that by losing massively in the general elections, these state governments had lost the mandate of the people. That called for fresh elections in these states. Indira was not asked to campaign in these elections. The then Congress President K. Brahmananda Reddy—who was elected through Indira's support after the resignation of D.K. Barooah post the 1977 election debacle—declared publicly that Indira Gandhi was not consulted while preparing the election manifesto. She was not consulted for the upcoming presidential election either. The Congress President extended support to Janata party's presidential candidate, Neelam Sanjiva Reddy, without consulting Indira.

Pranab often wondered in his diary about what these 'paragon of propriety' were doing during the 21 months of Emergency? They were senior ministers in Indira's Cabinet before and during Emergency. He concluded that these 'big leaders' were nothing but 'paper tigers'. And so, it was no surprise that things deteriorated so quickly under their watch. They lacked the courage to speak out against Indira while she held power, but were quick to criticize her as soon as she left office.

Both within the party and in Parliament, Indira and the people who stood by her were being pushed to a corner. All kinds of allegations were raised in Parliament, mostly by private members, against Indira and her supporters which included Pranab. These wild allegations were allowed to go into the records undenied, as the ministers in the government who were in possession of government files and papers did not attempt to deny or correct these allegations. Congress members were mostly mute spectators. Pranab occasionally tried to intervene, but was mostly unsuccessful. Congress MPs would avoid him in Parliament, except Indira loyalists like A.R. Antulay, Saroj Khaparde and Pratibha Singh. Two CPI MPs, Bhupesh Gupta and Kalyan Roy, remained his close personal friends.

RISING FROM THE ASHES

It was during this period of struggle and hardship that Pranab became Indira's close confidante. As old bonds were falling away, new bonds were created. Within the party, Indira continued to be marginalized and humiliated.

Though an idea of 'collective leadership' was mooted, in effect Indira was excluded from the 'collective leadership'. The Congress Working Committee (CWC) meetings became a platform for anti-Indira leaders to express their venom. They were lukewarm in their protests against Janata government's persecution through several inquiry commissions, with some even tacitly supporting it.

Several decades later, when the Congress suffered its worst electoral debacle in 2014 with just 44 seats in the Lok Sabha, Baba told me that the situation in 1977 was far worse. I did not fully understand why he said that. In 1977, Congress got 154 seats as opposed to just 44 in 2014. So, how could the situation be worse? Did he mean the inquiry commissions, and the vindictive attitude of the Janata government? After going through his diaries from that period and studying that period, I have now understood the true import of his words. After 2014, there was no serious challenge to the Congress leadership from *within* the party. Despite the departure of a few leaders and the presence of some internal factionalism which has historically existed within the Congress, there was no significant challenge to Sonia's leadership or any deliberate attempt to marginalize the Gandhi family within the party. On the contrary, the party organization stood solidly behind the then Congress President Sonia and Rahul Gandhi. But post Emergency, Indira had to not only fight the Janata party and the huge wave of public outrage against her, but also the strong anti-Indira forces within the party itself. This ultimately led to the split and the formation of Congress (I). Sometimes I wonder, if Congress did not have a leader with the dynamism, grit, political astuteness and charisma of Indira back then, would the party have slowly disintegrated into oblivion? Perhaps not. Perhaps, some new leadership would have emerged. But that's a question that will remain unanswered.

According to Pranab, the ideal situation would have been to take control of the party from within. But that seemed difficult, as most of the people who were once close to Indira had deserted her. Out of 21 CWC members, including the nominated ones, only five were with Indira. Pranab along with Antulay and D. Devaraj Urs argued for a split. Pranab told Indira that though the majority of members in CWC and CPP were against her, thousands of Congress workers were looking towards her for leadership. As Congress workers continued to face daily harassments from members of the Janata party, there was no one to raise their voice.

In December 1977, Indira resigned from the CWC and CPP. A steering committee was instituted to hold a national convention on 1–2 January 1978 in Delhi. It was decided that the invitation would be issued in the name of the four CWC members who were with Indira—Narasimha Rao, Buta Singh, A.P. Sharma and M. Chandrasekhar. The fifth and the eldest CWC member, Kamalapati Tripathi, would preside. Invitations were sent to all senior Congress leaders, CWC members, including Congress President Brahmananda Reddy. An appeal was issued to all Congressmen across the country to attend the convention. More than 5,000 delegates attended the convention. On 2 January, a short resolution drafted by Pranab was passed with thunderous applause electing Indira Gandhi as Congress president. Thus, the Congress (I) was born.

The first major challenge before Indira and the Congress (I) was contesting Assembly elections in four major states in less than two months (in February 1978) after the party's formation—Karnataka, Andhra Pradesh, Maharashtra and Assam. In Karnataka, where there was a Congress-led government by Devaraj Urs, a defection was engineered by another Congress MLA, K.H. Patil. This resulted in the collapse of the government. Brahmananda Reddy held Urs responsible for this and suspended him from the party. The results of these elections were astounding. Congress (I) scored a massive victory in Karnataka winning 149 seats, the Janata party was a distant second with 59 seats, while the other Congress—referred to as Congress (O)—just got 2 seats. In Andhra Pradesh, Congress (I) won 175 seats, Janata party won 60 and the Congress (O) won 30 seats. In Maharashtra, the votes split between Congress (I) and Congress (O) with each getting 62 and 69, respectively. The Janata party emerged as the single largest party with 99 seats. It was a spectacular victory for Indira Gandhi. Within one-and-a-half months of the split, and a year after her shattering defeat in the Lok Sabha elections, the Congress (I) formed full-fledged governments in two states and a coalition government with Congress (O) in Maharashtra.

However, things did not go as per script in Assam where the Congress (I) managed to win only 8 seats. Congress (O) and Janata party won 26 and 53 seats, respectively. The defeat in the state can be attributed primarily to the fact that the Congress organization and most of its senior leaders, including 10 Lok Sabha members from the state, remained with the Congress (O). Only one Rajya Sabha MP, Tilak Gogoi, joined the Indira camp. Further, the sympathy of the party and its supporters was with the former Party President D.K. Barooah. Hiteswar Saikia, the blue-eyed boy of Barooah, and a popular leader with a strong support-base among the youth, was hostile towards Congress (I). However, he later shifted to the Indira camp and went on to become the CM of Assam.

Pranab and others from the Indira camp faced hostile crowds in Assam. In Silchar, and Jalukbari in Guwahati, Pranab was attacked by stone-pelting youth and got injured. Even though it was difficult to do public meetings without organizational support, nevertheless, Pranab along with Ashok Bhattacharya (a youth leader from Tripura) toured the state extensively. He recalled how they would carry a small stool, a portable speaker and microphone in the car. They would stop the car whenever they noticed farmers working in the fields. They would take out the stool, climb on top of it and start delivering speeches to the farmers, who remained oblivious to the ramblings of these two men. I wonder how many former ministers or MPs (Pranab was then MP from Rajya Sabha) today would do such a thing. In my own very short political life, I have seen meetings being cancelled and 'leaders' not turning up because they felt that the crowd was not large enough. Success and recognition do not come easily.

Baba shared an amusing anecdote with me from that period, which involved him and Tilak Gogoi. Both of them went to meet the *pradhan* (head) of a village, and were invited for lunch. Soon, they were joined by many other people from the village. Gogoi engaged in conversation, while simultaneously eating. In keeping with Indian hospitality, his plate was replenished even before he finished the food completely. He continued eating, and more rice was added to his plate. This cycle continued uninterrupted. Baba later said, 'My eyes would travel from his face to plate whenever the lady of the house refilled it.' It was not that Gogoi was eating out of hunger or greed. Rather, he was engrossed in conversation and continued to eat mechanically. But no matter how much the mind is preoccupied, the body has its limits. By the time Gogoi realized it, it was too late. He was so full that he couldn't even move. He needed support to get up and was advised to lie down for a while. He later blamed Baba, questioning, 'Why didn't you intervene, Dada?' Baba replied, 'How could I stop you? You were so busy eating and talking that you didn't even look at me. I couldn't have said anything loudly because that would've appeared rude.' Luckily, nothing untoward happened! After a couple of hours of rest, they moved on to their next meeting.

After these elections, things changed drastically for Congress (I). A large number of Congress MPs from the other camp joined Indira. As a result, Congress (I) effectively became the main opposition party both in the Lok Sabha and Rajya Sabha. In November 1978, Indira returned to the Lok Sabha from Chikmagalur in Karnataka. The Janata party used all its might to make her lose. There was no dearth of abuse and personal attacks. George Fernandes, the election in-charge from Janata party, put up posters saying that she was a 'cobra who would bite voters', but the people of Chikmagalur decided to ignore his advice and voted for Indira.[31] Veteran Communist leader, S.A. Dange, sent a 'condolence' telegram to George after Indira's victory.

After the election victory, Indira visited England

---

[31]Ghose, Sagarika, '"Chikmagalur Can Never Forget Indira Gandhi"', *The Times of India*, 8 May 2018, https://tinyurl.com/3zv6abvv. Accessed on 27 September 2023.

accompanied by Rajiv and Sonia. Pranab and Geeta also accompanied Indira. This trip was a great success. Despite the hostile British media, she was received by PM James Callaghan as well as the then Leader of Opposition Margaret Thatcher. Pranab often recalled that at a dinner hosted by the Indo-British Friendship Society, Michael Foot, deputy PM of Britain (who later became the PM) made a prophetic remark: 'Life of Indira Gandhi is not a closed chapter. Many more glorious achievements are to be added to it.'[32]

Many decades later, a couple of days following Baba's demise, Sonia called me one evening simply to enquire about my well-being. Perhaps to lighten my mood, she spoke about this trip. She remembered my mother 'with her beautiful long tress of hair'. She mentioned that while she already knew my mother from before, this particular trip served as an opportunity to break the ice between them. She proceeded to share some interesting anecdotes (nothing related to politics) related to this journey and Ma.

The victory in Chikmagalur proved to be a turning point for Indira. It also marked the beginning of the end for the Janata party, whose vindictiveness and lack of political foresight knew no end. Within a month, they used their majority in Parliament to get her expelled, and sent her to jail for allegedly committing breach of privilege and contempt of the House. Incidentally, Vajpayee (then a minister in the Janata government) in his political wisdom advised that a softer approach of reprimanding would be enough. But Morarji Desai and Charan Singh wanted a stern action and decided to send her to Tihar jail. In

---

[32]Mukherjee, Pranab, *The Dramatic Decade: The Indira Gandhi Years*, Rupa Publications, 2014, p. 206.

the process, the Janata Party dug its own grave. Congress workers launched massive mass agitation programmes throughout the country and people's sympathy for Indira soared by leaps and bounds. She was released from prison on 26 December, after spending a week in detention.

However, this was not the end of Indira's troubles. Soon, relations with Devaraj Urs started to sour because he believed that the astounding victory of Congress (I) in the Karnataka Assembly elections, and even Indira's own victory in Chikmagalur, was due to his popularity. After becoming CM, he refused to step down as state party president. Internal factionalism was at its peak and Urs started issuing statements against the Congress (I) leadership. Pranab was given the task to assess the situation.

Recalling those days, senior Congress leader (and later CM of Karnataka), M. Veerappa Moily—who was then an MLA from Karkala Assembly segment of Chikmagalur Lok Sabha constituency—once told me how he and Pranab traversed the length and breadth of Karnataka during that time. After spending more than one-and-a-half months in Karnataka meeting party leaders, workers, influential people and the general public, Pranab gave the report to Indira and suggested that instead of appeasing Urs, they should build the party organization without him if necessary. He felt that though a large number of MLAs were with Urs, the majority of grassroots party workers and the public were favourably inclined towards Congress (I). His hard-line stance was criticized by some in the party, but ultimately a show-cause notice was issued to Urs.

Urs responded by breaking away from Congress (I) and forming his own Karnataka Congress. Pranab has written about this saying, '[Urs'] divorce from Congress (I) was a shot in the arm for Congress (O), which was fast running out of the steam. Their reaction was hysterical. Not satisfied with congratulating Urs for his "bold step", they offered him party leadership on a platter. Overnight, Congress (O) became Congress (Urs), with Devaraj Urs at its helm.'[33] He told us how Vajpayee made a humorous barb in Parliament, '*Congress I Congress U, Kabhi Mai, Kabhi Tu* (Congress I Congress U. Sometimes Me Sometimes You).' Incidentally, within six months, Urs was wiped out from Karnataka in the Lok Sabha elections with Congress (I) winning 27 out of 28 seats.

Pranab, along with the local leaders of Congress (I), decided to hold a convention in Bangalore (now Bengaluru) on 15 July 1979. A huge number of Congress workers across the state attended the convention. While addressing a public meeting after the convention, Indira received the news of PM Morarji Desai's resignation. They immediately flew back. A few days later, Charan Singh was sworn in as the PM. The Janata Party was nearing the end of its two-and-a-half year rule. The final act of the drama was unfolding and the curtain was about to close. Less than a month later, Charan Singh tendered his resignation and advised the President to declare fresh general elections.

By then, there was a mass exodus of leaders from Congress (O) to Congress (I). Brahmananda Reddy himself joined the party in November 1979. Many of them came back through Pranab, who categorically told them that they were most welcome to join back but should not expect party nomination for the upcoming election. He was quite against giving tickets to the 'deserters'. Indira

---

[33]Ibid. 222.

Gandhi told him one day, 'Pranab, don't be so rigid. Choose people who could run the government.' Baba later told me that from that statement, he understood two things. First, they were going to win. Second, mere loyalty cannot be a substitute for efficiency and experience required for governance. A leader needs to rise above petty personal grudges and take decisions that ensure smooth running of the government.

THE GLORIOUS COMEBACK

When elections were declared, Pranab insisted on contesting from Bolpur in West Bengal. Indira was totally against the idea of him contesting. So was my mother. My mother might not have been politically very savvy but had a wealth of common sense. She also harboured no illusions about her husband's status as a leader of the masses. Bolpur was a strong bastion of the Left and since 1952, the Congress had never won there except once. She rightly feared that Baba would lose. But Pranab could be quite obstinate and like any politician, he too harboured the ambition to win a seat in the Lok Sabha and return to Parliament with a popular mandate. So, despite strong objections from two important women—his wife and his leader—he contested.

The results were along expected lines, he lost by nearly 68,000 votes. Though the Congress did exceptionally well in other states, winning 351 of the 529 seats; in West Bengal, the Congress won only four seats out of 42. While the votes were being counted and the trends began to emerge, Pranab received a phone call from Geeta, who informed him that Indira had asked him to return to Delhi immediately. Geeta later recounted Indira's precise words, 'Tell him not to wait for the outcome, we are all aware of what it will be. Ask him to come back to Delhi right away.'

A disheartened Pranab returned to Delhi and went to Indira's residence straight from the airport, where he got a dressing-down of his life from her. She was seated at one end of a long dining table taking a foot bath (as she was suffering from cold) and he stood at the other end. There was no one else in the room. Pranab was severely reprimanded for being obstinate on contesting from Bolpur against her explicit advice, and was told that such stubbornness nullified all his other hard work. The admonishment went on till what felt like eternity. Sanjay walked in at some point and said, 'Mummy, at least let him sit.' The suggestion was ignored and Indira Gandhi continued, 'Even your wife did not believe that you would win, but still you insisted on contesting!' After a while, she calmed down and sent him back with a basket of fruit for 'Geeta and the children'.

Pranab was naturally devasted. He was not only worried about losing the election, but was also anxious about his future relationship with Indira. He knew that she did not take kindly to those who went against her explicit advice, so he was concerned about what their equation would be in the future.

His hopes of being included in the Cabinet seemed impossible. As the media speculated about the possible candidates for the Cabinet, his name featured nowhere, as it was taken for granted that a person faced with an electoral defeat would not be considered.

In the meantime, several newly elected members of Parliament started coming to meet him. Many of them told him that they were asked by Indira to do so. Pranab thought that perhaps Indira did not want him to feel too dejected after his loss. That must have provided him with some relief about his future relationship with her, although he still didn't hold any expectations of being included in the Cabinet. He decided that he would not speak to Indira about it as he felt too embarrassed to broach the topic after his defeat.

On 10 January 1980, Indira Gandhi was elected leader of the party at a meeting of the CPP. Pranab was present at the meeting, as he was still a member of the Rajya Sabha. On 12 January, Kamal Nath came to see Pranab and told him about some people likely to be inducted in the Cabinet, including Abu Barkat Ataur (A.B.A.) Ghani Khan Choudhury, a senior leader from West Bengal, and one of the four MPs who won from the state. Kamal Nath asked Pranab if he had discussed his Cabinet inclusion with Indira or Sanjay, to which Pranab replied in the negative. Pranab later wrote in his book, 'I had a hunch that Kamal Nath wanted to know my mind.'[34] Sanjay called him that evening saying that it was already decided to include him in the government, but he was not sure whether it would be in the first round or the subsequent expansion. Meanwhile, Pranab got a call from Indira's office asking him to meet her. When they met, she asked him to talk to the then CM of Sikkim Nar Bahadur Bhandari and work out a scheme for the merger of his party with Congress. She also sought his opinion about certain individuals whose names were doing rounds in the media as possible inclusions in the new Cabinet though she did not mention the reason for her

---

[34]Ibid. 226.

enquiry. There was no other discussion.

On 14 January, Indira was sworn in as PM for the third time. However, even on the night before the swearing-in, Pranab didn't know if he would be included in the Cabinet. On the day of the swearing-in, Pranab received a call from R.K. Dhawan, private secretary to Indira Gandhi, requesting him to be present at Ashoka Hall in Rashtrapati Bhavan by 11.00 a.m. When he reached the venue, he saw that there was no seat reserved for him in the row of ministers waiting to be sworn in. He looked at Indira who realized that something was amiss. Dhawan came running to Pranab and asked him to wait. It seemed that in the recommended list of ministers sent to Rashtrapati Bhavan, Pranab's name was at the end. While all the other names were typed, his name was scribbled by hand. The President's Secretariat had missed it. As a result, there was no chair earmarked for him. Indira quickly wrote another letter by hand, which was delivered to the President's Secretary. Pranab was seated between Narasimha Rao and R. Venkataraman, and was sworn in as a Cabinet minister.

The whole sequence of events seemed mysterious. Naturally, the media went wild with speculations as Pranab's inclusion was perceived as a last-minute decision. One newspaper even wrote that he was included due to astrological reasons, as Indira was advised by an astrologer to have 22 ministers in her Cabinet.

I could not fathom why Pranab's name was handwritten and not typed. When I asked him about this, he said that there was lot of pressure on Indira to not include him in the first round of ministers. So, she wanted to keep it a secret till the last moment and added his name by hand just before the list was sent to the President's Secretariat. I then asked him who was exerting that pressure? He did not respond.

So, who was so powerful in the Congress to exert such influence on Indira that she had to keep it a secret till the very last moment? Only one name comes to mind: Sanjay Gandhi. It was perhaps Sanjay who did not want Pranab to be included in the first round of ministers to be sworn in. There are subtle indications of this in the account provided by Pranab in his book. First, Kamal Nath's (who was in Sanjay's innermost circle) visit to 'ascertain his mind' regarding his conversation with Indira. Second, Sanjay's phone call assuring him of inclusion but uncertain about the timing. Since the swearing-in ceremony was scheduled for the next day, if he was to be included in the first round, Sanjay would have known and informed Pranab instead of giving a vague assurance. Third, Kamal Nath informed Pranab that he was advocating for the inclusion of Ghani Khan in the Cabinet. But despite everything, Pranab was included and his name was scribbled down in the list at the last moment.

But why would Sanjay try to oppose Pranab's inclusion in the first round of ministers? After all, as per Pranab, they shared an excellent rapport. The reason may have been purely political. West Bengal had only won four seats out of 42. Ghani Khan, who never lost an election, was the primary candidate from the state for ministership and in all fairness, could not be deprived. But to have two Cabinet ministers (especially one who had lost) from a state that gave Congress just four seats was not politically prudent. Indira was well aware of the challenges she would face in accommodating Pranab in the Cabinet following his defeat, which probably fuelled her anger towards him. She would have faced tremendous pressure, not just from Sanjay but also from various other quarters, including other states, had she declared her intention to include Pranab in the Cabinet. Hence, the secrecy. But she did it.

Indira broke past conventions. It was the first time in post-Independence India that a person who had lost an election was immediately inducted as a Cabinet minister. Though it may not have been the most sensible move politically, she did not leave her most trusted, and perhaps one of her most efficient lieutenants behind.

Pranab soon became the number two in the Cabinet presiding over Cabinet meetings in the absence of the PM. If a first-time Cabinet minister could become the second most influential member of the Cabinet, his induction by any logic could not have been accidental or for 'astrological' reasons.

There is another twist in the story. After the swearing-in, my mother confidently declared that she had always known that Pranab would be included in the first round. According to her, Indira had informed her but specifically instructed her to not disclose it to anyone, not even Pranab. 'He needs to learn a lesson,' Indira had said. It was definitely a lesson for Pranab, as he must have experienced a whirlwind of conflicting emotions for a few days between the announcement of the election results and the swearing-in ceremony. After years of hard work, it was undoubtedly a joyous occasion for him to witness the party's success and his leader's vindication. However, on a personal level, it was devastating because despite the party's triumphant return, he couldn't reap the rewards of his efforts due to his election loss. As for my mother, I'm certain she agreed with Indira that 'he needs to learn a lesson'. After all, which wife doesn't relish saying 'I told you so' to her husband, especially when she knew that everything would turn out fine in just a few days? My father didn't believe, or perhaps chose not to believe, that Indira had confided in her. After all, which husband wants to be proven wrong by his wife, especially in an area considered his expertise? Reflecting on those days, I recall Ma being calm and relaxed while Baba was stressed and low. I believed my mother.

Pranab was made the minister of commerce, with additional charge of steel and mines. Unfortunately, his diaries from 1978 to 1985 got destroyed due to a flooding in the basement of our house in GK. Those diaries would have been an invaluable source to learn about the time that Pranab always described as the best period of his life. However, I found an interesting entry made on 14 November 2014 in context of the inauguration of the 34th edition of the India International Trade Fair, held every year in New Delhi. He noted, 'I first started this fair as commerce minister and now it has emerged as one of the largest trade fairs in Asia and [is] being recognised as a major event in international calendar of events. This year more than 700 participants are there from India and other countries.' After 34 years, Pranab was going to inaugurate the event as the president of the country.

Pranab was also appointed the leader of the House in the Rajya Sabha by Indira Gandhi. In the very first session, he had to get a government bill passed. While this was not a problem in the Lok Sabha as Congress (I) had majority, in the Rajya Sabha it had only 69 members in a House of 244. The proposed Bill—'The Prevention of Blackmarketing and Maintenance of Supplies of Essential Commodities

Bill'—was actually an ordinance promulgated by the outgoing caretaker government of Charan Singh, which the current government wanted to make into a regular Act. Strangely, the same people who initiated the ordinance in the previous government opposed it now. The other major political parties including the Left, and Congress (Urs) also opposed it. Pranab ensured the passage of the Bill in Rajya Sabha by ensuring the support of DMK and AIADMK, reaching out to each and every independent MP personally, and by issuing a strict whip. He also made sure that some of the members from the opposite camps, who were in support of the Bill but would not openly vote for it, remained absent. Though she did not have any voting right in Rajya Sabha, Indira was present in the House during voting to render support for Pranab. When the result was declared, she congratulated him with a happy smile. Baba later told me how the members (including those who vehemently opposed the Bill) congratulated him after its passage. It was a tricky situation, but he had managed it well. It established his reputation not only as a good debater, but as an astute political manager. It showcased his skills to ensure passage of government bills which enabled the government to fulfil its promises to the people of the country and to carry forward its agenda.

In 1982, Pranab was given charge of the Ministry of Finance. It was extremely challenging as he had to present the Union Budget in just one-and-a-half months. The voracious reader that he was, the stress of the Union Budget did not prevent him from his usual habit of reading. While reading a book, if he found something that he thought might be of relevance or interest to Indira, he would mark the page(s) and send it to her. So, on one occasion, he sent her a book. The following day, he received a note from Indira which said, 'I am worried that my finance minister has the time to read books while he is preparing to present the national budget.' Nevertheless, her concerns were alleviated when Pranab presented the Budget on time.

However, this was not the end of the story. During the discussion on the Budget, Ravindra Varma (a member of the Lok Sabha from Janata party) alleged that the Budget was 'leaked' and that it had been shared with the International Monetary Fund (IMF). To prove his point, he started reading from a document in his hand. There was uproar in the House. A tense PM sent for Pranab from the Rajya Sabha. Pranab reached the House, observed the situation for a few minutes and asked the PM to relax. He told her that he would clarify it in his reply the next day. The following day, Pranab told the House and the member concerned that the text and the data Varma was quoting were absolutely correct. But Varma made a small mistake, he got confused between the years 1981 and 1982. Pranab told the House that the member was quoting from last year's Budget, which had been shared with the IMF as a normal practice, and which was in public domain in any case. Much to the glee of the Treasury Benches, an embarrassed Varma apologized to Pranab and vowed to take the person who had provided him with this 'bombshell' of an information to task.

The IMF was a contentious issue at that time. Pranab's predecessor in the Ministry of Finance, R. Venkataraman had negotiated a hefty loan from the IMF. At 5 billion SDR (Special Drawing Rights), it was the largest loan taken by any country till then. The balance of payment situation was precarious and India would have defaulted in its international payment obligations had it not taken the loan. The Opposition was up in arms fearing that the country's sovereignty and independent decision-making power would be severely compromised due to this. Parliament sessions were full of tumultuous days in which it was difficult to conduct the business of the House. No wonder then that after the Cabinet reshuffle, when Venkataraman was shifted to the Defence Ministry, he told Pranab, 'I pass on my sleepless nights to you.'[35]

But Pranab was not unduly worried. As he writes in *The Turbulent Years,* 'Having previously handled the trade and commerce portfolio, I was aware that exports were now on an upswing. I knew that our fundamentals were strong and exports would continue to grow, enhancing our foreign-exchange earnings and strengthening our position to negotiate.'[36] Surprisingly, after the Budget presentation, Pranab received support from an unexpected quarter. Member of Parliament from Opposition Janata party, Dr Subramanian Swamy, said, 'This is certainly not a budget with an IMF imprint.'[37]

Pranab was right. The position improved, the economy was handled well and India did not need to take the final instalment of the IMF loan amounting to $1.1 billion. India created history, yet again. It became the first country to not take a fully sanctioned loan. A cartoon from that period that remained a favourite of Pranab's, and which I still

---

[35]Mitra, Sumit, and Prabhu Chawla, 'An In-Depth Analysis of PM Indira Gandhi's Attempts to Carry Out Her Campaign Promises', *India Today,* 15 February 1982, https://tinyurl.com/mtxujk9b. Accessed on 4 October 2023.

[36]Mukherjee, Pranab, *The Turbulent Years: 1980–1996,* Rupa Publications, 2016, p. 40.

[37]Ibid. 42.

have, depicts a triumphant Indira Gandhi telling a pipe-puffing Pranab: 'Poor fellow, let him keep it Pranab.' The 'poor fellow' was a miserable IMF officer slumped on a desk, tears rolling down his cheek, holding $1.1 billion in a pouch.

In the same Budget, Pranab introduced the portfolio investment scheme to facilitate NRI (Non-Resident Indian) investment in India, a reform measure that was announced a decade before Narasimha Rao and Manmohan Singh set the ball rolling to open up the economy and encourage foreign investments. Perhaps, it was ahead of its time and the Indian industry was unwilling to let go of protectionist measures to safeguard its interests. A major controversy was created when Swraj Paul, a British NRI industrialist, brought shares in Escorts and DCM. It was feared that Paul was trying to take over the companies, and the government and its Finance Minister were accused of favouring him.

Around the same time, a Kolkata-based media group started a campaign against Pranab accusing him of unduly favouring Reliance Industries. It was a noisy session in Parliament and many questions were raised. Recalling those times, Baba told me that he was so disgusted that he wanted to resign from the government. But Indira dissuaded him from doing so. She told him that such propagandas to malign him only proved that he was becoming relevant in politics. His resignation from the government would only fulfil the desire of his detractors. She advised him that to be a long-term player in politics, he needed to be far more resilient to such attacks. This lesson came in handy many times in the future course of his political life. It's good that he did not resign. In

1984, *Euromoney*, a leading international financial journal, declared him as one of the five best finance ministers of the world for that year.

After Baba's death, while going through his papers, I found many short notes, letters, documents related to different states and ministries that were marked to him by the PM and her office. Indira had involved him in varied tasks that were far beyond the scope of his official responsibilities as a minister. But it was not just work. There were personal notes as well. Pranab had sent her a book by Alvin Toffler with a note. The book was kept but the note was returned with a remark, 'Thank you. I have read Toffler's other two books.' He also sought her permission to quote a verse from Chanakya's *Arthashastra* at the end of his Budget speech. He sent a photocopy of the *shloka* with its Hindi translation and with a request scribbled at the margin, 'If P.M. approves, I would like to put that shloka at the end of my budget speech. It is from Kautilya's *Arthashastra.* Translation in Hindi is given here.' The reply came back promptly: 'I have no objection.'

I also found a note, dated 7 July 1982, written by Indira:

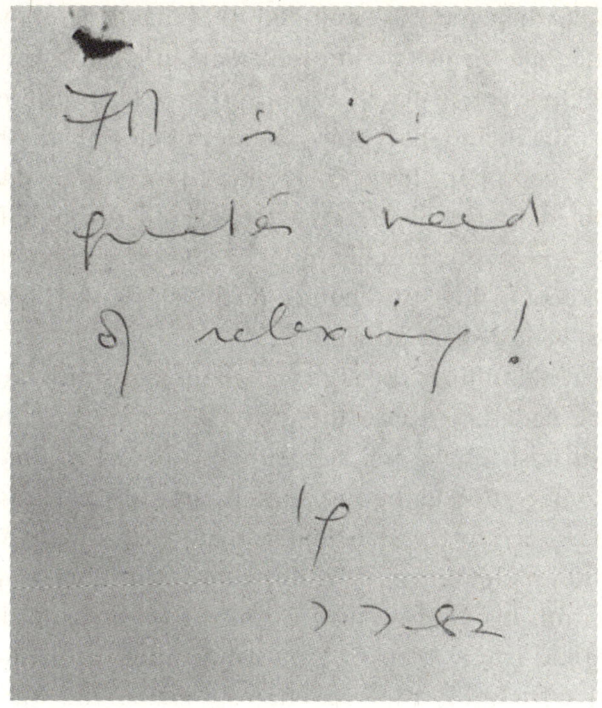

This is in
greater need
of relaxing!

This note was sent with a 'toy'. It was a small metal base holding hundreds of tiny magnetic chips that could be shaped into multiple forms. It was actually pretty relaxing and addictive. It was with Pranab for 30 long years and was always kept on the table at his residential office. Unfortunately, it got misplaced while shifting to Rashtrapati Bhavan.

In the papers that were kept in his Kolkata residence, I found a letter by Indira addressed to a gentleman called Prithwish Shaha, dated 7 September 1983. Shaha had lodged a complaint with Indira, stating that Congress MLA Subrata Mukherjee had collided with his car, driven by his son (Kunal) and had even supposedly assaulted Kunal.

However, when Indira responded to Shaha, she mentioned that she had heard a different version of the incident. Nonetheless, she assigned Pranab to investigate the matter further. She included a copy of her letter along with Shaha's five-page complaint letter to Pranab. Interestingly enough, I stumbled upon this letter while sorting through Baba's papers, and coincidentally, my cousin was present at the time. Recognizing the name Prithwish Shaha and the address, I showed her the letter.

After skimming through it, she burst into laughter and proceeded to share the story with me. As it turned out, Prithwish Shaha was her father-in-law and Kunal (the person allegedly roughed up by Subrata) was her husband. She then recounted what had actually transpired. At that time, Subrata had recently gotten married and was enjoying a drive with his newly-wed wife. On the other hand, Kunal, a strapping young man of 23, was joyriding in his father's car with a friend. In their mischievous exuberance of youth, they deliberately refused to give way to Subrata's vehicle and continuously obstructed him.

A frustrated Subrata somehow managed to get in front of Kunal's car and applied the brakes, which damaged both the cars. A heated argument followed. Kunal, fearing the wrath of his father for damaging his car, put the entire blame on Subrata. An enraged father then wrote this complaint letter to Indira. Other than the strange coincidence of finding the letter in presence of my cousin, who got married to Kunal 10 years after this incident, what surprised me was that the PM of the country took immediate cognizance of a complaint made against one of her party MLAs. She even assigned one of her senior Cabinet ministers to look into the matter. Anyway, the matter was sorted out. Many years later, when none of the key protagonists, except for Kunal, were alive anymore; a thin-haired, middle-aged but handsome Kunal sheepishly admitted that he was in the wrong.

Pranab's relationship with Indira was unique. Years after the Indira Gandhi era, when Pranab resigned from the CWC and the Congress to file his nomination as a presidential candidate, Sonia Gandhi said in her farewell speech that she would miss his tantrums. Little did she know, or maybe she did, that Pranab's habit of throwing tantrums was cultivated during the reign of her mother-in-law. Sometimes, I wonder how the 'iron lady' of India could have so much patience and tolerance for her cheeky young lieutenant. But she did. There are numerous stories, and Pranab never tired of talking about those days.

On one occasion, he actually tendered his 'resignation' to Indira. It so happened that H.K.L. Bhagat, union minister of information and broadcasting in 1983–84, met Pranab with a delegation of newspaper owners with a suggestion to withdraw 20 per cent tax on newspaper advertisements. Pranab, the then finance minister, had a dislike for any proposal that would cause a loss to the exchequer. So, he turned it down.

Later in the day, he was called by the PM. Pranab was in the habit of writing down the points he intended to discuss during his meeting with the PM. So, he jotted down those points on a sheet of paper and proceeded to meet her. As he was waiting outside the PM's office, Bhagat came out. Pranab had the impression, whether correct or not, that Bhagat was smirking at him. His temper started to rise. He assumed that Bhagat had gone to the PM to complain against him and the PM had agreed to roll back the tax. That was perhaps the reason behind Bhagat's apparent 'smirk'. When he entered, the PM asked him about the issue of the advertisement tax. Pranab lost his cool, and replied to her that if she wanted him to roll back the tax he wouldn't be able to do it. In the heat of the moment, he took out a piece of paper from his pocket and handed it over to her saying, 'Here's my resignation.' At that dramatic moment, R. Venkataraman walked in. He immediately sensed that there was tension in the air and enquired about the matter. To a shocked Venkataraman, Indira replied, 'Pranab has resigned. I have never seen a stranger resignation letter in my life.' She started reading out, 'No. 1: Sri Lanka; No.2: situation in North East and so on.' Pranab had, in his anger, handed her the list about the points to be discussed. Venkataraman burst out laughing. Indira then told a sulking Pranab that she was not asking him to roll back the tax, but just wanted to know more about the issue. And obviously, the 'resignation' was not accepted.

Pranab always maintained that the Indira Gandhi era was the golden period of his life. His complete loyalty towards his leader and her trust in him created a rare bond that he cherished throughout his life. That was a time when he was simultaneously learning, refining and putting into practice his political, parliamentary and administrative skills under her guidance. Indira's indulgence towards him did make him a bit cocky, a fact he acknowledged in his later years. However, at that moment, he was basking under her protection and tutelage.

But that did not last for long. As we know, Indira Gandhi was brutally assassinated by two of her security guards on the morning of 31 October 1984.

chapter 5

Birth of a Controversy

'I am alive today, I may not be there tomorrow [...] I shall continue to serve until my last breath and when I die, I can say that every drop of my blood will invigorate India and strengthen it [...]'[38]

These were Indira Gandhi's words during her last rally in Odisha, a day before her assassination. Many believed that she had a premonition about her death. Indira had a sense, premonition or not, that her life was at risk and was quite aware of the possibility of her assassination.

From the beginning of the 1980s, the movement for greater autonomy for the state of Punjab became increasingly virulent and calls for a separate state of Khalistan (seceding from India) seriously challenged the unity, territorial integrity and security of the nation. Punjab was rocked by violence; attacks and counter-attacks; assassinations and disruptions of normal life. The government had intelligence reports that Jarnail Singh Bhindranwale—the secessionist leader of the Khalistan movement—and his followers had taken control of the Golden Temple, the holiest of Sikh shrines, and were

[38]*Selected Speeches of Indira Gandhi: January 1, 1982-October 30, 1984 Volume 5*, Publications Division, Ministry of Information and Broadcasting, Government of India, 1986, p. 495.

residing in it. The holy precinct was being used by the militant group to hoard arms and as a base for conducting militant activities. A decision was taken to flush out the militants by army action. The decision to launch Operation Blue Star was taken at a meeting of the Cabinet Committee on Political Affairs, which comprised the PM, Narasimha Rao, R. Venkataraman, P. Shiv Shankar and Pranab Mukherjee. Pranab later reminisced, 'I still vividly recall Mrs Gandhi telling me, "Pranab, I know of the consequences." She understood the situation well and was clear that there was no other option. While being aware that her own life was at risk, she still took a conscious decision to go ahead in the best interest of the nation.'[39]

In between Operation Blue Star and Indira Gandhi's assassination, there was a happy occasion in our family. My elder brother, Abhijit, got married on 14 July 1984. Indira and Rajiv attended the wedding reception at my father's official residence, 2 Jantar Mantar Road. I remember Indira ji telling my mother that she would like to come over for dinner one evening for Bengali food. To the eternal regret of my parents, that could never happen. I had just passed out of school that year. I had been seriously pursuing dance since my childhood. Indira ji knew about it. On that evening, she said to Baba, 'As your daughter is culturally inclined, you should send her to Sorbonne. Paris is the best place for her.' My father didn't take that advice. I went to St Stephen's College in Delhi instead. No regrets!

On 31 October 1984, I was in the college library when a friend informed me of an assassination attempt on Indira

---

[39]Mukherjee, Pranab, *The Turbulent Years: 1980–1996*, Rupa Publications, 2016, p. 35.

and advised me to return home without delay. Normally, I would take the youth special buses to commute to Delhi University and back. But that day, my friend insisted that we should take an auto, and he accompanied me till home. While travelling, we could feel the unmistakable tension in the air and could see small crowds gathering at places. What followed was one of the most shameful chapters in the history of post-Independence India. Hundreds of innocent Sikhs were murdered, their houses burned, their shops looted in the capital city right under the watch of the Delhi Police. At home, Ma was crying inconsolably!

Pranab did not come home that night, but instead returned the following morning. When we saw him, my mother's tears finally dried. We couldn't bring ourselves to look at his face. He was devastated.

Pranab was addressing a rally in West Bengal with Rajiv Gandhi when the news of the attack on Indira reached them. They decided to cancel all the meetings and rush back to Delhi. From the venue of the meeting at Kanthi, they drove to Kolaghat. The two-hour drive to Kolaghat seemed exceedingly long. Rajiv wanted to drive but Pranab persuaded him not to do so. Rajiv sat in front of the car, while Pranab, Ghani Khan and Rajiv's PSO (personal security officer) sat at the back. While travelling in the car, they tuned in to the BBC station on the radio. They received news from there that Indira had been targeted with a total of 16 bullets. Rajiv asked his PSO how potent these bullets were. When informed that these were very powerful, Rajiv turned to Pranab and others and asked, 'Did she deserve all these bullets?'[40]

[40]Ibid. 69.

On reaching Kolaghat, a chopper took them to Kolkata, and from there they flew back to Delhi on a special Indian Airlines plane. At Kolkata, they were joined by Balram Jakhar, Shyamlal Yadav, Uma Shankar Dikshit, Sheila Dikshit, two secretaries of the Rajya Sabha and Lok Sabha and a few other officers. Immediately after take-off, Rajiv went to the cockpit. After a while, he came back and announced, 'She is dead.' Later, Pranab wrote in his book, 'There was absolute silence. Tears started rolling down my face, and I wept inconsolably, managing to compose myself only after some time and with great effort.'[41]

What transpired in the aircraft has been the subject of much conjecture since then. It was generally believed that Pranab, by virtue of his position as number two in Indira's Cabinet, had staked claim to be the interim prime minister. Since then, his relationship with the Gandhi family was seen through the prism of this speculation. Supposedly, that was the reason why the Gandhis never trusted him again. According to the media, in 2004 and again in 2009 when Sonia chose Dr Manmohan Singh over Pranab as the PM in UPA-I and UPA-II governments, the 'trust deficit' was brought in by what purportedly happened in the aircraft back in 1984. There was perhaps some trust deficit on Rajiv's part, and later on with Sonia too, but it was definitely not due to Pranab's alleged desire to become the PM. It was factually incorrect and Rajiv (and presumably Sonia) knew it too.

Among his papers, I found some handwritten notes, dating back to 1985, in which Pranab gave a detailed account of the events that unfolded on the airplane and his personal assessment of the 'trust deficit'. These notes

---

[41]Ibid. 70.

also shed light on why he was subsequently dropped from the Rajiv Gandhi government that was sworn in on 31 December 1984.

Pranab wrote that after Rajiv announced that Indira was no more, Pranab broke down. It took him some time to regain his composure. Rajiv returned to the cockpit. There was pin drop silence in the plane. The silence was broken by Balram Jakhar who inquired about the criteria used to choose Gulzarilal Nanda as the interim PM on two previous instances. He questioned whether it was because Nanda held the position of home minister. Pranab pointed out that the criterion was not the portfolio that he held, but rather his position in the Cabinet as number two. Uma Shankar also agreed with Pranab. Then Jakhar, Dikshit and Ghani Khan went to the rear of the plane. Pranab kept sitting.

Despite the burden of sorrow weighing on his heart and mind, he pondered over the next course of action, contemplating how to ensure smooth transfer of power. He wrote in his notes, 'I thought that Indira ji wanted Rajiv to be PM and it is my duty to ensure Rajiv to be installed as PM.' He also thought that if Rajiv took over immediately, no one in the party would have any objection. Given the circumstances and the gravity of the situation, there was no scope of any squabble within the party.

As he was pondering over these thoughts, Jakhar asked him to join the discussion and enquired about his opinion on Rajiv taking over immediately. Pranab readily endorsed this suggestion. Ghani Khan suggested returning to Delhi to discuss and make a decision. He questioned whether an 'outsider' (a person outside the Cabinet) could be made PM, as Rajiv was not a minister at that time. He further said, 'If anybody from the existing ministry is to takeover, then it should be you [Pranab] or PV.' Pranab replied that if the CPP chose Rajiv as its leader, no one should have any objection. He told them, 'I do not fear anything from the president's side as he would have no option but to go with the decision of the party which has a majority in the Lok Sabha.' He further pointed out that on earlier occasions when Nanda was sworn in as the interim PM, the situation was very different as both Pt Nehru and Lal Bahadur Shastri had passed away due to natural causes. Here, a PM had been assassinated. A sudden and unexpected void had emerged, causing a sense of fear and uncertainty. To address that, it was best to make Rajiv the PM without any delay and without an interim PM. Balram then asked Pranab to talk to Rajiv. Pranab went to Rajiv and requested him to take over as the PM. Rajiv then asked, 'Do you think I can manage?' Pranab replied, 'Yes, you can. Besides we are all there to help you. You will have everyone's support.'

So, as per Pranab's own account, he never staked any claim. On the contrary, he thought that under the circumstances, it was best to dispense with the interim PM all together. But we are all familiar with the convoluted manner in which rumours can circulate and develop a life of its own. Perhaps, his observation that Nanda was made interim PM not due to his portfolio but due to his position as number two in the Cabinet was interpreted as his desire to assert himself as the second-ranking member of the Cabinet.

P.C. Alexander, principal secretary to Indira Gandhi, who played a major role in Rajiv becoming the PM, later wrote:

> A group of individuals, with malicious intent, later spread a canard that Pranab Mukherjee had staked

> his claim to be sworn in as interim PM and had to be persuaded with great difficulty to withdraw his claim. The obvious objective was to create discord between Rajiv Gandhi and Pranab Mukherjee. But I should record here the true fact that Pranab Mukherjee had readily endorsed the suggestion I made to him.[42]

In Delhi, another scenario was being played out by a different set of people like P.C. Alexander and Arun Nehru (Rajiv's close friend) who also had the objective of immediately making Rajiv the PM. Alexander gives a detailed account of the events that unfolded in his memoirs. According to him, Arun Nehru and others wanted Rajiv to be sworn in immediately by the Vice President, since the President was abroad and had not yet returned to Delhi. As the relationship between then President, Giani Zail Singh and Indira Gandhi had become strained after Operation Blue Star, it was feared that he might not agree to have Rajiv sworn in as the PM. This same fear was expressed in the flight by Jakhar and others, which Pranab had dispelled. Additionally, since the President had not delegated his powers to the Vice President before travelling, the swearing-in by the Vice President would not only be unconstitutional, but would also send a very wrong message politically. Luckily, Alexander was of the same opinion. Rajiv too agreed with him rather than with Arun Nehru. When the President arrived, Rajiv was sworn in as the PM.

But this swearing-in was not without some confusion. Recounting the events of that day, Pranab notes, 'Rajiv's paper (for swearing-in) did not mention the word PM. So,

---

[42]Alexander, P.C., *Through the Corridors of Power*, HarperCollins Publishers, 2004, p. 217.

I corrected it and wrote the word "Prime" before the word "Minister".' Then, more commotion followed. Initially, it was agreed that the entire Cabinet would be sworn in. However, this was later revised, and it was decided that only three people would be sworn in along with Rajiv—Pranab, Narasimha Rao and Shiv Shankar. This sudden change put the Cabinet Secretary in an embarrassing situation, as he had already invited the majority of the council of ministers to attend the swearing-in. Several of them had already arrived at Rashtrapati Bhavan. However, he had to request them to return and inform the remaining members not to come. Then at Rashtrapati Bhavan, Rajiv decided to induct Buta Singh as well. So finally, four ministers were sworn in with Rajiv Gandhi as the PM. Pranab did not return home that night. From Rashtrapati Bhavan, he went straight to 1 Akbar Road where he spent the night 'grieving, meeting people, sharing memories and pondering about the future'.[43]

The future was not very bright for him. After Congress's landslide victory in the general elections later that year, creating a record of winning 404 seats out of 514, Rajiv Gandhi was sworn in as the PM for the second time on 31 December 1984. This time, Pranab was dropped from the Cabinet.

'DROPPED LIKE A HOT POTATO'

Pranab did not get any indication from Rajiv that he was going to be dropped. He wrote in his notes that he met

---

[43]Mukherjee, Pranab, *The Turbulent Years: 1980–1996*, Rupa Publications, 2016, p. 77.

Rajiv on 25/26 November and had asked him 'bluntly' if he would like to change him from the finance ministry? Rajiv replied, 'Who can replace you in finance? I do not find any one.' Pranab noted, 'On that day he was extremely warm and cordial and after 5 weeks of that conversation he dropped me like a hot potato.' He continued, 'Even when I met him on 29 December when the result was almost declared and he thanked the people at a press conference—at that meeting he never gave me any indication. Rather he asked me that why do I want to take hard measures for resource mobilization.' Pranab wondered what had happened between 29 and 31 December that led to Rajiv suddenly dropping him. This was a 'mystery' to him. Even Alexander seemed to be in the dark, as around 27 December he had met Pranab and discussed the presentation of the Budget.

However, Pranab did not think that something drastic had happened between 29 and 31 December. He was of the opinion that Rajiv had made up his mind well in advance to exclude Pranab, even before the swearing-in had taken place. However, he kept his cards close to his chest and did not give any indication to anybody.

The media was in a frenzy, circulating various speculations and rumours. Some claimed that Pranab staked claim to become the PM, while others said he wrote a letter to the President (a letter that didn't exist in actuality). There were also rumours of him negotiating for the position of deputy PM, but that he was snubbed by Narasimha Rao. Additionally, it was alleged that his house was raided and his passport was impounded.

Very recently, a former bureaucrat friend of mine asked me whether our house was raided at that time. When I told him that our house was never raided at that time, or before or after, he looked doubtful and said a very 'reliable source' had told him this. I retorted that in this matter the 'reliable source' could not have known better than me, as my father's house happened to be my house as well. I suppose, I would have noticed if my house was raided.

Pranab thought, rightly or wrongly, that the story of him staking claim in the flight back to Delhi on 31 October was first planted by Ghani Khan. He wanted to understand Pranab's position, when he suggested that either Narasimha Rao or Pranab should be made the interim PM. Ghani Khan may have had apprehensions of the potential consequences if his suggestion became public. Therefore, he pre-emptively decided to spread a different, more damaging story, suggesting that Pranab had asserted his claim. This narrative was then amplified and embellished by some people close to Rajiv in those days.

All sorts of rumours were spreading like wildfire, and the news of Pranab being dropped from the Cabinet only added fuel to it. Rajiv didn't do anything to counter these rumours. Perhaps, his reasons for dropping Pranab were far more complex and could not be disclosed publicly. Therefore, he allowed the rumours to spread.

In an interview with *Sunday* in March 1985, when he was asked why Pranab was dropped, Rajiv said, 'The Finance Minister has to be very tough. He can't be goody-goody. I don't think he (Mukherjee) was tough enough.'[44] The description of Pranab as 'goody-goody' and the justification seems weak. A person who was vilified during Emergency for 'raid-raj' can certainly never be described as 'goody-

[44]*Sunday*, Vol. 12, 10–16 March 1985, p. 24.

goody'! Even on 29 December 1984, as per Pranab, Rajiv enquired about his motivation to implement hard measures for resource mobilization. He was definitely not dropped because he was 'goody-goody', but rather for reasons that were likely the opposite.

Pranab had personally penned a detailed analysis, explaining the multiple reasons behind his removal. When Rajiv entered politics, after Sanjay's death, a new power circle emerged around him. These people were members of Rajiv's social circle. With Rajiv's political ascendency, this group started wielding political influence. It was clearly evident in the way Arun Nehru, who did not have any official position in the party or the government, ended up playing a major role in Delhi on the day of Indira's assassination. By Pranab's own admission, unlike some of his colleagues in the government as well as in the party, he never tried to cultivate a relationship with Rajiv's circle. He thought he shared a cordial relationship with Rajiv, but that never really extended to his friend circle. By his own admission, Pranab was not a very social person and was too busy with his work. Pranab felt that this group, perhaps, influenced Rajiv to some extent in his decision to drop Pranab from the Cabinet. Incidentally, Rajan Nanda, the then managing director of the Escorts group, was part of Rajiv's social circle. In the war with Escorts and DCM on one hand and the Pauls on the other, the NRI portfolio investment scheme came under attack. In a debate in Parliament, Rajiv stated that the maximum limit of NRI shareholding in Indian companies should be capped between 1–2 per cent. Pranab, after consultation with Indira, had made it an aggregate of 5 per cent. Pranab felt that this could have been one reason for Rajiv's friends being unhappy with him.

Other than the influence of his friends, Pranab believed that Rajiv was attempting to create a perception of distancing himself from the past.

Though Pranab was only a few years older than Rajiv, symbolically, due to his closeness to Indira, Pranab represented a different era.

However, Pranab records the main reason for his removal as follows:

> When I introspect, I find that he is justified in not including me in the Cabinet. He noticed during two months of our working together that I had my own mind and I cannot be easily pursued to toe others line. Perhaps he did not like my assertiveness in the Cabinet meetings and CPB meetings. When others did not speak and went with the current, I opposed and spoke what I felt was just and proper […] Rajiv realized that I am a tough nut and perhaps it would not be easy for him to work with me.

As I was reading these notes, a recollection of an experience I had flashed through my mind. Before the Assembly elections in Telangana in 2018, I was appointed by the then Congress President Rahul Gandhi as a member of the screening committee for selection of candidates. For one particular constituency, I strongly advocated for a candidate from the Mahila Congress. I was then the head of the Mahila Congress in Delhi. All the other members in the election committee from Telangana, including the PCC (Pradesh Congress Committee) President and the Chairperson of the screening committee favoured another candidate. In the first Central Election Committee (CEC) meeting, the decision for this particular constituency got postponed due to my very vocal opposition. During the next committee meeting, I thought that if the PCC President and all the others from the state were in favour of the other candidate, why should I push so much? After all, I was an outsider and was not really familiar with the ground realities. When the discussion for this constituency came up, I kept quiet. After everyone spoke in favour of the other candidate, Rahul looked at me and asked, 'Do you have anything to say?' I replied that though I still had reservations about the constituency, I would go with the voice of the majority. The other candidate was finalized. After the meeting, Rahul said to me, 'Sharmistha, I like your attitude.' When I reported the matter to Sushmita Dev—the then All India Mahila Congress (AIMC) President who was close to the Gandhis—she said, 'You did the right thing. You made your point, but then let the matter go.' She added, 'Gandhis don't like being pushed beyond a point.'

If my father were in my position, the situation may have unfolded differently. Anyone even remotely familiar with Pranab would agree that he would not have given up so easily, simply because he had limited knowledge of the state's ground realities. He would have fiercely advocated for his candidate, presenting compelling arguments supported by facts and figures. He would have delved into the constituency's history, geography, caste dynamics and even analysed election data for the last 50 years. Pranab would have thoroughly assessed the pros and cons of both candidates, considering their family backgrounds and political affiliations. He would have also taken into account the power dynamics within the constituency and the PCC. In short, he would have left no stone unturned.

Countering his arguments was no easy task, as he always presented strong reasoning and supported it with factual details. A similar situation arose between him and Rajiv during those two months, when the party had to select candidates for the Lok Sabha. There were two contentious candidates—one that Pranab opposed and another that he supported. In his notes about these meetings, Pranab later wrote, 'Perhaps he [Rajiv] did not appreciate my tone and manner of protesting.'

Other than these factors, there were other instances when Rajiv may have felt that Pranab was trying to subvert his authority. As Pranab writes in his book:

> For example, an interview that I gave on 31st October 1984—in which I stated that the economic policies of the government would be continued—was interpreted as questioning the authority of the Prime Minister. While I had given the interview to quell any uncertainty about India in the international markets following the assassination of Mrs. Gandhi, it was portrayed as presumptuous and unmindful of Rajiv's authority.[45]

An entry from Pranab's diary, dated 15 August 1989, reveals more:

> Shiv Shankar came to meet me at 9.30 am. He told me the situation in which I was dropped from the Cabinet. According to him, Rajiv told him all the senior ministers were against me and advised him not to include me in the Cabinet. (sic) They thought that one day, I might emerge as his political rival. According to

[45]Mukherjee, Pranab, *The Turbulent Years: 1980–1996*, Rupa Publications, 2016, p. 100.

> him, apprehension about my challenging his authority was the deciding factor.

Regardless of whether Pranab would have emerged as a political rival, his non-subservient attitude during his early days of working with Rajiv might have been enough to further drive home the point. His meticulous homework on any subject that he dealt with, his assertive nature and strong belief in taking action when necessary were Pranab's strengths, but it did not serve him well in his interactions with Rajiv. Perhaps, this was also the reason that Sonia was apprehensive about Pranab when she assumed control. However, both Sonia and Pranab learnt to negotiate the issue over a period of time and formed their own equation. In a personality-centred political culture, supreme leaders may find it a bit wearisome to work with people who have a strong mind of their own backed by a formidable combination of knowledge, experience and expertise. Such a person would never blindly toe the line. By Pranab's own analysis, this was the basis of the 'mistrust' between him and Rajiv–Sonia, and I tend to agree with him.

POLITICAL WILDERNESS

On 19 January 1986, Pranab was dropped from the CWC, the highest decision-making body within the party, and from the CPB. For Pranab, being dropped from the CWC was more painful than being dropped from the Cabinet. As a Congressman, he considered being a member of the CWC the highest recognition possible within the party. He had been a CWC member continuously for eight years.

Incidentally, he was invited for breakfast on 18 January by Arun Nehru, which prompted him to write in his diary,

'I don't know why he called me. Arun Nehru is no friend of mine.' He went on to write that they discussed the present political situation where Pranab gave his views 'very clearly'. While Pranab did not explicitly link the breakfast meeting to his subsequent removal from the CWC, upon reading it, I felt that perhaps Pranab's 'clear views' were conveyed to the 'high command' and that they were not appreciated.

The indications of Pranab being sidelined by the new dispensation were evident for quite a while. In March 1985, Pranab was appointed the state president of the WBPCC. In May–June 1985, the Kolkata Municipal Corporation elections were due. Despite limited amount of time for preparation and internal conflicts within the party, the Congress put up a strong fight but ultimately lost to the CPI (M) by a margin of just one seat. The party has not been able to better the performance since then. But Pranab's detractors within the party sensed an opportunity, and he was replaced by Priya Ranjan Dasmunsi as the WBPCC president.

In the Rajya Sabha, Pranab was no longer the leader of the House and functioned as an ordinary member. He was not given many chances to speak. As he was not a member of the Cabinet anymore, there was no question of consulting him on government issues. A public snub came during the centenary session of the Congress in Mumbai in December 1985. Rajiv first asked Pranab to move the main centenary declaration at the session. Pranab suggested that Narasimha Rao do it, as Pranab's command of Hindi was not strong. Rao was fluent in many languages. So, it was decided that Rao would move the resolution and Pranab would second it. As Pranab started his speech, seconding the resolution, it was cut short abruptly by an announcement of lunch break. It was unprecedented in the history of the Congress that a person's speech, seconding the main resolution, was disrupted in this manner. Pranab felt deeply humiliated and believed that it couldn't have been accidental.

Pranab had always been a proactive person. Despite being sidelined within the party, he organized a series of events in West Bengal titled, '*Shatobarsh-er Alok-e Congress* (Congress in the Light of the Centenary)'. But that was perceived as 'parallel activity' and he was asked to stop the programmes. Pranab did so immediately.

In Delhi, there was growing dissent within the Congress. This was not an unfamiliar situation. Whenever there is a transition of power, there are often clashes between the old guard and the new. The divisions within the party were particularly intense during Indira's tenure as PM, resulting in the Congress party splitting twice. Prior to Rahul Gandhi assuming the role of Congress president (and subsequently resigning), there were widespread speculations in the media about tensions between the old guard led by Ahmed Patel and Rahul and his close associates.

However, during Rajiv's time, dissent was negligible, as his popularity was at an all-time high and truly represented the hopes and aspirations of a new, forward-looking India. Perhaps, 'unhappiness' rather than 'dissent' would be a more suitable term to use. Veteran leader Kamalapati Tripathi felt that he was being sidelined and took to expressing his grievances by writing frequent letters to Rajiv. Leaders who felt ignored by the new regime rallied around Tripathi. Pranab had been close to Tripathi and his family since his days as Tripathi's deputy in the Shipping and Transport Ministry. It was speculated that Pranab was the one drafting those letters. Though Pranab always denied drafting the letters, there might be some truth in it. Pranab once mentioned to me that after his reconciliation with Rajiv, the latter once jokingly remarked that he knew Pranab was the one drafting some of those letters. 'Who else would quote Shakespeare?' Rajiv said.

In April 1986, *The Illustrated Weekly of India* carried a 12-page story that included an interview of Pranab titled, 'The Man Who Knew Too Much'. It created quite an uproar in political circles. The story insinuated that Pranab knew things that could harm the party, government and Rajiv personally, and claimed that he was waiting for an opportune moment to reveal it. Pranab felt that Pritish Nandy, the editor of the publication and Pranab's interviewer, was deliberately out to create mischief. As he mentioned in his book:

> The questions in the interview had been deliberately framed to compare Mrs. Gandhi's rule to Rajiv's, and I could not but give honest responses. Some of my anguish at being dropped from the CWC and CPB and being treated as an outcast also came through. However, I made it absolutely clear that there was no move to split the party, there was no question of destroying a national institution like the Congress and the party would survive all dissent.[46]

On 26 April 1986, Pranab was expelled from the party for six years. He was at Tripathi's residence when he heard the news of his expulsion on television.

In an interview with *India Today,* Rajiv was asked by T.N. Ninan about his reasons for expelling four leaders, especially Pranab.

---

[46]Ibid. 196.

TNN: What exactly did they do? Was it just the interview that Pranab Mukherjee gave to *The Illustrated Weekly of India*?

RG: Well, a series of things.

TNN: What specifically?

RG: I have told them specifically.

TNN: Did you think that the interview went beyond the limits of party discipline?

RG: Certain words in it, yes. And some other actions also.

TNN: Why did you pick on Pranab Mukherjee? There were others who wrote you letters.

RG: He didn't write me a letter.

TNN: He said he's written to you on the Muslim Bill.

RG: I haven't got that letter. I don't know where is it [...][47]

The letter that Pranab wrote to Rajiv pertained to the Muslim Women (Protection of Rights on Divorce) Bill, which the government tabled in Parliament in response to the landmark Supreme Court verdict in the Shah Bano case.

In April 1978, Shah Bano Begum, a 62-year-old Muslim woman filed a petition in a court in Indore asking for maintenance from her husband Mohammed Ahmad Khan, a lawyer based in that city. Married in 1932, they

---

[47]Ninan, T.N., 'I'm Sure the People in Punjab Want Peace: Rajiv Gandhi', *India Today*, 31 May 1986, https://tinyurl.com/3w4nt254. Accessed on 29 September 2023.

had five children from the marriage. Subsequently, the husband married another woman and threw out Shah Bano from their house. In 1975, he divorced Shah Bano by uttering 'Triple Talaq'. Shah Bano filed the petition seeking maintenance under Section 125 of The Code of Criminal Procedure (CrPC) 1973, which is a provision of maintenance of wives, children and parents. It puts a legal obligation on the husband (with sufficient means) to provide maintenance for his wife, similar to alimony, even after a divorce in case the wife is not in a position to maintain herself or till she remarries.

Khan contested it on the grounds that under Muslim Personal Law in India, the husband is required to provide maintenance only during the *Iddat* period—the waiting period of usually three months after the death of a husband or a divorce, post which the woman can marry again. Khan was supported by the All India Muslim Personal Law Board, which argued that courts cannot interfere in matters under Muslim Personal Law.

The matter reached the Supreme Court of India, and in a landmark judgment in 1985, a five-judge bench of the Supreme Court led by the then CJI Y.V. Chandrachud upheld an earlier High Court judgment granting maintenance rights of Shah Bano by her husband. Delivering the judgment, CJI Chandrachud said that Section 125 was enacted in order to provide quick and summary remedy to a class of persons who are unable to maintain themselves. It's a moral edict and morality cannot be clubbed with religion.

Chief Justice of India Chandrachud also made some pointed observations in the context of the Uniform Civil Code (UCC). As stated in Article 44 of the Constitution of

India, UCC is a directive principle of state policy that calls for having common civil laws for all citizens of India in matters of marriage, divorce, succession, inheritance and adoption. The Supreme Court added:

> It is also a matter of regret that Article 44 of our Constitution has remained a dead letter [...] There is no evidence of any official activity for framing a common civil code for the country. A belief seems to have gained ground that it is for the Muslim community to take a lead in the matter of reforms of their personal law. A common Civil Code will help the cause of national integration by removing disparate loyalties to laws which have conflicting ideologies.[48]

It further observed, 'It is the State which is charged with the duty of securing a Uniform Civil Code for the citizens of the country, and unquestionably, it has the legislative competence to do so.'[49]

This judgment is also significant in the context of ensuring gender parity in personal laws. With the passage of Hindu Code Bills—a series of laws passed in the 1950s—and through subsequent amendments, Hindu women were given equal rights in personal matters. The Hindu Succession Act, 1956 gave equal rights to daughters for inheritance. Hindu Marriage Act, 1955 outlawed polygamy.

---

[48]Mahapatra, Dhananjay, 'Rs 20/Month Alimony to Shah Bano Brought Spotlight on Ucc in 1985', *The Times of India*, 29 June 2023, https://tinyurl.com/ynrj2pd4. Accessed on 15 November 2023; Mohd Ahmed Khan v. Shah Bano Begum and Ors, 1985 AIR 945, 1985 SCR (3) 844, Supreme Court of India, 23 April 1985, https://tinyurl.com/5n7muh4p. Accessed on 15 November 2023.

[49]Ibid.

The Hindu Adoptions and Maintenance Act, 1956, encouraged adoption of girl child. These laws apply to all Hindus, Jains, Buddhist and Sikhs. Members of other religions and some tribal communities continue to be governed by their personal laws.

The Shah Bano verdict became a matter of major controversy with a section of Muslims opposing it vehemently, saying that it interfered with the Muslim Personal Law in India. In an attempt to mollify the Muslim opinion, the Rajiv Gandhi government, despite its numbers in the Lok Sabha, did not make the UCC a reality. Instead, it passed the controversial Muslim Women (Protection of Rights on Divorce) Act, 1986 which nullified the Supreme Court judgment. It made maintenance obligatory only during Iddat period and took Muslim women out from the ambit of Section 125 of CrPC.

I found a draft of the above-mentioned letter in Pranab's papers after his passing. This was the letter that Rajiv said he never received. It is self-explanatory, and though it does not contain the name of the addressee, it is clear from the text whom it was addressed to. However, a question comes to mind. Pranab wrote that letter and presumably sent it as well. But Rajiv said that he didn't receive it. So, did some people around Rajiv, in his office, deliberately withhold the letter from him? There are no clear answers.

I have added the full text of the letter below, which was written before the Bill was tabled in Parliament, as I feel that it clearly reflects Pranab's views on the UCC.

My Dear ______,

I am writing this note in connection with the Bill-Muslim Women's (rights after divorce) likely to be taken up in the last week of this month or first week of next month.

The proposed amendment of Cr.P.C. in the context of the judgement of the Supreme Court in Shah Bano case has created a sensation amongst the common people throughout the length and breadth of the country. Personally I feel, that decision of the Govt. to change Cr.P.C. in the light of the Supreme Court judgement, was not correct one. This particular decision of Supreme Court was welcomed by a large section of right thinking people of this country.

The demand for a uniform civil code to strengthen the forces of secularism is an old one. Even in the mid-fifties, when the Hindu Code Bill was passed in Parliament, this demand was raised on the floor of both the houses of Parliament.

Three decades have passed since the passage of the Hindu Code Bill.

Now instead of attempting to introduce the uniform civil code for all citizens of the country, the proposed amendment of Cr.P.C. introduced by the Govt. has created unhealthy atmosphere in the country. Fundamentalism is raising its ugly head. The Muslim community is also sharply divided on this issue which has been visibly demonstrated by contradictory positions taken by two of your Cabinet colleagues on the floor of the house. Various political parties have taken different stands on this issue. In the Congress Parliamentary Party also, it seems there is no uniformity of views, despite your personal intervention in the discussion. Whole country is agitated on this issue.

It would have been desirable if the Govt. would not have taken any stand to nullify the judgement of the Supreme Court by this proposed amendment. But if the Govt has taken a stand for whatsoever reasons, in the circumstances, I would suggest that in this issue, Members of Parliament should be allowed to exercise their rights to vote freely. Continuation of Govt does not depend on this issue. This is not a money bill, nor the defeat of the Govt in this issue would amount to no confidence against the Govt. Hence it would be desirable that whips should not be issued to the party members when this Bill will be taken up for consideration in both the houses. If the members by exercising their own judgement takes (sic) a decision either way, it would help to clear the atmosphere which unfortunately has been vitiated.

I would request you to kindly consider this suggestion and allow the Congress Members to vote freely.

With regards,

Yours sincerely
Pranab Mukherjee

Contrary to Pranab's suggestion, Rajiv issued a three-line whip for Congress MPs to vote for the Bill. As I learnt from his diary, Pranab voted against the Bill.

During a discussion with my father on the Triple Talaq Act passed by BJP in 2019, he mentioned to me that it was wrong on the part of the Rajiv Gandhi government to nullify the Supreme Court judgment in the Shah

Bano case. Uniform Civil Code is one of the directive principles as enshrined in our Constitution. Despite an unprecedented majority in the Lok Sabha, Rajiv, instead of enacting a progressive legislation towards fulfilment of the objective of UCC, pushed a regressive Act that nullified the Supreme Court judgment. Further, Pranab felt that even politically it was a blunder for the Congress. By nullifying the Supreme Court judgment, seemingly under pressure from the conservative sections of Muslims, the Congress got the 'minority appeasement' tag that it could never shake off, and which has now reached colossal proportions through Right-wing propaganda. He further explained that Congress had always been a Centrist party accommodating people both from the left and the right of the axis. Congress's actions had the unintended consequence of driving right-of-the-centre voters towards the BJP.

GREATEST POLITICAL BLUNDER

After being expelled, Pranab floated his own political party Rashtriya Samajwadi Congress (RSC). By his own admission, both in public and private, it was a complete disaster. In the later years of his life, Pranab came to believe that it was the greatest political blunder of his life. The party brought together some disgruntled leaders like A.P. Sharma, R. Gundu Rao, Prakash Mehrotra and others. Though Kamalapati Tripathi criticized the formation of the new party, his son Mayapati joined it. Few MLAs from West Bengal including Sisir Kumar Bose (nephew of Netaji Subhas Chandra Bose), Ananda Mohan Biswas, Samar Mukherjee, Sukhendu Sekhar Roy and few others joined in.

The party contested its one and only election, the West

Bengal Assembly polls in March 1987, with catastrophic outcomes. The party could not win a single seat, and many of its candidates lost deposits. Pranab did not contest, but he was the face of the campaign. Pranab's overestimation of his strengths, overlooking the fact that he was not a mass leader, was not the only factor at play. The timing of his actions was also not favourable. Rajiv's personal popularity was at its peak. There were no reasons for people to get disgruntled with the Congress yet. Further, the Left Front was firmly established in its bastion.

Reflecting on that period, Baba confided in me that another factor was that people simply could not accept that Indira Gandhi's closest lieutenant would break away from her son. The fact that Pranab did not voluntarily leave the party, but was expelled, did not cut much ice with the voters.

After this defeat, RSC simply faded away. As he wrote in *The Turbulent Years*:

> Most of my colleagues at the centre rejoined Congress and I, in turn, withdrew into a shell. I was thoroughly disenchanted with politics and chose instead to write my memoirs. I was thus in hibernation from April-May 1987 to January 1988. I continued in the Rajya Sabha till July 1987 but was hardly active. I intervened only once during the Budget debate. I lost contact with my old colleagues and would often sit in the Central Hall of Parliament all alone, puffing my pipe. A couple of people who did make an effort to stay in touch were Najma Heptulla and G.K. Moopanar.[50]

---

[50]Mukherjee, Pranab, *The Turbulent Years: 1980–1996*, Rupa Publications, 2016, p. 104.

Pranab was ousted from the Congress and faced a significant loss in the Assembly elections, all at the age of 52. Yet, it was too early to retire. In a span of two decades in politics, he had seen and experienced the height of power. Now the wheel of fortune had turned and placed him at the lowest abyss in his political journey. Even during the post-Emergency defeat, there was no dearth of work. Now, he simply didn't know what to do with his time. Pranab had always been a workaholic. Senior journalists, bureaucrats or politicians who had worked with him, all have anecdotes to share about how they would get appointments during wee hours, sometimes after midnight, and see him diligently reviewing and clearing files or writing drafts for a political resolution.

For a person who thrived on working for 18 hours a day, 24x7, having no work could be a real torture. Pranab deeply regretted the fact that he lost a few productive years of his life owing to his falling out with Rajiv.

In his personal life too, Pranab faced a terrible loss when his father passed away on 26 September 1986, at the age of 97. Though he was old, due to an extremely disciplined and healthy lifestyle, he was in reasonably good health and sound mind almost till the very end. Pranab was deeply attached to him. He was the only person in the family with whom Pranab could talk freely about politics and take advice. Pranab was deeply saddened by his father's passing. I could not attend the cremation, as I was in Delhi. But I later learnt from him and some other family members that very few people had attended the funeral. With a dip in Pranab's political fortune, most of his 'friends' too had disappeared.

This was also the time when our family dog, Hippo,

bit him. Hippo had the unique distinction of biting every member of the family, at least once, on some pretext or the other (never viciously though). My father, always being out of the house, deprived Hippo of the opportunity. Now, Hippo had his chance. His 'to-do' list was complete.

During this period, it was Pranab's love for books and reading that perhaps saved him from falling into depression. An avid reader, Pranab devoured books. His reading interests were diverse, ranging from politics to history; literature to philosophy; social science to biographies and autobiographies. He is the only person I have met in my life who loved reading the Constitution of India, not as part of his job or a reference, but as 'leisure' reading. He also wrote two books on the Indian economy during this period—*Beyond Survival: Emerging Dimensions of Indian Economy* (1986) and *Off the Track: A Few comments on Current Affairs* (1987).

Looking back, this was the only time other than his post-presidential retirement period when I saw him not overwhelmingly busy. I wish I had spent more time with him during this period. But I was in my own world of dance, tutorials and boyfriends back then.

However, everything was not so grim, especially on the family front. During this period, we had a rare family holiday—much awaited and much needed. This was something that could have never happened earlier due to Pranab's hectic schedule. We went for a few days to Puri, known for its famous Jagannath temple. Two of my friends from Delhi, who also happened to be daughters of a close family friend, joined us. As per the usual ritual of nicknaming the kids in a Bengali family, the elder and the younger were called 'Badi' and 'Chhoti', respectively. A couple from Kolkata, Swapna and Priyabrata Deb, who were close friends of my parents, joined us with their younger son, Gautam. One day, Badi, Chhoti, Gautam and I went to visit the Jagannath temple with my father. For some reason, the other elders in the family didn't join us. Badi was wearing a skirt with an elastic waistband, a crucial detail to understand the events that unfolded later. Anyone familiar with the Jagannath temple would know that its vicinity is infested with hordes of monkeys. These monkeys could be quite a nuisance, snatching away food packets and purses from the unsuspecting pilgrims. As we were walking towards the temple, a monkey came running towards us, and pulled down Badi's skirt with a vicious tug. As Chhoti, Gautam and I began laughing uncontrollably, Badi just shut her eyes and started screaming at the top of her voice. It was left to an acutely embarrassed Pranab to then restore Badi's 'dignity' by attempting to pull her skirt up. But the monkey gave another tug and pulled it down again. This continued for a few seconds before the monkey mercifully left us and ran away. Pranab was not amused, and scolded us throughout our car ride back for laughing at our friend's plight. Much to his dismay, when the incident was reported to others, they too burst out laughing. By then, Badi had recovered sufficiently from her shock and joined in as well.

RETURNING TO THE FOLD

After that eventful trip to Puri, Pranab's luck took a positive turn. Perhaps, it was due to the blessings of Lord Jagannath or the encounter with the monkey. He soon returned to the Congress. This was facilitated by Santosh Mohan Dev from Assam, who was a union minister in Rajiv's Cabinet. Santosh had been a good friend of Pranab's since 1978 when he had contested for a Rajya Sabha seat. Though he belonged to the Reddy Congress then, Pranab had helped him get surplus votes from Congress (I). Though Santosh did not win that particular election, he and Pranab became lifelong friends. When I contested Assembly elections from Delhi in 2015, Santosh was one of the very few people whom Pranab personally tried to reach out to campaign for me. Unfortunately, by then he was in an advanced stage of Alzheimer's. Though he could not campaign for me, his daughter Sushmita Dev did so. She was then an MP from her father's constituency, Silchar in Assam. Incidentally, Sushmita is a dear friend of mine. She told me that during elections, Santosh would request Pranab to call a few miscreants in his constituency and allocate them duties outside the state so that they couldn't create mischief, and vice-versa.

Santosh was in-charge of the Assembly elections being held in Tripura in February 1988. He told Rajiv that Pranab had good influence in Tripura, and it would help if he campaigned for the party. Rajiv enquired what prevented Santosh from contacting Pranab directly. Rajiv told him that as the election in-charge, he could take a call on the people he wanted to invite for campaigning. Santosh pointed out that as Pranab had been expelled from the party for a period of six years, he couldn't take that call. Also, a lot had been publicly said from both sides, which simply could not be brushed under the carpet. So, it was decided that AICC Joint Secretary A.R. Mallu be sent to Pranab with a request for him to campaign for the party.

Pranab, by his own admission, was desperate to get back to the Congress. He readily agreed. The next day, it was announced by the AICC that Pranab would campaign in

Tripura. When asked by a journalist whether the expulsion had been revoked, the question was skilfully side-stepped by saying 'only Congress persons are campaigning for the Congress party in Tripura'.[51]

Later, Pranab learnt that even Sheila Dikshit had tried to persuade Rajiv to bring Pranab back into the party. Pranab was a bit surprised because he hardly knew Dikshit at that time and their interactions were minimal. But he did share a cordial relationship with her father-in-law, Uma Shankar Dikshit, and speculated that it might have been because of him.

Sometime after the Tripura election, Pranab was made the chairperson of the Economic Advisory Cell in the Congress in 1987. According to senior Congress leader Anand Sharma, after Pranab's return from Tripura, he was asked to address a press conference at the AICC headquarters. Sharma was in-charge of communications at the AICC at the time. Sharma told me that Rajiv had called him personally and informed him that Pranab would be addressing a press conference. He asked Sharma to ensure that proper respect be given to him. However, despite 'proper respect' being shown to him, it took some time for Pranab to get properly rehabilitated within the party. What he really craved for was to become a member of the CWC, but it eluded him—though he was invited for the extended CWCs as a special invitee.

It was only after the defeat of the Congress in the general elections of 1989 that his relationship with Rajiv began to improve. Rajiv started taking inputs from Pranab on the grave economic situation in the country, with no

---

[51]Ibid. 106.

money to repay international loans or import essential commodities. Yashwant Sinha, the then finance minister, had to mortgage India's gold reserves to raise funds. Pranab prepared a paper for an important CWC meeting in February 1991 in which he advocated for major economic reforms that could influence the economic thinking of the party.[52] Though generally regarded as conservative in his economic approach, on reading the note, it appears that Pranab was actually one of the early advocates of reforms. As he mentioned in the note, 'In order to generate resources for the development, Government must join radical economic reform in line with international trends of de-regulation, competition and decentralization.'[53]

In hindsight, Pranab always felt that the misunderstanding between him and Rajiv resulted from the coterie around Rajiv. They deliberately fuelled the discomfort and distrust by exaggerating and, sometimes, distorting statements and actions attributed to Pranab and some others previously close to Indira. Rajiv himself admitted to this in an interview with Aroon Purie in 1991.

> **AP**: Earlier, you tended to do away with people Mrs. Gandhi had used, people like Pranab Mukherjee and Dhawan and then, you reverted back to them. Is that some learning process you went through?
>
> **RG**: Many things said about them I found weren't true.[54]

---

[52]Ramesh, Jairam, *To the Brink and Back: India's 1991 Story,* Rupa Publications, 2015, p. 15.

[53]Ibid. The full note is attached as an Appendix to the book.

[54]Purie, Aroon, 'Indications Are We Should Get a Clear Majority: Rajiv Gandhi', *India Today,* 31 May 1991, https://tinyurl.com/ynk5bs4b. Accessed on 5 October 2023.

I once asked my father if he harboured any resentment towards Rajiv for subjecting him to the worst phase of his political life. He replied that politics, and life, were not about holding onto grudges. He imparted some fatherly advice: 'You can't hold on to grudges and anger. Holding on to negative emotions only harms you and no one else.' As I was going through a turbulent phase in my personal life at that time, I thought that he was probably making an oblique reference to that.

Much later, when I was going through his diaries, I realized that he practised what he preached. He expressed his emotions and frustrations within the pages of his diaries, and then proceeded to let them go. About his relationship with Rajiv, he said that both of them had made mistakes. Rajiv let others colour his vision about Pranab and believed whatever they said about him. Pranab was equally candid about his own mistakes. He felt that he may have come across as overly assertive—which was often mistaken for arrogance—during the initial months and, later, became excessively frustrated and too impatient too soon. He also felt that he should have been more guarded in his words while speaking to others, not just journalists but politicians as well. Many of his erstwhile colleagues had been jealous of him during the Indira regime. During Rajiv's time, they seized the opportunity to misrepresent Pranab's words and reported them to Rajiv or his close circle, falsely attributing to him statements that he had never made. Pranab also acknowledged that forming his own political party was a mistake. Narasimha Rao had once remarked that if Pranab hadn't taken that step, he could have rejoined the Congress much earlier. Pranab concurred with his view.

Notwithstanding these issues, Pranab was always highly

appreciative of the measures initiated by Rajiv during his brief tenure as PM, which lasted only five years. Rajiv had a vision to transform India into a technologically advanced nation and position it as a global leader in digital technology in the twenty-first century. He dreamt of revolutionizing the telecommunications sector with the help of experts like Sam Pitroda. Rajiv also initiated a grassroots movement to empower people through local self-governance in both rural and urban areas, which eventually materialized through the 73rd and 74th Constitutional Amendment Acts during the Narasimha Rao government. Additionally, he empowered the youth and made their voices relevant in national politics by reducing the voting age from 21 to 18. His efforts to negotiate peace through accords with troubled states like Punjab and Assam were also significant achievements. They showcased his dynamic and forward-thinking leadership. But Pranab was critical of Rajiv on two issues: his handling of the Shah Bano case and the opening of the locks of Babri Masjid.

THE LAST MEETING

A few months after Pranab's return to the Congress, hectic preparations for the 1991 general elections began in full swing. On 20 May 1991, Pranab received a message from Rajiv to meet him at the airport. Rajiv was travelling around the country campaigning for the elections, which were being held in phases. On that day, the third phase of voting had ended. Rajiv was enroute from UP to Odisha before heading to Tamil Nadu, and was only passing through the capital. Pranab and M.L. Fotedar went to the airport to see him. In Pranab's own words:

> Rajiv was disheveled and dirty due to the hectic campaigning schedule. A foreign news channel had asked for an interview with him. On an impulse, I suggested that Rajiv should come with us, bathe and change, and then give a ten-minute interview to the channel before proceeding on the campaign trail. Rajiv agreed. He went to 10 Janpath, changed and then went to 24 Akbar Road. He gave the interview and left for the airport.[55]

Pranab did not know that he was seeing Rajiv for the last time. On 21 May 1991, Rajiv's life was tragically cut short by his brutal assassination by the Liberation Tigers of Tamil Eelam. Pranab received the news of Rajiv's assassination around 9.30 p.m. and rushed to 10 Janpath. Congress leaders and workers were gathering there. He spent the night at the lawns of 10 Janpath. For Pranab, it was a sense of déjà vu as just about six and a half years ago, on 31 October 1984, he had spent the night at the lawns of 1 Akbar Road after Indira's assassination.

Rajiv was only 47 then. The nation had lost one of its brightest, young and dynamic leaders; Congress had lost another PM; and the Gandhi family had lost yet another of its members to terrorism. Pranab felt that when Rajiv deployed Indian Peace Keeping Force in Sri Lanka, he, like his mother, knew that he was playing with fire. Yet, like his mother, he put the interest of the nation above the fear for his own life.

Pranab deeply regretted not having worked closely with Rajiv for a longer duration. He considered it extremely unfortunate that a leader who was maturing politically

---

[55]Mukherjee, Pranab, *The Turbulent Years: 1980-1996*, Rupa Publications, 2016, p. 125.

and had the potential to successfully lead India into the twenty-first century had his life cut short by a brutal assassination. Even during his presidency and in the years following it, Pranab would visit Veer Bhumi, the memorial of Rajiv Gandhi, on Rajiv's birth and death anniversaries to pay his respects. He continued with this practice till the outbreak of Covid-19.

chapter 6

The Second Innings

Rajiv Gandhi's assassination sent shockwaves throughout the country. For the Congress, it was not only a grave tragedy but an emergency. As the country was in the middle of a general election, the party had to make a quick decision to appoint a new leader.

On 22 May 1991, a CWC meeting was convened hurriedly in which it was unanimously decided to request Sonia Gandhi to take up the mantle of the Congress president. Sonia refused, not once but twice. There were many other contenders—the dynamic Sharad Pawar, charismatic N.D. Tiwari, crafty Arjun Singh and the savvy Maharaja of Gwalior, Madhavrao Scindia. But Narasimha Rao, the veteran Congress leader and a senior minister in the Cabinets of both Indira and Rajiv, became the Congress president.

There have been many accounts as to what exactly happened before finally appointing Rao as the Congress president and whether Sonia had a role to play in it. Though at that time Sonia was averse to joining politics, she had married into India's first political family for long enough to understand the implications of appointing a Congress president (who might become the next PM of the country within a month) in the middle of a national election.

Hence, despite her personal grief, she could not have been indifferent to it. As per K. Natwar Singh, then a close associate of Sonia's, Rao became the Congress president and subsequently the PM with her approval.[56]

When the election results were announced, though falling short of the majority, the Congress emerged as the single largest party by winning 232 seats of the 487 seats it contested. Within the party, the power struggle began between Rao and Pawar for leadership of the CPP. Two days later, the CPP unanimously elected Narasimha Rao as its leader. Recalling the meeting, Pranab wrote:

> I was one of the biggest supporters in the run-up to the CPP meeting on 20 June 1991 where he was elected as the leader. I actively lobbied among MPs I knew personally, and garnered for him support of both Lok Sabha and Rajya Sabha MPs from the North-East, West Bengal, Bihar, Orissa, etc. Immediately after his election as leader of the CPP, P.V. asked me to give him a list of probable ministers. I did, and most of the names I suggested found a place in his Cabinet.[57]

On 21 June, exactly a month after Rajiv's assassination, there was another Congress government at the Centre with Rao as the PM. Recently, as I was writing this book, a senior journalist informed me that in the list prepared by Pranab, he did not mention his own name out of politeness, assuming that he would be included. However, Pranab was in for a big disappointment—his name was not included in

---

[56]Singh, Natwar K., *One Life Is Not Enough: An Autobiography,* Rupa Publications, 2014, pp. 288–89.

[57]Mukherjee, Pranab, *The Turbulent Years: 1980-1996,* Rupa Publications, 2016, p. 137.

the list of ministers. He was so confident of being inducted in the Cabinet that he got all dressed up and kept waiting for the call from the Cabinet Secretary. But it never came.

Though quite junior to Narasimha Rao in age, Pranab considered himself a close friend of the former. Their relationship spanned over many years. As both were voracious readers, their conversations would often go beyond politics to discussions on literature, philosophy and world history. As early as 1974, Rao invited Pranab to speak in a seminar on famous Bengali writer Sarat Chandra Chattopadhyay in Hyderabad. Both of them stood by Indira and worked together after the post-Emergency election debacle. Rao was very fond of my mother and would often visit our house to enjoy vegetarian Bengali meals. He had an excellent personal equation with her. If Ma ever said, 'Let me ask Pranab', Rao would jokingly retort, 'This is between you and me. Why are you dragging Pranab?'

While being dropped from Rajiv's Cabinet caught Pranab unawares, considering his long association and cordial relationship with Rao, non-inclusion by Rao left a sense of personal hurt. Nevertheless, a politician needs to have the ability to absorb disappointments. Pranab, by then a spokesperson of the party, held a regular press briefing at the AICC 'without displaying his emotions'.[58] However, he did not attend the swearing-in ceremony.

After the swearing-in, Pranab received a call from Rao, asking him to meet the next day. Pranab did not want to go but he went, after much persuasion from his wife and his close associate Sukhendu Sekhar Roy. Rao offered him the post of deputy chairperson of the Planning Commission.

---

[58]Ibid.

Pranab replied that he would think over it. Rao retorted, 'You can think for as long as you want, but I expect you to join on Monday.' Pranab did not have a choice. He did not want to ruin his long relationship with Rao. Further, the prospect of enduring another phase of political wilderness without any work seemed daunting. So, Pranab accepted.

One of the main theories circulating about Pranab's non-inclusion in the Cabinet is that it was due to the people perceived to be close to Sonia, who were not in favour of Pranab being included. Though I never had any discussion with him on this, my personal opinion is that Sonia would have been too grief-stricken to pay attention to Cabinet formation. However, it is possible that Rao himself believed Sonia would not approve of Pranab's inclusion in the Cabinet. And so, as a precautionary measure, he chose not to include Pranab. He did not want to take any actions at the start of his tenure as PM that could irk 10 Janpath, Sonia's residence, which remained Congress' centre for power even after Rajiv's death.

Many years later, during my days in politics, a senior Congress leader told me that Rao did not include Pranab in the Cabinet, as he feared that the presence of the heavyweight but Left-leaning and conservative Pranab could create a clash between him and the new Finance Minister Dr Singh, whom Rao brought in to implement his economic reforms agenda. When I reported this to my father, he brushed it aside saying that logically, it didn't make sense. He pointed out that he could have been allocated a 'non-economic' ministry. He asked, 'Then why did PV appoint me as Deputy Chairperson of Planning Commission, and later as commerce minister?' In both cases, he had to work closely with the finance minister. In

Top: Pranab addresses a Delhi Pradesh Congress Committee (DPCC) meeting in the early 1970s. *(Sitting from left to right)* Savita Behn, Radha Raman, Bansi Lal Mehta and Amar Nath Chawla

Bottom: Love and mutual respect—Baba and Ma in the 1970s

Top: With Baba and Ma at Baba's first ministerial bungalow—15 Pandit Pant Marg—in the early 1970s

Bottom: Ties forged in blood—Prime Minister Indira Gandhi with Sheikh Hasina (left) and Geeta in the mid-1970s

A pipe-smoker who could read the political 'tobacco' leaves: Pranab in the early 1980s

Top: The 'chair' represents responsibilities, not power—Pranab at work in the 1980s

Bottom: A riot of colours—Ma poses as Krishna during Holi celebrations in the 1980s, as Baba looks amused.

Top: Dadu's birthday celebrations sometime during the early 1980s. My elder brother Abhijit feeds him a sweet, as Ma and Thakuma look on.

Bottom: Prime Minister Indira Gandhi and Finance Minister Pranab Mukherjee share the stage at the inauguration of the National Bank for Agriculture and Rural Development (NABARD), an initiative of Pranab as finance minister in 1982.

Top: Words of wisdom from his mentor—Prime Minister Indira Gandhi in a discussion with Pranab during an event in the early 1980s, as other leaders look on.

Bottom: Bonding beyond bitterness—With Prime Minister Rajiv Gandhi in the 1980s

Top: Prime Minister P.V. Narasimha Rao is flanked by India's future prime minister, Dr Manmohan Singh, and future president, Pranab Mukherjee, during the 46th meeting of the National Development Council in September 1993.

Bottom: In support of her husband—Geeta speaks at a meeting on the Future of India after GATT in 1994

Top: A proud parliamentarian—President Dr A.P.J. Abdul Kalam felicitates Pranab for being the only sitting member to complete 108 sessions of the Rajya Sabha out of its 200 sessions, in 2003. Prime Minister Atal Bihari Vajpayee is also seen.

Bottom: A Congressman for life—Pranab holds the Congress flag high during the election campaign at Jangipur in 2004

Celebrating half a century of love and companionship: The Mukherjee family comes together to celebrate Pranab and Geeta's fiftieth marriage anniversary in July 2007 at 13 Talkatora Road. *(Sitting left to right)* Me, Shaunak (Abhijit's son), Baba, Shuchismita (Abhijit's daughter) and Ma. *(Standing left to right)* Indrajit, Sugandhi (Indrajit's wife) holding Brishti, Abhijit and Chitralekha (Abhijit's wife).

Top: Straight out of a National Geographic documentary. On a visit to Chile's Frei Base with Defence Minister Pranab Mukherjee and other members of the delegation in South Shetlands, Antarctica, in October 2005.

Bottom: Defining moments in India–US bilateral relations. Pranab is greeted by US President George W. Bush during his visit to Washington DC in March 2008.

Top: A close and warm working relationship—with UPA Chairperson Sonia Gandhi

Bottom: Something to smile about—Pranab shares a light moment with Rahul Gandhi

Top: A stormy political relationship—with Mamata Banerjee, founder Chairperson All India Trinamool Congress and chief minister of West Bengal

Bottom: Lifelong friends across the political divide—with former Chief Minister of West Bengal, Jyoti Basu

Top: Pranab hands over his nomination papers for the presidential elections to Vivek Kumar Agnihotri, Rajya Sabha secretary general and returning officer, in June 2012. Also seen are Prime Minister Dr Manmohan Singh, Congress President Sonia Gandhi, Samajwadi Party Chief Mulayam Singh Yadav and Congress leader Pawan Kumar Bansal.

Bottom: Brishti, Sugandhi, Indrajit and I feeling ecstatic after the announcement of Pranab's presidential nomination in 2012

Pranab performs Durga Puja at our ancestral home in Mirati

Pranab seeking blessings from his elder sister, Annapurna

Family time at Rashtrapati Bhavan: Baba, Ma and me

that particular situation, there was higher probability and potential for conflicts.

The most likely explanation of his exclusion was perhaps technical considerations. Pranab's term as a Rajya Sabha member had ended and at the time of government formation, he was not an MP. As per rules, that does not prevent a person from becoming a minister, or even PM, as long as he gets himself elected within six months. But the situation back then was rather unusual. Rao himself didn't contest the 1991 election. As a result, when he became the PM, he was not a member of either House of Parliament. He intended to appoint Dr Singh as the finance minister, who was again not an MP. To appoint a third member in the Cabinet who was not an MP would definitely not have been politically prudent. His government, which was a minority government, would have faced immense criticism right at the start. Rao made his reform agenda a top priority and chose to induct Dr Singh rather than accommodating Pranab.

Pranab being an astute politician himself must have understood Rao's predicament. He overcame his disappointment and applied himself with full dedication to his new assignment.

As the deputy chairperson of the Planning Commission, Pranab's job was to formulate the eighth five-year plan. His diaries from those days are full of details of meetings with various CMs and other ministries, allocation figures, reasons and formulae for allocating funds, details of centrally-sponsored schemes (CSS), resource-sharing between the Centre and the states, etc. The content was quite monotonous, and I frequently found myself fighting to stay alert after reading a few pages.

However, even the most tedious of readings can have its rewards. Here's an amusing anecdote I stumbled upon. It seems that during the National Development Council (NDC) meetings between the CMs of various states, the then CM of Arunachal Pradesh Gegong Apang had the habit of making tortuously long speeches. To tackle the issue, Pranab promised Apang an extra ₹1 crore of central assistance to his state for every five minutes he reduced from the duration of his speech. It worked like magic. In the next NDC meeting, Apang made the shortest speech of his life to the loudest applause from the other CMs. I don't think the promise was kept, though, because nowhere in the world can the length of a speech ever be a criterion for fund allocation. But Apang got the message and kept his speeches short since then, much to the relief of the other members.

Though the other CMs complained about insufficient funds allocated to their respective states (a normal ritual), they appreciated Pranab's innovative solution to the problem. During his days in the Planning Commission, Pranab devised a system called the 'Gadgil–Mukherjee Formula' that took 'performance' as a criterion for allocating resources to states for the first time. This continued until the replacement of the Planning Commission with the NITI Aayog in 2015.

In April 1992, the seventy-ninth session of the Congress was held at Tirupati. The PM, who was also the Congress President, declared that elections would be conducted for the CWC members. The core body of the CWC consists of 23 members: 12 elected members including the party president and the CPP leader, and 11 members nominated by the Congress president. The last organizational election of the

Congress was held 19 years ago, in 1973. The preferred method for appointing even the elected CWC members, was by reaching a consensus among different leaders within the party. In the absence of a consensus, an election for the CWC is held. Rao received praise from the media for his decision to hold the CWC elections, which was seen as a step towards democratizing the party and increasing transparency in the process of constituting the CWC.

Pranab decided to contest for the CWC. He observed in his diary the it was a bitter campaign, vitiating the atmosphere of the session. He wrote, 'Siddhartha [Shankar Ray] and Mamata [Banerjee] launched a vicious campaign against me. However, Somen [Mitra], Subrata [Mukherjee], Manish [Tewari], Ramesh [Chennithala], Pradyut [Guha] and Pratibha Singh did their best for me.' He lost, but could get some consolation from the fact that he was among the three people who, despite their defeat, managed to get more than 200 votes. The other two were Purna Sangma and Captain Satish Sharma. Many other Congress stalwarts like J.B. Patnaik, Bhajan Lal, Buta Singh, Hiteswar Saikia, Kalpnath Rai and Y.S. Rajasekhara Reddy also lost. Pranab further observed, 'Ganging up of leaders of big states like UP, MP, Maharashtra and Gujarat decided the victory in their favour. As a result, no one from smaller states like WB, Odissa and NE could win.'

The Tirupati session witnessed fierce competition between the pro-Rao and anti-Rao groups. Despite his 'democratization' attempt, Rao was rather dismayed by the election results. His bête noire Arjun Singh won with the highest number of votes. Some other members of the anti-Rao camp, including Sharad Pawar, won handsomely. The constitution of the CWC was not what he had wanted.

Rao then took recourse to a rather Machiavellian strategy. He made his people, who had just won the election, resign on the grounds that no woman or Dalit had been elected to the CWC. Pressures were put on others to follow suit. He then reconstituted the CWC in which he included all those who were elected, including Arjun Singh and Sharad Pawar. The justification to ask for resignations was rather weak. He could have easily appointed women and Dalits in the nominated category. But by making his opponents resign and then reappointing them, he took the thunder away from their victory. Now, they were dependent on Rao for their continuation in the CWC.

This tendency to seek resignations was demonstrated once more, before the Cabinet reshuffle the following year as Pranab wrote in his diary on 16 January 1993:

> High drama of resignation took place. PM invited his ministers for dinner at his home. There, the proposal of resignation enmasse was raised by Santosh Mohan Dev and Rajesh Pilot. [They] got signatures of all those who attended the dinner. I was not invited. Later on, I came to know from others. It was aimed at giving PM a free hand for reshuffling.

The next day, Pranab received the much-awaited call from the PM inviting him to join his Cabinet. It was after eight years that Pranab became a Union Cabinet minister again.

WHEN POLITICS CHANGED FOREVER

Since the time he was last in the Cabinet, a lot of water had passed under the bridge. His personal life was a mixed bag. He lost his father on 26 September 1986, but reached a significant milestone in his life by becoming a grandfather. My elder brother's daughter, Puja, was born in 1988 and son, Arjun, was born four years later in 1992.

In his political journey, Pranab had reached rock bottom when he was expelled from the party, though he was back to its fold again. Like his political life, the nation too went through a turbulent phase. Two PMs had been brutally assassinated. India had experienced yet another coalition experiment at the Centre under two PMs and two years of unstable governments. Caste politics in India strengthened with V.P. Singh's decision to implement the Mandal Commission report, granting 27 per cent reservation for jobs for Other Backward Castes (OBCs) in the central government and public sector undertakings. Most importantly, the menace of communal politics was baring its fangs. This culminated in an incident that shook the world: the demolition of Babri Masjid on 6 December 1992.

The site of the Babri Masjid had been a contentious issue since long. The presence of a mosque that was built in 1528—after the alleged destruction of a temple at the site believed to be the birth place of Lord Ram by the Hindus—infuriated a large number of devotees. It was a matter of faith, an emotive issue.

In December 1949, the Babri Masjid had been locked following the appearance of idols of Lord Ram inside the mosque. Nevertheless, the devotees started offering puja. In 1950, in response to a suit filed by local petitioners, a local court granted the parties permission to conduct pujas, but ordered the inner courtyard gates to remain locked. That is how things stood for over three decades, whereby the lock remained in place but puja was performed outside the locked gate.

After 36 years of status quo, in February 1986, under the Congress government at UP and the Rajiv Gandhi government at the Centre, the locks were opened through the orders of a district judge in Faizabad. Representatives of the local administration in Ayodhya personally appeared before the District Court, stating that removing the lock from the main gate of the disputed structure would not create any law-and-order problem.[59]

This move was seen by many as an attempt by the Congress to arrest eradication of Hindu votes, as a result of the nullification of the Supreme Court judgment in the Shah Bano case. However, it led to further polarization. Following the unlocking, prominent personalities from the Muslim community formed the Babri Masjid Action Committee. Vishwa Hindu Parishad (VHP), that had earlier launched a movement for constructing a temple on the disputed site, intensified the movement and was fully supported by the RSS and the BJP. The BJP took up construction of the Ram Janmabhoomi temple as an electoral plank and it appeared for the first time in its election manifesto in 1989. That same year, the VHP announced its intention to do *shilanyas* (foundation laying ceremony); and bricks (specially manufactured for the purpose) were transported from different parts of the country to Ayodhya to lay the foundation stone for the temple. The shilanyas was performed by VHP on 9 November 1989 at the disputed site. Rajiv launched the Congress election campaign with a rally at Faizabad with the promise of *'Ram Rajya'*.

---

[59]'1986: Babri Masjid Unlocked', *Frontline*, 15 August 2022, https://tinyurl.com/bmmh66kk. Accessed on 9 October 2023.

In the elections, the Congress suffered a major debacle coming down to 197 seats from 404 seats in 1984, while the BJP increased its tally from 2 to 85. Rajiv's image as a secular, progressive, forward-looking leader took a beating and his clean image was further damaged by the Bofors controversy. Political scientist Zoya Hasan wrote in her book *Congress after Indira*:

> Senior Congress leader from Uttar Pradesh, Kamalapati Tripathi, warned that this craven approach would destroy the unity and integrity of the country and the only course open to the party was mass mobilization to counter the VHP moves. Needless to say, the party leaders did not heed this advice as it was keen to undercut the BJP's temple campaign with its own gestures to appease Hindu sentiment but it backfired as the Sangh Parivar rapidly seized the initiative.[60]

The next two years were a period of political instability at the Centre with two PMs in two years—V.P. Singh and Chandra Shekhar. The country witnessed massive agitations with students protesting over Singh's decision to implement the Mandal Commission report. Social justice aside, the reservation for OBCs could potentially consolidate the OBC votes for Singh.

The BJP's answer to this was to organize a mammoth Ram Rath Yatra from Somnath in Gujarat to Ayodhya in UP. A brainchild of the then BJP President L.K. Advani, the idea behind the Yatra was to consolidate the Hindu votes by intensifying the Ram temple movement. The Yatra took

---

[60]Hasan, Zoya, *Congress after Indira: Policy, Power, Political Change (1984-2009)*, Oxford University Press, 2014.

off on 25 September 1990 from Somnath in Gujarat and planned to cover 10,000 km before culminating at Ayodhya. The building of Ram temple at the disputed site became a clarion call for the BJP. Through the Yatra, Advani managed to bring the building of Ram temple at the disputed site of Babri Masjid into the forefront of political discourse in national consciousness.

'Politics in India will be changed forever,' Pranab noted in his diary, commenting on the Yatra that left behind a trail of communal violence. He wrote that religious fervour once ignited could go beyond control. While mentioning the communal riots preceding and during Partition, he lamented that 'lessons from history are often ignored to serve partisan interest'.

Even though Advani was arrested in Bihar in October during the Yatra, his followers reached Ayodhya. During a clash with the police, the UP government under CM Mulayam Singh Yadav issued an order to open fire that killed some volunteers, but not before some of the *kar sevaks* managed to climb the mosque and hoist saffron flags atop. In the 1991 Legislative Assembly elections in the state, the BJP formed the government with Kalyan Singh as CM. Rao was the PM at the Centre.

In October 1992, the VHP gave a call for *kar seva* (religious service) to be performed by lakhs of devotees right next to the Babri Masjid on 6 December. Being a seasoned politician, Rao must have realized the implications of temple politics. However, his response was rather ambivalent. According to Rao's biographer Vinay Sitapati, Rao had asked his Home Secretary Madhav Godbole to prepare a secret contingency plan to secure the mosque by central forces. The report suggested as an option the imposition of President's Rule in UP by invoking Article 356. However, it recommended that if this course of action was to be taken, it should be executed prior to 24 November. This precaution was advised to prevent any potential conflicts with the kar sevaks, who were expected to assemble in larger numbers as the date (6 December) approached. Additionally, it aimed to minimize any damage to the existing structure in case of mob violence.[61]

However, Rao did not take any action. In his book, Sitapati cites several reasons as to why Rao did not resort to the imposition of President's Rule. He also gives an account of how Rao opened secret backdoor channels of communication with senior BJP, VHP and RSS leaders in order to secure assurance that the Babri Masjid structure wouldn't be damaged.[62] But obviously, those failed too. Rao also perhaps believed in the 'solemn' assurance given by the Kalyan Singh government to the Supreme Court that no damage would be done to the existing structure. However, that trust was misplaced.

On 6 December 1992, Babri Masjid was demolished by frenzied kar sevaks in the presence of senior BJP leaders, while the rest of India received the news with a sense of utter shock and disbelief.

Following the destruction of Babri Masjid, PM Rao faced severe criticism, even from his own colleagues. Pranab was supportive of the PM in public. In a Cabinet meeting following the demolition, in which Sitaram Kesri broke down, Pranab said, 'There is no reason to be melodramatic. All of you were members of the Cabinet and some of you

---

[61]Sitapati, Vinay, *Half-Lion: How P.V. Narasimha Rao Transformed India*, Penguin/Viking, 2016, pp. 231–43.
[62]Ibid.

were members of CCPA (Cabinet Committee on Political Affairs). Responsibility is collective; the onus cannot only be on the Prime Minister or Home Minister.'[63] Pranab also wrote that Rao did not have many options. He could not have dismissed an elected government under Article 356 in mere anticipation of breaking down of law and order, that too while heading a minority government.[64]

However, in his diary, he was far more critical of Rao. On 7 December 1992, he wrote, 'PV failed miserably by not taking a bold and timely decision. He should have handled the situation firmly. This failure on part of political leadership will cause great harm to the nation.' He was even more scathing in his criticism of Rajiv Gandhi. He wrote:

> Fanaticism encouraged by BJP-RSS is the immediate cause of this sordid, dastardly act but at the root of this lies the monumental stupidity of Rajiv Gandhi and Arun Nehru in unlocking the temple in 1986. Rajiv and his cohorts indulged in this game and Advani-Joshi combine want to serve their narrow partisan objective by unleashing fanatic forces. Not just Muslims in India, lives and honour of Hindus in Bangladesh and Pakistan will be jeopardized.

As noted in his diary, in a private meeting with Rao, Pranab openly expressed his thoughts and shared his candid opinions. He asked Rao how he could let this happen? Couldn't he have found some senior experienced political leaders to handle the situation or to advise him on this? Did he realize the repercussion of this both within the country

---

[63]Mukherjee, Pranab, *The Turbulent Years: 1980-1996*, Rupa Publications, 2016, pp. 154–55

[64]Ibid. 154.

and internationally? Pranab further wrote, 'He was sitting with an expressionless face. I felt sad and sorry for him. But I said what I had to say.'

'CALL' OF DUTY

A month after this outburst, Pranab was invited to join Rao's Cabinet. Always mindful of details, Pranab noted in his diary that he had to 'wait for the call for eight years and sixteen days'. The 'call' eluded him on two earlier occasions—31 December 1984, when Rajiv Gandhi formed the government after the 1984 elections; and 21 June 1991, when Narasimha Rao formed the government. Pranab was flooded with congratulatory messages and visitors. He noted in his diary, 'Total number of calls and visitors exceeded thousand. All the governors, chief ministers, Congress leaders and leaders from other parties phoned and congratulated me.' He continued, 'PM was quite candid and told me that he depends on me substantially.'

Pranab was allocated the portfolio of commerce. Along with the new responsibility, he continued to hold his position as deputy chairperson of the Planning Commission for the next three years till the end of the government's tenure. He felt happy being back in government after a gap of eight years.

However, barely six months after assuming office as a Cabinet minister, Pranab had to resign. He lamented in his diary that nothing in his life had happened smoothly. This time, the unexpected hurdle came in form of the then Chief Election Commissioner (CEC) T.N. Seshan. When Pranab joined the Cabinet in January 1993, he was not a member of either House of Parliament. As per the rules, a minister has to get himself elected to either House within six months of his assuming office. Pranab decided to contest from West Bengal, where some seats were falling vacant in July.

However, all elections in West Bengal, including Rajya Sabha, were postponed due to a dispute between Seshan and the state government over the appointment of the state chief electoral officer in West Bengal. Earlier, Seshan had postponed by-elections in Tamil Nadu, followed by deferment of other elections and by-elections of Parliament and state assemblies, including those of Rajya Sabha and Legislative Councils. Seshan felt that the government, both at the Centre and state levels, was trying to interfere and undermine his authority. Whereas, governments and political leaders, including Opposition members, felt that the CEC was overstepping his jurisdiction. Pranab was really upset over these developments and expressed his frustrations in his diary, 'Seshan [is] acting like a bull in a China shop. His arrogance, ego and unstable mind is totally incompatible with his high office.'

Pranab's diary entries give a glimpse of the high drama of those days. On 25 July 1993, he noted that the CEC had declared an indefinite postponement of Rajya Sabha elections. On 27 July, the CEC notified that Rajya Sabha election in West Bengal was to be held on 14 August. On 30 July, Pranab filed nomination. On 2 August, CEC postponed all elections again. Sharad Pawar, who was contesting from Legislative Council in Maharashtra, filed a case in Bombay High Court and got a stay. On 3 August, Rajesh Khaitan (Congress MLA and a lawyer) filed a suit in Calcutta High Court and obtained a stay. On 4 August, a caveat was filed in the Supreme Court. On 12 August, the

Supreme Court stayed all High Court orders and asked the CEC to declare fresh election dates. On 13 August, the CEC notified that Rajya Sabha elections would take place on 17 August and Assembly by-elections on 2 September. On 17 August, Pranab was elected to the Rajya Sabha from West Bengal.

He was much relieved. Even keeping aside the nerve-wracking anxiety over the uncertainty of the election, it was not an easy election for Pranab. Due to intense factionalism within the West Bengal Congress, a party candidate had lost by one vote in an earlier Rajya Sabha election. The party had 41 MLAs in the Assembly. Pranab needed 42 first preference votes to win. He not only needed to keep the flock together, but had to get an extra vote. He emerged a clear winner with 48 first preference votes. He spoke to the PM after the votes were counted and noted that 'he was quite happy'.

Pranab was elated to be back in the Upper House. He took oath in the Rajya Sabha on 20 July 1993 'after six years and seven days'. Much to his satisfaction, he was given the same seat that he used to occupy six years ago—the middle seat in the front row just opposite the Chairperson (Rajya Sabha), as he noted in his diary.

On 30 August, Pranab took oath as a minister for the sixth time since the beginning of his journey as an MP in 1969. He noted down in his diary the earlier dates of his oath taking ceremony:

1. 5 February 1973: Deputy Minister, Industry
2. 10 October 1974: Minister of State, Revenue and Expenditure
3. 14 January 1980: Minister Commerce

4. 31 October 1984: Minister Finance
5. 17 January 1993: Minister Commerce
6. 30 August 1993: Minister Commerce

This was his third stint as the union minister of commerce. However, there were major changes in the approach to economic policy and philosophy between the two decades. From the controlled economy of the 1980s, India had already begun its process of economic liberalization. In Pranab's own words, as commerce minister, his focus had to shift from 'import substitution' to 'export promotion'.[65]

Within one year of assuming charge, he managed to register a growth of 4 per cent in exports.[66] One of his most significant achievements, during his two years as commerce minister, was the signing of the historic World Trade Organization (WTO) Agreement— which ratified the establishment of the WTO—on behalf of India on 15 April 1994 at Marrakesh, Morocco. However, soon after the agreement was signed, the BJP, Left parties and the Janata Dal joined hands to attack the government and launched a massive propaganda campaign against the government. Numerous allegations were made, claiming that India would lose its sovereignty and would become re-colonized. These allegations also included baseless concerns about the unavailability of affordable common drugs, withdrawal of agricultural subsidies and the forced reliance on patented seeds from foreign companies, preventing Indian farmers from using indigenous seeds.

Pranab was considered a 'villain'. His effigies were burnt. In Bengal, women affiliated with the Left parties

[65]Mukherjee, Pranab, *The Turbulent Years 1980-1996*, Rupa Publications, 2016, p. 163.
[66]Pranab's diary, 21 March 1994.

vigorously beat the effigy to their satisfaction with brooms before igniting it. At that time, Pranab found a most unexpected ally who came to his support—his wife. Recently, while going through some old photographs, I was pleasantly surprised to find a photograph of my mother speaking at a meeting which had a big banner in front of the podium—'Future of India after GATT' (in Bengali). I presume she was speaking in favour of her husband. Perhaps, she could not digest the ignominy of her husband's effigy being beaten with brooms, so she stepped up to support him.

Unlike my mother, I was least interested in GATT and was totally involved in my profession as a Kathak dancer, a vastly different world from my father's world of politics. He rarely attended my performances, preferring instead to utilize the time to clear his files or attend meetings. To be honest, he did not have much interest in Indian classical dance and music. His love for music remained confined to Rabindra Sangeet and Bengali folk traditions, especially the famous Baul and Kirtan. During any general conversation on politics or current affairs, whenever my father would feign annoyance at my ignorance, I would counter him by asking questions on Indian classical music, challenging him to tell me the difference between *teental* and *jhaptal*[67]; or the specific time of day (or night) when a particular *raga* is performed. Of course, he was unable to answer!

Naturally, our professional paths never crossed, except once when I was asked by the Rajya Sabha secretariat to perform on the occasion of a farewell dinner for outgoing members. In those days, it used to be a fairly common

[67]Rhythmic cycles in Indian classical music

practice to have cultural programmes on such occasions, though I don't know if it is still continued. I had actually forgotten about this show till I read an entry in his diary, dated 18 March 1994: 'In the cultural function, Munni presented a good performance of Kathak dance. PM, Vice President, Najma [Heptulla] and Sikander Bakht specially mentioned her in their speeches.' He must have been a proud father that day!

Around this time, Margaret Thatcher, the former PM of the United Kingdom (UK) visited India. Pranab hosted a lunch for her. Usually, he kept us away from his official engagements. But this time, knowing that I would be thrilled to meet Thatcher, he asked me to join the lunch. When he introduced me to Thatcher, she said to me, 'You have the beauty and grace of a dancer. Are you a dancer?' I was floored to say the least, and was on cloud nine for the rest of the lunch. After the lunch, I bragged to my father, 'See! Just by looking at my "beauty and grace" she could discern that I am a dancer.' Baba made a face and replied that all visiting dignitaries are briefed by their respective embassies about the key guests attending an event. 'They must have briefed her about you, being the hosts' daughter,' he said. Though my balloon was effectively punctured, I spent the rest of the day calling up my friends and boasting about Thatcher's compliment. Needless to say, I highlighted the 'beauty and grace' aspect while conveniently omitting the 'briefing' part.

This period was also marked by yet another important 'development': Pranab gaining notoriety for his volatile temper. It is likely that it all began during this time and continued over the years. On 15 March 1994, he wrote in his diary:

> Today in RS [Rajya Sabha] I made an ass of myself simply by losing my temper. I do not know what to do with my temper. Work of months can be ruined in a minute when I lose my temper and this is happening time and again. My preparation was good. I could score over the Opposition with logic but I simply spoilt everything. I cannot but only curse myself.

This sort of confession on his inability to control his temper was a recurring theme in his diaries. It indicates that while he was aware of his shortcoming, he wasn't able to do much to overcome it. He was fighting a losing battle, as being short-tempered is probably imbedded in our genes and runs in the family. I too am terribly short-tempered, and so is my elder brother.

There are many stories of Pranab losing it in the House, in Cabinet meetings and also stories from journalists who would face his wrath if they were not adequately prepared. 'Don't come to me with half-baked information' was one of his most frequently-used lines!

One incident that I particularly enjoyed is of a journalist who had to write a report on parliamentary committees. His editor instructed him to speak to Pranab, then the leader of the House in Lok Sabha. The journalist was young, and knowing Pranab's reputation, was already quite nervous. He met Pranab and asked him his questions. Pranab snapped at him, 'You don't know anything.' He then asked his Personal Secretary Pradyut Guha to come back with a book. He also told Pradyut on which shelf it was kept. Pradyut returned with a thick volume on parliamentary committees. The book was given to the journalist with the instruction to read it and come back for the interview only after he had finished reading it.

The crestfallen journalist went back to his editor and reported the incident showing him the book. The editor simply said, 'Read the book and go back.' The poor fellow had no choice but to finish the book within a week and return for the interview. This time, Pranab gave him his interview, not only answering all his questions but also explaining to him in detail the significance and workings of parliamentary committees. This journalist's wife, also a journalist, told me how they had to thoroughly prepare on any subject before going to speak to Pranab about it.

I asked the journalist friend whether they minded it. She said, 'No, because you always came back learning something from him [Pranab]. If he felt that you were genuinely interested in a subject, he would explain it to you with all the patience of a professor.' Before joining politics, Pranab was a lecturer in a college. In a way, that continued in his political career too, especially in his later years. Anyone who approached him with a genuine question, whether a journalist or a parliamentarian across party lines, would receive patient explanations on complicated bills, parliamentary procedures or even India's foreign policy. He was always willing to help, as long as he was not being deliberately targeted.

Pranab did not tolerate fools, including his daughter. I too had to face the music often, especially after I joined politics. Some of his Cabinet colleagues were not spared either. Once in a meeting with UPA allies, Mamata Banerjee was at the receiving end of it. She was by then the CM of West Bengal and was insisting on a five-year moratorium on debts of West Bengal on the ground that it was incurred during her predecessor's (Left government) time. Pranab tried to explain to her that political parties may come and go, but the obligation of the government remains and needs to be fulfilled by the successor government. The issue had been going on for some time. Through the Finance Ministry and the Planning Commission, Pranab gave a special package to West Bengal but could not fulfil all her demands as doing that would have invited similar demands from other states. Pranab had repeatedly explained it to her and to her Finance Minister, but Mamata had her own unique approach to doing things and could be quite stubborn about certain matters. Pranab reached his breaking point this time and reprimanded her so harshly that she reportedly burst into tears saying, 'Even my mother never scolded me so harshly.' Sonia asked Kumari Selja to console Mamata, while asking Pranab to calm down. In fact, in the Lok Sabha, where Pranab's seat was next to Sonia's, she would often be seen handing over a glass of water to Pranab, asking him to calm down whenever he lost his cool.

There's yet another humorous episode that relates to a crucial meeting with Opposition leaders. Pranab was trying to resolve a logjam in Parliament, when his mobile phone kept ringing non-stop. Thinking it might be an important call, Pranab answered it only to be told by the caller from a telemarketing agency that he was eligible for a pre-approved loan from a bank! Ironically, Pranab was the finance minister then. He was so furious that he reportedly threw the phone on the table. When the worried Opposition leaders enquired about and learnt the cause of his anger, they made every effort to suppress their laughter. It was left to Sushma Swaraj to pacify him.

Later, Swaraj told me during a function at Rashtrapati Bhavan after Pranab became the president that he was being missed in Parliament. I jokingly asked her if she missed his bad temper too. She countered me by saying that though 'Dada' lost his temper, he was never mean or nasty. He never held on to his anger and would calm down within a few minutes. She also told me that he would always apologize if he was in the wrong. Once, Pranab was enraged when Opposition leaders were creating a ruckus in the House and rebuked them by saying, 'Behave like mature leaders and not petulant children.' The Opposition staged a walkout amid pandemonium in the House. When the House reconvened, Pranab apologized for using 'unparliamentary language' and requested the Speaker to expunge the statement from the records.

Despite his outbursts, Opposition leaders held him in high esteem because he had the ability to see the other side of the argument and concede to logical demands of the Opposition. Perhaps, that was one of the reasons why he was considered a builder of consensus on tricky issues.

POLITICIAN–DIPLOMAT

Pranab was appointed as India's external affairs minister (EAM) on 10 February 1995. His move to the MEA was expected. Even as commerce minister, he led the Indian delegation to the fourty-ninth session of the United Nations General Assembly (UNGA) in September–October 1994. Before that, he was leading most of the delegation level talks with different countries visiting India.

In May 1995, the eighth summit of the South Asian Association for Regional Cooperation (SAARC) was held at New Delhi. Pranab had to use his diplomatic skills to counter Pakistan's attempt to insert certain amendments in the draft declaration. He observed in his diary:

> They wanted to bring bilateral contentious issues, regional concept in NPT and human rights violation in the region as reported by international agencies. All these were directed against India. When I heard this before the dinner, I spoke to the FM [Foreign Minister] of Bangladesh and Sri Lanka to talk to FM Pakistan and prevail upon him not to insist on these amendments. I spoke to FM of Bhutan, Nepal, Maldives and explained at length why suggestions of Pakistan were unacceptable to me. I also decided to hold the morning session at 11 am instead of 9 am. I was told in the morning that in the drafting committee no progress was made. So, I cancelled the formal meeting at 11 am and sat with the Foreign Ministers in informal meeting. I explained at length on each point of Pakistan why it cannot be accepted at all. At 1.30 pm, Pakistan reached out and agreed to the text of the New Delhi Draft Declaration as recommended by us with minor changes.

He ended the entry on a self-congratulatory note: 'Everybody praised my handling of the situation and issues.' Pranab learnt this art of prolonging the negotiation, when required, from Indira. 'Tire them out,' she would say.

In the same month, he represented India in the 'Victory Day' celebrations in Moscow to commemorate the victory of the Allied forces over Nazi Germany in the Second World War. This was to be followed by a visit to London for the Victory in Europe (VE) Day celebrations to mark the end of the Second World War in that continent. Pranab had his reservations about India attending these celebrations. He argued with PM Rao, saying:

> While there was no doubt that the Second World War was a victory over the fascist forces, Netaji Subhas Chandra Bose had worked with Germany and Japan to advance the cause of India's freedom. He had established the Indian National Army, which valiantly fought against the Allied forces. After the 1937 general elections, the Congress had formed governments in several provinces. All these governments resigned in protest in 1939 against the unilateral announcement of India's participation in the war on the side of the Allies by Viceroy Linlithgow. During the war, the Congress party, under Mahatma Gandhi, had launched the Quit India Movement on 9 August 1942. The government had banned the Congress following the launch of Quit India movement. Its leaders were put in jail and the people's agitation suppressed ruthlessly.[...] Knowing all this, how can our government celebrate victory in the Second World War as a Victory Day?[68]

Interestingly, 20 years later, as the president of India, he gave the same reasons again for his unwillingness to attend the Victory Day celebrations in Moscow in 2015 to then Foreign Secretary and now EAM, Dr S. Jaishankar. Pranab, being a former member of the Congress, expressed his reluctance to attend the event. He highlighted Congress's opposition to the British government's decision to join the Allied Forces without consulting the Indian leaders. Pranab proposed that either the PM or the Foreign Minister should be the ones to attend instead of him. However, the Foreign Secretary suggested otherwise. Pranab wrote in

[68]Mukherjee, Pranab, *The Turbulent Years: 1980-1996*, Rupa Publications, 2016, p. 176.

his diary on 17 March 2015: 'FS remarked, "[T]o improve relation with Russia after Obama visit as Republic Day guest, your visit will have much better impact as they have huge confidence in you since long than any present leader in the government. Moreover, PM will visit Russia twice this year." It was really a candid observation.'

Pranab, deep down, harboured a dislike for attending these 'Victory Day' celebrations. He couldn't overlook the immense cost of the war—both in terms of material resources and manpower loss—imposed on India by the colonial rulers without any consideration of the views of Indians. Perhaps, he was haunted by childhood memories of the devastating Bengal famine of 1943, an entirely man-made catastrophe caused by the British government's wartime policies without any consideration for the suffering of their oppressed subjects. This famine claimed the lives of millions and left countless others impoverished. However, regardless of his personal sentiments, diplomacy and exigency prevailed. Pranab went for the events both in 1995 as EAM, and later as the president in 2015.

During his visit to London in 1995 to commemorate the VE Day parade, Pranab was invited to a banquet hosted by Queen Elizabeth II. He was, perhaps, the only EAM invited to the banquet and was seated with Katharine, the Duchess of Kent on one side, and the British Foreign Minister on the other. The Duchess of Kent reminisced about her visit to Kashmir during her honeymoon.

In another meeting with the Queen, during the Commonwealth Heads of Government Meeting (CHOGM) in Auckland, New Zealand, in November 1995, the Queen commented that the Indian PM was once again not present.

Pranab quipped, 'Your Majesty, that does not speak of our lack of interest in the Commonwealth. I am mandated to declare in this conference India's decision to substantially enhance our contribution to Commonwealth fund. My Prime Minister has conveyed his warmest regards to Your Majesty.'[69]

The same year, Pranab visited the US for a week. He termed the visit as 'highly successful'. It was significant, as it was for the first time the then US Secretary of State Warren Minor Christopher agreed to consider Kashmir as a bilateral issue. Pranab wrote:

> I put across our views on issues clearly, with candour and forthrightness, which they liked. For the first time, USA secretary of State recognized Kashmir dispute as bilateral. I could meet a cross section of people who influence decision making process in the country. I had meetings with the editorial boards of US news and world reports, Chicago Tribune, Wall Street Journal, and gave interviews to Washington Times, Washington Post, National public radio. I spoke to academicians and think tanks, and addressed Chicago and New York Councils of Foreign Affairs, Chicago University, Business Schools, Heritage Foundation etc. Another feature was that they made extraordinary security and protocol arrangements for me throughout the visit.

During this visit, Pranab had an 'accidental meeting' with the then President Bill Clinton. As he was going to meet the National Security Advisor (NSA) Anthony Lake, President Clinton was walking to the White House from Pennsylvania Avenue. The protocol officer introduced

---

[69]Ibid. 181.

Pranab to the President. They shook hands and exchanged pleasantries. Clinton profusely thanked the Government of India (GoI) for the hospitality extended to the First Lady Hillary Clinton during her visit. When Pranab shared this story with us, I mentioned how remarkable it must have been to 'unexpectedly bump into the President of America while walking'. Pranab responded by saying that in the realm of international diplomacy, nothing is 'accidental'.

On this trip, Pranab also visited Chicago. Nearly a century ago in 1893, a young, unknown Bengali monk from India—with nothing in his possession other than the blessings of his Guru, and a burning desire to spread the age-old wisdom of India's philosophy, encompassing the message of unity and universalism—captivated his audience when he greeted them as 'Sisters and Brothers of America'. Pranab was an ardent admirer and devotee of Swami Vivekananda. He met the Mayor of Chicago, and on his request, the Mayor agreed to put a plaque to commemorate Vivekananda's historic speech and name a street after him. On 11 November, a plaque was installed in the reconstructed hall (where the event was held in 1893) within the Art Institute of Chicago, and a stretch of the busy Michigan Avenue that passes in front of the Art Institute was named Swami Vivekananda Way.

Pranab went back to Chicago in January 2012, this time as the chairperson of the National Implementation Committee set up to celebrate the 150th birth anniversary of Swami Vivekananda. He unveiled another Vivekananda Memorial Plaque with engraved brass relief and an embossed image of Swami Vivekananda on it. On behalf of the GoI through the Ministry of Culture, he also set up the

Swami Vivekananda Chair at the University of Chicago and signed the 'Vivekananda Memorial Program for Museum Excellence' with the Art Institute of Chicago.

Pranab was also the chairperson for the National Implementation Committee to celebrate the 150th birth anniversary of another global icon from Bengal—Rabindranath Tagore. During the same visit, Pranab inaugurated an exhibition of Tagore's paintings at the Art Institute of Chicago. Both Swami Vivekananda and Rabindranath Tagore were iconic personalities whom Pranab revered. It was with a sense of profound gratitude and personal joy that he fulfilled his duties as the chairperson of implementation committees for both the celebrations. A friend of mine, who was residing in Chicago at the time and had attended the events, informed me that in his speeches, Pranab emphasized the significance of Vivekananda and Tagore's messages and values in today's world. He clarified that his intention was not just to glorify India's past but also to celebrate her future.

His tenure as the EAM also gave Pranab the opportunity to meet the immediate family of Netaji Subhas Chandra Bose. Like millions of Indians, Pranab too was an ardent admirer of Netaji. The meeting with Netaji's wife and daughter held a special significance. On behalf of the GoI, Pranab was to discuss the extremely sensitive matter of repatriating Netaji's ashes back to India. As of the time of writing, his ashes still remain housed in the Renkoji Temple in Japan since his tragic demise in a plane crash on 18 August 1945.

Pranab met Netaji's wife Emilie Schenkl, his daughter Anita Bose Pfaff and Anita's husband Martin Pfaff in the picturesque medieval town of Augsburg, Germany on

21 October 1995. He was accompanied by the then Indian Ambassador to Germany, Satinder K. Lambah. Contrary to the reports of some 'Netaji experts', Pranab was given a warm welcome and a dinner 'that continued till late' by Schenkl and family. Pranab wrote in his diary:

> We discussed in details about the ashes of Netaji. They are convinced about the genuineness of the ashes but Anita is afraid of her cousin Amiya Bose who does not want to recognize the ashes. She wants to carry them along. I invited them to join the centenary committee and to visit India in December '95.

Despite attempts of various governments, the effort failed due to the hostile attitude of a large section of the Bose family, members of the All India Forward Bloc (AIFB) and some other political parties, who refused to accept Netaji's death in a plane crash. Pandit Nehru tried, but couldn't do it because many in the Bose family refused to accept the death. Bose's younger brother, Sailesh Chandra Bose, wrote to Indira Gandhi in 1982 with a request to pass an order not to bring back the ashes, as he believed there was no convincing proof that they were genuine.[70] Bose's nephews, Amiya Nath Bose and Subrata Bose, both members of the Forward Bloc, had written a similar letter to V.P. Singh.[71] During PM Rao's tenure, another attempt was made.

In 1994, Netaji's Centenary Celebration Committee was formed with PM Rao as its chairperson and Pranab as deputy chairperson. In its very first meeting, the first agenda was

---

[70]'Explained: Why Netaji Subhas Chandra Bose's Remains Are Still in Japan', *Firstpost*, 16 August 2022, https://tinyurl.com/4p5rhx7r. Accessed on 3 October 2023.

[71]Ibid.

to bring back Netaji's ashes from the Renkoji Temple and to build a memorial. But it was turned down by the other members of the Committee. As late as 2006, referring to this meeting, Subrata Bose, then MP of the AIFB said in a parliamentary debate in the Lok Sabha on 3 August 2006:

> The record shows that when this agenda was taken up, there were some who boldly opposed it. I am certainly grateful to hon. Shri Atal Bihari Vajpayee, he was then I think the Leader of Opposition. I am also grateful to hon. Kumari Mamata Banerjee who was the Member of that Committee. We also recall with gratitude late Shri Chitta Basu and Shri Samar Guha. All those Leaders raised their voices against this proposal. The Chairman and the Deputy-Chairman had no other alternative but to drop it.[72]

After this meeting with Netaji's family in Germany, Pranab broached the subject of repatriating Netaji's ashes again during a meeting with several members of the Bose family at Netaji Bhavan in Kolkata. He had to face the wrath of the members, who refused to accept the ashes as those of Netaji.

I personally faced some of this hostility. After the Modi government's decision to declassify the Netaji files in 2015, I participated in multiple news channel debates as a media panellist representing the Congress. Some select representatives of the Bose family and self-proclaimed 'Netaji experts' made wild and unfounded insinuations and allegations, including a direct accusation against Pranab for attempting to 'bribe' Emilie Schenkl during his visit to

---

[72]'Lok Sabha Debates: Further Discussion on The Report Of Justice Mukherjee Commission Of ... on 3 August, 2006', *iKanoon,* 3 August 2006, https://tinyurl.com/b44znjrd. Accessed on 5 October 2023.

Augsburg in October 1995. The bribery accusation revolved around an alleged offer made by Pranab to Schenkl, stating that if she recognized the ashes kept at Renkoji Temple as Netaji's, the Indian government would compensate her or fulfil any request she had. This bribery allegation made me furious, often leading me to lose my temper. I questioned why nobody had brought up the issue right after the meeting, and filed a complaint regarding this grave accusation of the Indian EAM attempting to offer a 'bribe' to Netaji's wife, if it was indeed true. Additionally, why wasn't this matter addressed while Schenkl was still alive, and why was nobody interested in hearing Anita Bose Pfaff and her husband's account of the incident, considering they were present during the meeting?

There were no answers, but the advocates of conspiracy theories relentlessly trolled me on social media. Not only was this 'bribery' proposition absurd, but it was also incredibly disrespectful. Even Pranab's fiercest opponents would agree that, despite any other flaws he may have had, he was not an uncouth person.

When I asked my father about this, he said:

> Of course, on behalf of Government of India and on my personal behalf, I assured them that if they required any assistance they could count on the Government of India. Why shouldn't Government of India offer its help and support to Bose's family? There was no question of any quid-pro-quo. If some nephews and nieces of Netaji want to interpret this as offering bribe, then it's their problem, not mine.

If the 'bribe' allegation was true, there was no reason for Anita to meet Pranab again. But I learnt from Pranab's diary that he was supposed to meet her on 27 February 2000 at 6.00 p.m. in Delhi. But unfortunately, Pranab had to cancel the appointment and rush to Kolkata immediately, as his brother-in-law Kamalesh Das had succumbed to cancer that afternoon. However, Pranab met Anita many times in later years, even when he was the President.

The recently declassified files on Netaji not only debunk the myths about Netaji's death, but also document the objections raised by some members of his family. Today, they seem to be finally convinced that Netaji died in a plane crash on 18 August 1945, and the ashes kept at Renkoji Temple are indeed his. Even the current government has acknowledged this fact. In response to an RTI query, the Ministry of Home Affairs stated, 'After considering the reports of Shah Nawaz Committee, Justice GD Khosla Commission and Justice Mukherjee Commission of Inquiry, the Government has come to the conclusion that Netaji had died in the plane crash on 18.8.1945.'[73] It is ironic that the people who previously regarded the findings of the Justice Mukherjee Commission of Inquiry as the absolute truth, are now vehemently rejecting it. As everyone seems to have finally accepted the truth now, there should be no further delay in putting an end to the exile of one of the greatest sons of Mother India, and he should be brought back home with due honour.

---

[73]'Explained: Why Netaji Subhas Chandra Bose's Remains Are Still in Japan', *Firstpost,* 16 August 2022, https://tinyurl.com/4p5rhx7r. Accessed on 3 October 2023.

BALLOTS AND BREAK-UPS

Pranab's tenure as the EAM came to an end with the defeat of the Congress in the general elections of 1996. The party, under the leadership of PM Rao, witnessed a fall of epic proportions and won only 140 seats from the earlier tally of 232 in 1991. Rao resigned as the PM. His fall was drastic and dramatic.

Soon after the loss, Rao was embroiled in several court cases following allegations of corruption. He resigned from the post of Congress president because he did not want newspaper headlines to read 'Congress President has been arrested', in the event of his arrest. He appointed Sitaram Kesri, an old time Congressman, as his successor as Congress president, in the hope that Kesri would remain loyal to him. But power does strange things to people. Kesri soon sidelined Rao. Once, Rao admitted to Pranab that making Kesri the Congress president was a blunder on his part that cost him dearly. However, Rao had another adversary within the party who posed a greater threat than Kesri.

The growing influence of Sonia within the party, and the bitterness that developed between Rao and Sonia over the years, sealed Rao's fate. He was ignored and marginalized within the party. He fought alone without any support from his party and former colleagues. Pranab was one of the very few Congressmen who kept in touch with him on a regular basis. In one of Pranab's meetings with him in March 1997, Rao told Pranab that he desired to be active but did not know how. Pranab advised him to speak out on issues. He agreed. However, that strategy did not work, as Rao was more in the news for his cases than for his viewpoint on important issues of the day.

Pranab was advised by people close to 10 Janpath to avoid maintaining contact with Rao, which he ignored. He wrote in his diary, 'Through ML Fotedar, she [Sonia Gandhi] advised me not to attend the CBI court when PV's case was to be heard in the court.' I don't know whether Pranab attended the court or not, but he and Geeta stood by Rao when he was arrested and later released on bail.[74] In fact, my mother stood surety for him in case Rao failed to appear before the court on 14 October. I found the document in my mother's papers after her death.

Rao's estrangement with 10 Janpath was so absolute that even death could not bridge the gap. When Rao died on 23 December 2004, the UPA-I was in power and Sonia Gandhi was the Congress president. To Pranab's utter dismay, and perhaps to the dismay of many other Congress men and women, Rao's body was not allowed inside 24 Akbar Road, the AICC headquarters. This was one action for which Pranab could never forgive Sonia. He repeatedly told me that it was disgraceful on part of Sonia and her children to refuse to allow the mortal remains of a former PM and Congress president inside the Congress headquarters. Pranab personally implored Sonia to unlock the gate, but she remained silent and unyielding. Pranab carried a profound sense of hurt on behalf of his friend, which stayed with him until the end of his life.

In 2019, when Pranab was awarded the Bharat Ratna by the Modi government, the absence of the Gandhi family at the award function raised many eyebrows. When I commented on this to my father, he replied, 'What's the

[74]On 9 October 1996, Rao was arrested by CBI in case No. RC. 1 (S)/90-SIG/SPE/CBI, New Delhi under section 120-B IPC. Read with Sections 195, 469 and 471 of the IPC.

big deal! They did not allow PV's body to enter AICC. This [not attending the award ceremony] is nothing compared to that.'

In July 2020, he had made a few entries in his diary regarding the celebration of Rao's birth centenary. He expressed his satisfaction with the Telangana PCC's decision to commemorate Rao's centenary year. However, he believed that this celebration should have been organized by the AICC, and it is likely that the AICC refrained from doing so due to Sonia's strong dislike for Rao. A couple of days later, he wrote that while he appreciated senior Congress leaders including Sonia Gandhi, Dr Manmohan Singh and Rahul Gandhi praising Rao as the 'architect of reforms of the Indian economy', he observed that this might have been 'prompted by concerns that legacy of a distinguished Congressman was likely to be highjacked by others like Telangana CM K Chandrasekhar Rao'. He went on to write, 'It is no secret that Mrs. [Sonia] Gandhi and her family, lamentably and to their eternal shame, treated the late PM with disdain. After his term as the PM ended, he was kept on the fringe of the organization and abandoned as he fought the challenges of the legal cases. Sonia and her cohorts did not allow his dead body to enter AICC.'

Since the centenary celebrations were held at the beginning of the pandemic, the then State President of Telangana Congress N. Uttam Kumar Reddy, requested Pranab to send a recorded speech on Rao, which he graciously fulfilled. Barely a month before his own passing, Pranab paid his last tribute to P.V. Narasimha Rao—his friend, prime minister and colleague of many years—through his own last recorded speech.

Rao paved the way for Kesri, who remained at the helm

of affairs for less than two years. However, it was significant, as during this period the country faced political uncertainty, marked by the downfall of two central governments. Additionally, the Congress West Bengal unit suffered a high-profile split orchestrated by Mamata Banerjee, resulting in the subsequent rise of the Trinamool Congress (TMC).

Pranab's diary of 1997 began on a worrying note, stating that uncertainty loomed large over the party and the central government. He wrote, 'Kesri is itching to be the Prime Minister, but does not know how.' After the defeat of the Congress, the United Front (UF) government was formed at the Centre on 1 June 1996, led by H.D. Deve Gowda, with outside support from Congress. However, the Congress withdrew support to the government on 30 March 1997. The move was sharply criticized in the media and even by many Congress MPs in the Lok Sabha, who were opposed to the idea of facing another election so soon.

It was generally felt that Pranab supported the move, as the letter to the President for withdrawal of support was drafted by him. The responsibility of formulating the Congress' defence for the act fell on him as well. But, in reality, Pranab was against the move. I read in his diary that in a meeting with Kesri on 22 January 1997, he clearly told him that it would be difficult for Kesri to operate after the withdrawal of support. He clarified that the Left parties would not support Congress, nor would other parties that were already in power in the UF government. After all, why would they support the Congress unless they received something extra in addition to what they already had? He further argued that all these parties were thriving on 'anti-Congressism' in their respective states, as Congress—and not the BJP—was the main opposition party there. It suited them to support the UF government rather than a Congress government at the centre. Even if Congress was able to successfully form a government, its tenure would be short-lived, lasting no more than a few months. Nevertheless, Pranab's reasoning failed to persuade Kesri. Pranab noted in his diary, 'Unbridled ambition of this man makes him blind to hard political realities.'

On the day the Congress decided to withdraw support from the Deve Gowda government, Pranab received a call from Kesri to meet him at 8.30 a.m. In Pranab's own words:

> [On reaching] I found ML Fotedar sitting there. Kesri ji told me that he has decided to withdraw support from UF. I asked him about the numbers [support of MPs]. He told me [that] he has tied up but did not disclose anything further. He asked me to draft a letter to the President withdrawing our support from the UF. I dictated the letter to the stenographer and the draft was ready by 11.30 am. He was to meet the President at 12 noon.

On 11 April 1997, the Deve Gowda government fell after losing a no-confidence motion in Parliament. However, as predicted by Pranab, Congress could not gather enough support to form the government. It was then decided that Congress would again extend its support from outside if the UF projected another leader as the PM. In addition, the Congress made a demand for the formation of a coordination committee consisting of members from both the Congress and UF. The second proposal was not accepted by the UF coalition.

On 20 April 1997, nine days after the fall of the

government, Pranab attended a CWC meeting as a special invitee. During this meeting, Kesri received a call from N. Chandrababu Naidu of the Telugu Desam Party (TDP), who was the convener of the UF. After speaking to him for a minute, Kesri handed over the phone to Pranab. Chandrababu told Pranab that the UF parties were not in agreement to have any coordination committee with the Congress and then handed over the phone to Jyoti Basu, who reiterated Naidu's stand. Pranab made it clear to him that there needed to be a certain mechanism in place, and that the Congress party's preference would be to establish a coordination committee with five members each from the Congress and the UF. Pranab wrote in his diary, 'During the day, Chandra Babu talked to me several times and said that UF parties were adamant, but I told him firmly in that case, there would be no agreement. In the evening, they agreed.'

Next day, on 21 April, I.K. Gujral was sworn in as the PM heading the second UF government. However, despite making a promise in the presence of President Shankar Dayal Sharma to establish a coordination committee between the UF and the Congress as a pre-condition for supporting the Gujral-led government, it never materialized. The Left and the Deve Gowda faction hindered its formation. Thus, from the beginning, the 'support' to the second UF government was on shaky ground.

On 23 August 1997, the Jain Commission, which was set up to investigate Rajiv Gandhi's assassination, released its interim report. The report indicated the possible proximity of the leaders of the DMK (a constituent member of the UF government) to leaders of LTTE, the outfit responsible for Rajiv's assassination. The Congress leadership demanded the ouster of the DMK and its three ministers from the

UF government. Gujral refused to do so on the ground that there was no evidence of any direct involvement of any DMK leader or its minister with the LTTE. Congress withdrew its support and the government fell, leading to the dissolution of the eleventh Lok Sabha on 4 December 1997. The country was confronted with the prospect of facing another general election in less than 24 months.

However, there was still one final act left in India's dramatic political theatre of the 1990s.

A TALE OF TWO LADIES

Four months before the fall of the second UF government, the eightieth Plenary Session of the Congress was held in Kolkata from 8 to 10 August 1997. This session was personally significant for Pranab, as he was elected as a CWC member for the first time in his life. Earlier in April, he was nominated as a CWC member by the Congress president, but he still decided to contest, winning with 503 votes.

The session was significant in Congress' history as Sonia attended the plenary, publicly indicating her intention to join politics. It was also during this session, that the firebrand Youth Congress leader from Bengal, Mamata Banerjee, openly rebelled against the Congress leadership by simultaneously holding an outdoor rally in Kolkata on 9 August. This ultimately led to the formation of the TMC a few months later, after breaking away from the parent Congress.

This was not the first time that Mamata had openly defied her party. In the post-Rajiv era, her relationship had been strained with the central leadership of Congress both under Rao and Kesri. During her tenure as union sports minister in Rao's government, she held a protest rally in Brigade Parade Ground in Kolkata against her own government at the Centre, on the grounds that some of her suggestions were not being implemented in the ministry. She resigned from the ministry as well. The open defiance and criticism of the Congress government by one of its own ministers caused great embarrassment for the government as well as the party. She was relieved of her portfolios but continued as a minister in the Union Cabinet without portfolio, till she was dropped in the Cabinet reshuffle of January 1993. Someone less influential would have faced serious repercussions. However, owing to her widespread popularity within West Bengal, no disciplinary action was taken against her. She even continued in her position as the Youth Congress president of West Bengal which she held till 1994.

She put Rao's government and the Congress party on the back foot once more on the issue of Terrorist and Disruptive Activities (Prevention) Act, or TADA. Enacted by the Rajiv Gandhi government, TADA was a contentious law involving two conflicting but vitally important viewpoints—a legal and institutional framework to tackle the menace of terrorism versus the protection of human rights. The Act needed to be renewed periodically, and to do so, a fresh mandate of Parliament was required in 1995. Many in the Union Cabinet and the party, including Pranab, were not in favour of renewing it but suggested replacing it with a more balanced Act, either through amendments or by introducing a new bill.

However, no one made a dramatic gesture like Mamata, who was then still a Congress MP. She walked into Parliament holding a placard that read—'Ta-Ta TADA'.

While Mamata's admirers may smile indulgently at her antics, she once again caused great embarrassment to the government and her party.

Many people, including some of the younger generation of Congress workers and leaders, tend to believe that Mamata was forced to leave the party due to intense factionalism within the West Bengal Congress. A logical corollary to this belief, bolstered by her success in demolishing the Left Front in Bengal in 2011, is that had the Congress central leadership and Pranab supported her in this battle of factionalism, she would have remained with the party and West Bengal would have had a Congress government led by Mamata. There is no doubt that there was extreme factionalism in West Bengal Congress. While going through Pranab's diaries of the period when he was the WBPCC president, or later, it was quite a challenge to stay updated on the constantly evolving dynamics of factional politics in the state, as well as the ever-shifting alliances and rearrangements among West Bengal Congress leaders. Nevertheless, it would be somewhat naive to think that just by giving her the reins of the party in West Bengal, Mamata would have been satisfied and remained with the Congress.

Two factors determined Mamata's inability to remain and operate within Congress—first, her own nature; and second, her single-minded political goal. Pranab once told me that Mamata is a law unto herself, which she had amply demonstrated by her actions over the years. She could not be bound by any party discipline, which is essential to operate within the framework of a larger national party, or even a regional party, unless she herself is the supreme boss.

More importantly, Mamata's one-point political

agenda was to fight and wrest power from the CPI (M) in West Bengal. She could not think or look beyond the state. To achieve that, she was not even averse to have an understanding with the BJP in Bengal. For the central leadership of the Congress, that was totally unacceptable. Mamata was looking for an opportune moment to quit the Congress so that she could totally focus on fighting the CPI (M) in Bengal through her own outfit, without any constraints from the shifting landscape of national politics after the demolition of Babri Masjid and Congress' response to it.

After the Babri Masjid demolition, a different political scenario emerged in India that shook the secular parties. They got alarmed not only at the rising popularity of the BJP but also at the extent to which Right-wing fanatics could go to fulfil its 'Hindutva' agenda. After the Babri Masjid demolition, an extended CWC meeting was called on 24 December 1992 in which the possibility of joint-action programmes with anti-BJP parties, including the CPI (M), were explored. Mamata strongly opposed any talk of understanding with the Left. Pranab wrote in his diary: 'Mamata is disturbed over the proposal of joint-action with the left parties. She fears that her agitational approach would receive a setback. Not just her, none of them [Bengal leaders] want joint-action with CPI (M). They feel that BJP will erode itself.'

How I wish that they were correct in their assessment!

In August 1997, Mamata went a step further and declared publicly that the BJP was not 'untouchable' and that she would do whatever was necessary in the state to fight the CPI (M). Even after her open defiance of the Congress by organizing the outdoor rally, the then Congress

President Sitaram Kesri told the media in Kolkata that no action would be taken against her. Senior Congress leaders tried to pacify her and bridge the gap between her and Somen Mitra factions in the West Bengal Congress.

Pranab met Mamata at her residence on 23 November 1997, but he felt that she was not willing to reconcile. In light of the upcoming general elections, the Congress was making vigorous efforts to maintain internal cohesion and establish alliances or engage in seat sharing with other regional political parties.

A last-ditch effort to reconcile with Mamata was made by Sonia Gandhi, who was becoming increasingly active within the Congress. A compromise formula was initiated. However, one of the conditions was that Mamata had to publicly withdraw her statement regarding the BJP and distance herself from that party. Pranab wrote in his diary on 20 December 1997:

> Yesterday a patch-up formula to solve the impasse in WBPCC was worked out. Last night Mamata was called by Sonia. Thereafter [Vincent] George[75] phoned Oscar [Fernandes] to get the approval of CP [Congress President] on dictated line. He also spoke to Somen to accept that. Somen was also requested by Kesri and he accepted it grudgingly. As per the formula: (1) Mamata was to be appointed as chairperson of the Electioneering Committee to conduct elections in West Bengal (2) The [current] PEC will be suspended (3) The Electioneering Committee would have equal numbers of both the factions (4) Mamata will withdraw her public stand on BJP (5) She would call on CP.

[75]Personal secretary to Sonia Gandhi

Leaders close to Mamata said that this was breached soon after, as Sitaram Kesri declared at a press conference in Hyderabad that Mamata had been appointed as head of the publicity committee (instead of electioneering committee) for conducting the elections.[76] However, it is important to highlight that Mamata had already filed an affidavit before the Election Commission to register TMC as a separate party on 17 December 1997, even as Sonia Gandhi was making efforts to reach a compromise.[77] More importantly, Mamata refused to publicly distance herself from the BJP. This was totally unacceptable to the Congress.

On 22 December 1997, Mamata was expelled from Congress due to her refusal to withdraw her statement about the BJP.[78] Pranab wrote on that date:

> She [Mamata] at a press conference declared that she would carry on with her Trinamool Congress. She refused to rescind her stand on BJP. It was one of the conditions that she would publicly declare her disassociation with BJP which she refused to do…how could she think that Congress will support her to overthrow left front government in Bengal with help of BJP?

As for Mamata, getting out of the Congress was necessary to fully concentrate on ousting CPI (M) from Bengal even if it meant fraternizing with the BJP. Mamata later became part of the NDA led by the BJP. In 1998, she became part of the

---

[76]Gupta, Monobina, *Didi: A Political Biography*, HarperCollins Publishers, 2012, p. 44.

[77]'Mamata Expelled From Congress, To Seek New Symbol', *Business Standard*, 23 December 1997, https://tinyurl.com/337d72df. Accessed on 5 October 2023.

[78]Ibid.

NDA, and in the second Vajpayee government in 1999, she joined the government becoming a Union Cabinet minister.

Pranab had a stormy political equation with Mamata. In 1992, during state organizational elections in West Bengal, Mamata lost narrowly to Somen Mitra for the post of WBPCC president. Mamata squarely blamed Pranab for her loss. Her supporters made scathing attacks on Pranab in the media, often crossing boundaries of decency by using unsavoury language. Pranab had a different version of the story which he wrote in his book, *The Coalition Years.*

Mamata's biographer, Shutapa Paul, wrote, 'Years later, when Pranab was rallying support to become the thirteenth President of India, Mamata would show that she had not forgotten or forgiven what had transpired during the West Bengal organizational election in 1992.'[79] Perhaps, Paul was right. Even before opposing Pranab's presidential candidature, Mamata and her associates tried to debar Pranab from contesting the Rajya Sabha elections in 1999 from West Bengal. As I learnt from Pranab's diary, Sovandeb Chattopadhyay, an MLA close to Mamata, filed an affidavit and a petition with the Election Commission in West Bengal seeking to disqualify Pranab from contesting the Rajya Sabha election. The petition was rejected. Then, they tried to field a seventh candidate which would mean that there would be a contest. The strength and configuration of the parties was such that six candidates for six available seats would have been elected uncontested. Unfortunately for them, they could not gather enough number of MLAs to support the nomination of the seventh candidate. The ploy failed.

---

[79]Paul, Shutapa, *Didi: The Untold Mamata Banerjee*, Penguin, 2018, p. 48.

Mamata's resentment against Pranab resurfaced when Pranab was awarded the Padma Vibhushan in 2008. Mamata criticized the decision to grant the award to Pranab, raising doubts about his contributions. However, this time, Pranab was in good company as Mamata's wrath was equally directed towards Ratan Tata who was awarded Padma Vibhushan the same year.[80]

I think the differences between Mamata and Pranab were perhaps due to the nature of the politics they practised and their field of operation. Mamata and her party leaders had always accused Pranab of being soft towards the Left. Without doubt, at a personal level, Pranab *did* have an excellent relationship with leaders of Left parties (especially Jyoti Basu) going back to his days in the Bangla Congress. Judging by that criterion, Pranab could be accused of being 'soft' on every political party in India whether it be the SP, BSP, JD (U), JD (S), RJD, DMK, AIADMK, TDP, BRS and even BJP, as he had an excellent rapport with leaders across party lines.

However, with regard to the Left, Pranab would have put it differently and probably termed it as 'political exigency'. While Mamata's primary focus remained on West Bengal and her efforts were directed towards removing the CPI (M) from power in the state, Pranab, as a leader at the national level, had to engage with the Left and other parties. He had to coordinate floor management in Parliament to support or oppose government bills, and address various other issues. This was particularly crucial during the UF governments when the Left (both CPI and CPI-M) was part

---

[80]'Mamata Criticises Awarding Padma Vibhusan to Pranab, Tata', *The Economic Times*, 27 January 2008, https://tinyurl.com/mrx9ezj2. Accessed on 5 October 2023.

of the coalition and Congress supported it from the outside; and later, in UPA-I when the Left supported the government from the outside. Not just at the Centre, the Congress needed support of Left parties on many occasions to keep the BJP and its allies at bay in other states as well.

An interesting entry in Pranab's diary regarding the 2002 presidential election, reveals not just the importance of 'timing' in politics but also the fact that unlike Mamata, for Pranab and the central leadership in the Congress, the primary opponent was the BJP and not the CPI (M). That year, the ruling BJP first wanted to nominate P.C. Alexander as the presidential candidate. Later on, it changed its mind and declared A.P.J. Abdul Kalam's name instead. It was a masterstroke by the Vajpayee government that put the Congress in a quandary. Earlier, the Congress had planned to convince the sitting President K.R. Narayanan to stand as a candidate of the United Opposition, or to back the then Vice President Krishan Kant. With Kalam's name being announced, Samajwadi Party (SP) Supremo Mulayam Singh Yadav, who had earlier agreed to support the United Opposition candidate, came out in Kalam's support.

There was immense pressure on Sonia Gandhi, from outside and within the party, to support Kalam. His stature and the fact that he belonged to a minority community, did not leave much choice for the Congress. Only the CPI (M) decided to oppose Kalam strongly on the ground that he was not well versed with constitutional matters, something that the political situation of the time demanded.[81]

The CWC met on 12 June 2002 to deliberate on the issue. While this was taking place at the Centre, a serious

---

[81]'Left Parties on the Presidential Elections', *Communist Party of India (Marxist)*, https://tinyurl.com/2xducv4w. Accessed on 23 October 2023.

political upheaval was unfolding in Maharashtra. The ruling coalition government of the Congress, Nationalist Congress Party (NCP) and few other parties faced a major challenge from its Opposition in the state: the BJP–Shiv Sena alliance. The government needed to survive a confidence motion on the floor of the Assembly and prove its majority on 13 June, the day after the CWC meeting. In the CWC meeting, Pranab said that there should be no 'tearing hurry' to announce the Congress party's stand on Kalam. He proposed waiting until the following day, as the Congress–NCP government in Maharashtra required the support of two CPI (M) MLAs. Therefore, it would be counterproductive to antagonize the Left just one day prior to the crucial floor test in that state. Pranab further wrote in his diary that Jaipal Reddy insisted that the media was eagerly waiting to know Congress' views. Pranab retorted, 'We cannot take decisions as per desire of media.' The next day, the Maharashtra government passed the floor test by a narrow margin of 10 votes. The same day, the Congress declared its support for Kalam's candidature.

There was one occasion when Pranab made a strong but silent statement about his ideological differences with the Left, in his own fashion. On 14 August 1997, a midnight session in Parliament was convened to celebrate 50 years of India's independence. Pranab wrote in his diary that he did not attend the session as Indrajit Gupta, one of the senior-most members of the CPI and the then home minister of the UF government was seated on the dais. Pranab's opposition to it was not due to any personal animosity, but due to a historical ideological difference between the Congress and the Left. Pranab wrote that Gupta and his party did not recognize 15 August 1947 as the day that India gained freedom. As per their communist belief, no country could be truly free unless it frees itself from the 'shackles of capitalism'. In 1947, as the entire nation was celebrating the historic moment of gaining independence after 200 years of colonial rule, the members of the undivided CPI went along with its stated position: '*Yeh azaadi jhooti hai* (This freedom is a false dawn).' Pranab found it ironic that a political party, which initially refused to recognize the independence of India and the Congress-led freedom movement had now become part of the government through the political process of parliamentary democracy (that emerged from that very freedom struggle) and was now part of the official government celebration as well.

Pranab had a good personal relationship with Mamata. He admired her fighting spirit, her connect with people and her sense of timing (which is so important in politics). For several years, I had observed Mamata di regularly visiting our home. She would dine with us, engage in conversations with my mother in her bedroom and occasionally enquire why I hadn't pursued a career in politics. Whenever she would come to meet Pranab, she would chastise Hiralal, Pranab's peon for many years, for serving Pranab too many cups of coffee. It's not good for his heath, she would say.

However, in politics, important decisions are taken by leaders on the basis of their political goals, and not on their personal relationships. Pranab had good personal relationship with Advani too, but that didn't mean that Advani would support his presidential bid. I fail to understand what political goal Mamata meant to achieve by vehemently opposing Pranab's candidature for the presidency, particularly since he was the only candidate from Bengal in post-Independence India, and she was formally part of the UPA-II government. It is still a mystery to me. When I asked Pranab about it, he just said that she's unpredictable. But he was confident that she would turn around and eventually support him in the presidential race. And she did. Perhaps, that is what Mamata Banerjee is—an enigma!

❧

While Mamata's behaviour may have been rather inexplicable, the increasing clamour within the Congress party to replace Kesri with Sonia Gandhi as Congress president seemed understandable. After the declaration of the results of the general elections in 1998, it became even more pronounced. The party won only 141 seats and its vote share plummeted from 39.5 per cent in 1989 to 25.9 per cent in 1998.[82] Pranab was personally dissatisfied with Kesri's leadership, as he believed that Kesri's political ambition did not align with his ability to lead the party or his political foresight.

Interestingly, Sonia's elevation as Congress president was quite a dramatic event, and Pranab had a role to play in it. Though Pranab's own relationship with Sonia was nothing remarkable, he believed that it would benefit the party if she assumed leadership. In his diary, he evaluated the pros and cons of Sonia taking over as Congress president. He wrote that she was intelligent and showed 'exemplary dignity' by refusing Congress presidentship after Rajiv's assassination. Being a member of the

[82]Mukherjee, Pranab, *The Coalition Years: 1996–2012*, Rupa Publications, 2017, p. 44.

Gandhi–Nehru family, she would be able to keep top-level factionalism at bay and keep the party united. In terms of drawbacks, he had concerns that her lack of political experience could make her vulnerable to the influence of a politically inexperienced group, just as her husband had been. But the most compelling reason in Pranab's mind in favour of Sonia was that he felt 10 Janpath would continue to remain a major power centre within the Congress. Even a senior and experienced political leader like Rao was not able to diminish its importance. Rather than remaining an outside source of power and influence, Pranab felt that it would be better if she took over officially so that authority, along with responsibility, could be streamlined and legitimized.

However, Congress leaders were faced with a complicated problem. In the Congress constitution, there was no provision for removing a president other than voluntary resignation. Senior party leaders including Dr Manmohan Singh, Pranab, A.K. Anthony and others tried to persuade Kesri to resign, but without any success. He issued a press statement indicating his intention to step down in favour of Sonia Gandhi, should she be willing to assume leadership. However, he later clarified that he would tender his resignation only after convening an AICC session. Kesri did not provide any assurance or indication of his intention to act quickly. Additionally, he did not send a formal resignation letter to the CWC.

Pranab was asked to find a solution to the deadlock. After studying the Congress Constitution carefully, he discovered a clause that says, 'In extraordinary situation, the CWC can resort to appropriate solutions not mentioned in the Constitution, but subject to the ratification of such a decision by the AICC within six months.'[83] Though it did not say anything specifically about removal of a president, the non-specific nature of the clause regarding an 'extraordinary situation' did not preclude it either.

On the morning of 14 March 1998, a large number of CWC members met at Pranab's residence to discuss a letter that Pranab had drafted, urging Kesri to promptly convene a CWC meeting in order to address the uncertainty that arose after his 'resignation'. All the CWC members present there signed the letter. Oscar Fernandes was given the unpleasant task of handing over the letter to Kesri, and of requesting him to immediately call a CWC meeting, failing which the requisitioning members of the CWC would call a meeting themselves and take appropriate action. Another resolution invoking the power of the CWC, under the specified clause to take appropriate action in extraordinary circumstances was drafted. It further thanked Sitaram Kesri for his offer to relinquish his office to Sonia Gandhi (as reported in the media earlier).

At the CWC meeting, Kesri refused to take any cognizance of the letter and walked out in a huff. Jitendra Prasada then presided over the meeting and a resolution to request Sonia Gandhi to take charge as Congress president was adopted unanimously. Sonia came to the AICC in the evening and assumed charge. The rest is history.

As the twentieth century was drawing to a close, its last decade witnessed a few landmark moments in Indian politics—the first minority government in post-Independence India headed by Narasimha Rao that lasted a full term and initiated major economic reforms; a

---

[83]Ibid. 39.

period of uncertainty that saw three general elections with three PMs; and thereafter, the electorate voting the first non-Congress government into power that lasted for full five years.

In his personal life, Pranab suffered some terrible losses. Within a span of six months, there were three deaths in the family. Pranab's elder sister Annapurna's son and my cousin died by suicide. Another sister Swagata's husband succumbed to cancer. Pranab knew him even before he got married to my aunt and depended on him substantially on family matters. But the most devastating loss for him, was the demise of his mother Rajlakshmi Devi on 22 November 1999 at the age of 89. Pranab wrote in his diary that he just sat next to her quietly, thinking of her suffering and the sacrifices she had made for the family. He felt sad that his mother could not be there with him to usher in the new millennium. For him and for us, it was truly the end of an era.

chapter 7

The Man for all Seasons

On 13 May 2004, Pranab finally succeeded in fulfilling a long-cherished dream of winning his first Lok Sabha election from Jangipur in West Bengal. In his political life of 35 years till then, Pranab was an elected member of the Rajya Sabha five times, but a victory by the direct mandate of the people eluded him. He had contested and lost two Lok Sabha elections earlier. Though the members of the Rajya Sabha enjoy the same powers and privileges as Lok Sabha members, except for voting or making amendments to finance bills, Pranab always harboured the aspiration to enter Parliament through the direct mandate of the people. He felt hurt and humiliated by his political detractors calling him a 'rootless wanderer', who had never won an election by popular mandate. Jangipur changed that. In his first post-election rally in the constituency, a visibly emotional Pranab expressed his gratitude to the people of Jangipur for taking this stigma off him.

His choice of constituency was rather unusual. A rural, underdeveloped hamlet bordering Bangladesh, Jangipur was a bastion of the then ruling party of Bengal, CPI (M). Since its delineation as a Lok Sabha constituency in 1971, Congress had won there only twice before—in 1971 and 1996. It was a Muslim majority constituency having 66.27

per cent Muslims, as per 2011 census. The only Hindu MP was a CPI (M) leader who won in 1977.

Upon reading his diaries, I learnt that he was also considering other constituencies in West Bengal as an option. But three factors tilted his decision in favour of Jangipur. First, he had a strong preference for rural constituencies, which he had also mentioned to me on multiple occasions. Second, the neighbouring constituency of Baharampur was a stronghold of Congress leader Adhir Ranjan Chowdhury. It was Adhir who insisted and convinced Pranab to contest from Jangipur. Third, his trusted aides and local leaders from the constituency, Samar Mukherjee and Mohammed Sohrab, conducted a survey in the constituency and returned with encouraging findings. Pranab later told me that even if he would have lost, the Congress would not have had to sacrifice a 'good seat' where they had a good chance of winning. It may sound paradoxical, but makes sense considering Pranab's inability to win Lok Sabha elections on earlier occasions and his resultant lack of confidence. After all, Adhir's influence in the area had not helped previous Congress candidates win elections.

However, Pranab felt that as his stature as a national leader had grown considerably since the last time he had contested the Lok Sabha elections in 1980, it could be a deciding factor. This would also keep the intense local factionalism within the Congress at bay. This was also reflected in the survey done by Samar and Sohrab. Pranab decided to take a leap of faith and succeeded this time.

However, it was not smooth sailing all the way. West Bengal is notorious for political violence and booth capturing by the ruling parties. On 10 May 2004, the day of polling, Pranab wrote in his diary:

> Got the report of booth capturing at Sekh Dighi High School. I rushed there and gave a dressing down to the presiding officer who in collaboration with CPI (M) allowed the CPI (M) goons to drive out the Congress agents and went on pressing the button. When I chided the presiding officer, the local CPI (M) cadres armed with swords etc gheraod me. However, the police intervened.

Sonia, like her mother-in-law, was not in favour of Pranab contesting the election. 'Even Ahmed Patel was also not comfortable with the idea. (sic) But both of them were pleasantly surprised when the results were declared,' Pranab wrote in his diary. His victory brought him immense joy, to the point where he felt comfortable poking fun at himself. At the opening session of the fourteenth Lok Sabha, Pranab welcomed the newly elected members of the Congress in the CLP (Congress Legislative Party) meeting by saying that he was welcoming them 'as the oldest Congress member in the Parliament and one of the newest members in Lok Sabha'. As he wrote in his book, everyone laughed.[84]

It was the Congress that had the last laugh after the election results. The pre-poll surveys by various agencies predicted a comfortable win for the NDA, led by then PM Vajpayee. In fact, PM Vajpayee was so confident about winning that he actually preponed the elections by a few months. However, the party's high profile 'Shining India' campaign failed to impress voters. The result was a fractured mandate. The Congress emerged as the single

---

[84]Mukherjee, Pranab, *The Coalition Years: 1996-2012*, Rupa Publications, 2017, p. 68.

largest party with 145 seats followed by the BJP with 138. The Congress went into elections with informal alliances and seat-sharing arrangements with various regional parties. Post elections, all these parties along with the Left parties came together to form the UPA. The Left parties with a record of 61 seats decided not to join the government but to support it from outside on the basis of a Common Minimum Programme (CMP).

As the president of the single largest party to win the elections, Sonia Gandhi was tipped to be the PM. She even had the full support of the coalition partners. The Constitution of India does not discriminate against any person from holding the office of PM irrespective of his/her origin, as long as the person is a citizen of India. But the BJP launched a rancorous campaign against the Congress regarding Sonia's foreign origin issue, and threatened to take it all over India.

Sonia renounced her claim to be the PM—a decision that took the entire nation, including her own party colleagues and coalition partners, by surprise. Pranab's diary entries from those days contain very sketchy details, perhaps indicating a lack of time owing to a busy and hectic schedule filled with meetings and consultations with various stakeholders.

On 17 May 2004, he wrote, 'Sonia Gandhi decides to withdraw from Prime Ministerial candidature. BJP's vicious campaign. Myself, Manmohan, Arjun, Ahmed Patel and Ghulam Nabi were called. We are stunned.' On 18 May, he wrote, 'Sonia Gandhi sticks to her decision. Countrywide agitation. Allies are also shocked. CPP meeting emotionally surcharged. Appeal to her to reconsider. Work up to 1 am.' On 19 May, almost with a sigh of relief, he wrote,

'Issues resolved. Manmohan Singh becomes PM designate. Manmohan and Soniaji met President and the President was pleased to give mandate to form the government to Manmohan Singh.'

Though at that time he didn't write anything more, on 31 December, while recounting major events of the year, Pranab wrote, 'Most surprising was the amazing sacrifice of Sonia Gandhi by refusing to accept the Prime Ministership of the country despite pressure from within the party and outside. Her decision saved the country from a bitter confrontation between BJP and Congress.'

THE PM INDIA NEVER HAD

Following Sonia's decision to withdraw from the prime ministerial race, there was intense speculation within the media and political spheres. The names of Dr Manmohan Singh and Pranab were being discussed as the top contenders for the position. I did not have the chance to meet Baba for a couple of days as he was terribly busy, but I spoke to him over the phone. I asked him excitedly if he was going to become the PM. His response was blunt, 'No, she will not make me the PM. It'll be Manmohan Singh.' He added, 'But she should announce it fast. This uncertainty is not good for the country.'

If Pranab harboured any disappointment about not being named the PM, it did not reflect in his diaries. He told journalist Suman Chattopadhyay that he did not have any expectation from Sonia to make him the PM. If there's no expectation, there's no disappointment as well.[85]

---

[85]Chattopadhyay, Suman, *Prathom Nagarik*, Karigar Publishers, 2017, p. 290.

Pranab knew that Sonia had a close relationship with Dr Singh. As Congress President in 1998 during the Vajpayee government, she appointed Dr Singh as the LoP in Rajya Sabha. Dr Singh either headed or was a member of almost all the important committees that Sonia had formed. In 1999, after the fall of the 13-month-old Vajpayee government, Sonia made a futile attempt to form the government. In her conversation with then President K.R. Narayanan, she reportedly proposed Dr Singh's name to lead her party's government as the PM.[86] There is every possibility that Pranab knew about it.

Before the Lok Sabha elections in 1999, Pranab wrote in his diary, 'Dr. Singh contesting from South Delhi. He is expected to win the seat. He is the likely PM candidate for Congress. It'll have a good impact on electorate.' Though his expectation of Dr Singh's victory and the impact on the electorate came to naught, as the BJP took the lead and formed the next government, it is quite clear that even in 1999, Pranab had foreseen the possibility of Dr Singh becoming the PM in the event of a Congress victory. Hence, it could not have come as a major surprise or disappointment to him when Sonia chose Dr Singh over him in 2004.

It is generally believed that Pranab had a chance to become the PM earlier in 1984 as well, after Indira Gandhi's assassination, and not just in 2004. Moreover, according to M.L. Fotedar, Pranab's name was suggested as PM on another occasion by none other than the then President R. Venkataraman. Fotedar wrote in his autobiography that after the fall of the V.P. Singh government in 1990, he went

---

[86]Kidwai, Rasheed, *Sonia: A Biography*, Penguin India, 2011, p. 123.

to meet Venkataraman to request him to invite Rajiv to form the government as the leader of the single largest party in the Lok Sabha. He further wrote, 'On this, the president directed me, with an emphasis of authority, that I may put it to Rajiv Gandhi that if he supported Mr. Pranab Mukherjee to be prime minister, he would administer the oath of office to him that same evening.'[87]

There is no way to ascertain the veracity of this claim. There is no mention of any such possibility in Pranab's diaries. I know that Fotedar had come to meet Pranab and presented him the book after its publication in 2015. Pranab must have read the book too, or at least glanced through it, but there is no mention of the content of the book in his diaries. It's unlikely that Venkataraman, himself a consummate politician, would propose such a thing. It is a well-known fact that Rajiv gave outside support to Chandra Shekhar to form the government. Nevertheless, I found it to be an interesting anecdote, perhaps to be taken with a pinch of salt.

So, did Pranab actually harbour the ambition to become India's PM? People have often asked me this question. I posed this question to my father many years ago, perhaps during the UPA-I era. It happened on a rare evening when Pranab arrived home early. There were no long queues of visitors waiting to meet him or too many files to be cleared. He seemed relaxed, and we engaged in a casual conversation. Although I don't recall the exact context, I enquired if he aspired to become the PM someday. His response was emphatic.

---

[87]Fotedar, M.L., *The Chinar Leaves: A Political Memoir*, HarperCollins, 2015, p. 259.

Pranab: Of course, I would like to be the prime minister. Any politician worth his salt has this ambition. But just because I want it does not necessarily mean I am going to get it.

Me: Why not? Do something, talk to Sonia Gandhi.

Pranab: And say what? I am not like you that if I don't get something I want, I create a ruckus.

Me [with indignation]: I create [a] ruckus when I don't get something?

Pranab: Yes! Ask your mother. She'll fully agree with me.

Sensing that the conversation was getting into uncomfortable territory, I quickly changed the topic without realizing then that my father had manoeuvred the change with the practised ease of a master politician. In our conversations over the years, I felt that he was not really comfortable talking about it. If I probed beyond a point, he would either change the subject deftly or would get irritated and snap at me.

However, I came to my own conclusions. Pranab definitely had the desire to be the PM, but he also came to terms with the fact that he was not going to become one. In the diaries of his early years in politics in the 1970s, he deliberated on personal qualities required to be a successful political activist. He wrote, '[To be] always alert, always active and develop objectivity, most importantly the ability to absorb disappointments are necessary.' Over the years, he learnt how to absorb disappointments. To begin with, Pranab was not born with a silver spoon. He had to struggle relentlessly to achieve the position he attained solely through his own merit and hard work. Indira Gandhi mentored him, but she did it because she found merit and grit in the young politician. Pranab had to earn her confidence. When Pranab started his political life, in all probability, he did not even think that he would reach Rashtrapati Bhavan one day. It could be that he lacked that unswerving ambition that makes a person move mountains to achieve their goals. He was quite aware of his limitations of not being a mass leader. He accepted the fact that he would never be the number one person in terms of trustworthiness with Sonia. He was also a deeply religious person who believed in destiny. Perhaps, he felt and accepted that it was not in his destiny to become the PM. He was grateful for what he got in life, rather than being bitter about what he did not get.

Strangely, I felt that he did not have any rancour against Sonia for not making him the PM, and definitely not against Dr Singh. Pranab had the ability to see an issue from the other person's perspective. During his presidential years, he told me that in the cut-throat world of politics, every one safeguards their interests first. Sonia was simply safeguarding her own interests and that of her family's, by choosing someone whom she trusted to not challenge her authority. What followed was an interesting conversation that is still etched in my memory.

Me: Would you have challenged her authority?

Pranab: Whether I would or wouldn't have is not the question. She probably felt that I would. She had the power to choose the PM. She did what she thought was right. What's there to argue about it?

Me: But you would have made a better prime minister…

Pranab: That's your subjective opinion. You think your father would have been a better PM. Manmohan Singh's daughters would have an entirely different point of view. Rahul Gandhi would think that his father was the best prime minister ever. Sonia Gandhi would think that her husband was even better than Indira Gandhi. That's not the way to evaluate.

Me: Who was the best prime minister in your opinion?

Pranab: Undoubtedly, Pt Nehru. He was a visionary, a statesman, builder of institutions, architect of modern India… No one can come near him.

Me: Not even Indira Gandhi?

Pranab: She had her strengths, but not a patch on her father.

Then he added with a mischievous smile, 'But if the daughter was the father, the entire Kashmir would have been ours.' He then proceeded to pick up a book, which served as the indication that the conversation had ended.

Even if Pranab felt any hurt or disappointment for not becoming the PM, it was assuaged by none other than Dr Manmohan Singh. Years later, when Pranab was no longer the president and Dr Singh was no longer the PM, at the book launch of Pranab's book *The Coalition Years*, Dr Singh said, 'He [Pranab] had every reason to feel a grievance that he was better qualified than I was to become the prime minister, but he also knew that I had no choice in the matter.'[88] His comment left the audience, which included Sonia and Rahul, in splits. Dr Singh further described Pranab as the 'most distinguished living parliamentarian and Congressman'. He went on to say, '[…] he is the greatest politician living in the country.'[89]

That night, Pranab was as happy as a child. He expressed his admiration for the former PM, describing him as a gracious gentleman.

WORKING THROUGH COALITIONS

Sonia Gandhi did not make Pranab the PM, but she did give him the option to choose his ministry. After Dr Singh's name was announced, I had the opportunity to meet Baba. Curious about his upcoming role, I enquired about which ministry he would be assigned to. With confidence, he responded that it would either be Home or External Affairs. He was the chairperson of the Parliamentary Standing Committee on Home Affairs during Vajpayee's tenure and was familiar with the ministry.

But he got neither Home nor External Affairs, and learnt about it at the swearing-in ceremony at Rashtrapati Bhavan on 22 May 2004. After the function, my mother, other family members and I returned home. Baba was to come back later on his own. I vividly recall sitting in the bedroom with my mother when he entered, appearing somewhat bewildered. 'They are giving me Defence now,' he said, looking at me. 'I don't know anything about the

---

[88]'Pranab Mukherjee Was More Qualified to Become PM but He Knew I Had No Choice, Says Former PM Manmohan Singh', *Outlook*, 14 October 2017, https://tinyurl.com/2u6z967u. Accessed on 6 October 2023.
[89]Ibid.

ministry. How am I going to handle it?' he added. When I asked him what had happened, he just shrugged and went off to his home office where a number of visitors were waiting to meet him.

Many years later, I learnt from his diaries what had actually transpired. On 20 May, two days before the swearing-in, he had to meet Sonia, Dr Singh and others regarding government formation and accommodating coalition partners. Pranab worked out a formula for ministerial berths for the alliance partners, depending on the strength of their numbers in the Lok Sabha. It was further decided to keep the big four—Finance, Home, External Affairs and Defence—and some other ministries like Petroleum, HRD, I&B, etc., with the Congress. After the meeting, Sonia asked Pranab to stay back. In Pranab's own words, 'She asked my preference of ministry. She said that she will accommodate me first and then others. I asked for Home or External Affairs indicating Home would be the first choice. She said she will give me my preference.'

But that changed within a day. Pranab noted in his diary that on 22 May, during the swearing-in ceremony in which he took oath after the PM, Dr Singh informed him that Sonia had had a change of heart and wanted him to hold the Defence portfolio instead of Home. Pranab further wrote, 'Home is a political ministry and a lot of work could have been done there. After the swearing-in, I asked Soniaji. She told me "Except you, I do not find anyone who can clear the mess at the Defence ministry." So what could I say? I had no choice.'

As I read this, I thought of another incident which took place three years later. In 2007, before the presidential election, there was speculation about Pranab's name as a possible Congress candidate. The Left parties had proposed his name to Sonia. Pranab was also keen. Sonia met Pranab and told him that she would happily nominate him as the presidential candidate, on the condition that Pranab finds a replacement for himself. She told him that he was indispensable for the government and in Parliament, and could not be spared. Pranab might have felt flattered by the compliment but it did not serve his purpose. Sonia knew how to deal a blow gently.

Over time, Pranab developed a close and warm working relationship with Sonia. Even though Pranab had played a crucial role in solving a critical impediment to her assumption of the role of Congress president, the relationship was distant in the beginning.

Pranab's personal loyalty towards any political leader began and ended with Indira Gandhi. After Indira, Pranab served the Congress but not any individual leader. Though he felt that her taking over would be beneficial for the party, it was not due to a sense of any personal loyalty towards her. Sonia must have had a strong intuition about it. But unlike Rajiv, she did not try to push Pranab to the periphery. Unlike Rajiv, she did not have the numbers either. When Sonia assumed leadership of the Congress after the general elections in 1998, the Congress tally in the Lok Sabha had come down to 141 seats. Even in 2004, though the Congress became the single largest party by winning 145 seats, Sonia perhaps needed every political mind within the Congress to stitch the alliance and keep it going. She was a pragmatic politician.

However, Pranab and Sonia's relationship had thawed much before 2004. Sonia could see the value in Pranab's knowledge of a vast range of subjects and his experience in both politics and governance, and she called upon his expertise as and when required.

Pranab felt that Sonia was intelligent, hardworking and keen to learn. Once he told me that unlike many political leaders, her biggest strength was that she knew and recognized her weaknesses and was willing to work hard to overcome them. She knew that she lacked political experience but worked hard to understand the complexities of Indian politics and society. For this, she not only depended on her political colleagues, but actively sought guidance from academicians, subject-experts and social activists. Pranab shared anecdotes with Sonia from the time Indira was in power, and discussed their approach to challenging political and governance matters. Another quality of Sonia's that Pranab noticed was her ability to listen. She delegated work and made various committees. On any issue, she would first listen to the viewpoints of the members and then decide. Sometimes, she would change her mind even after a decision was taken—a tendency which irked Pranab at times. But, on occasions, he wrote in his diaries, that it also showed her lack of rigidity. Pranab's earlier fear of Sonia relying too heavily on a coterie due to her lack of experience turned out to be unfounded. As per Pranab, Sonia had her close advisers but she did not follow anyone's advice blindly. He once told me that the Gandhis (Sonia and her children) do not trust anyone completely except each other. Given their experiences in life, perhaps, it is understandable.

Pranab and Sonia formed their own equation. Pranab had strong views on issues, and he did not hesitate to express those 'firmly' and 'frankly'—two words he often used in his diaries—during internal meetings. He did so during Indira's time as well. Indira modified her views many times after listening to Pranab's arguments. When she didn't, she would tell Pranab, 'You said what you had to say. Now go and do what I am telling you.' Once a decision was taken, even when it was contrary to his own opinion, Pranab did his best to implement it as per the decided party line. He accepted that Sonia was the boss and the final decisions on matters related to the party and the coalition were hers.

On her part, though Sonia could not trust Pranab enough to make him the PM, she came to value his sage advice and political management skills, especially during the crucial years of UPA-I and -II. During UPA-I, she introduced Pranab to Jacob G. Zuma, the visiting president of African National Congress (who later became president of South Africa) as 'the senior-most Congress leader, leader of Lok Sabha and who virtually runs the government'.

Sonia tolerated Pranab's temper-tantrums and handled it skilfully, even humouring him at times. There is an interesting entry in Pranab's diary, dated 22 November 2006. It was the beginning of the Parliament session. During a meeting on the upcoming session, Pranab lost his cool. Writing about the incident, he noted, 'Soniaji suddenly whispered in my ear "you are the boss of the Parliament". The way she said it, I could not help smiling and I calmed down.'

I came across another interesting entry written during Barack Obama's first visit to India as the US president. Obama later wrote in his memoirs *A Promised Land*, 'We are told of the handsomeness of men like Charlie Crist and Rahm Emanuel, but not the beauty of women, except for one or two instance, as in the case of Sonia Gandhi.'[90] Pranab was not the kind to comment on anyone's appearance or physical attributes, irrespective of gender. But, on the occasion of PM's dinner for Obama, he could not help but notice Sonia and later commented in his diary, 'Soniaji was looking really beautiful with her light make-up and select jewellery.'

However, there were also occasions of serious tension. On 5 April 2005, Pranab wrote in his diary that he was being 'given hell' by Sonia and others. The contentious issue revolved around the granting of an alleged 'clean chit' to George Fernandes, who faced accusations of multiple scams while serving as the defence minister during the NDA regime, which is when the Kargil War occurred. In response to the intense pressure of the Opposition over allegations of serious irregularities in the emergency procurements made during the Kargil War, the NDA government ordered a special CAG audit. Based on the CAG report, a Public Interest Litigation (PIL) was filed in the Supreme Court alleging a loss of ₹2,175 crore to the exchequer. In response to the PIL, in 2005 an Under Secretary at the Defence Ministry submitted an affidavit in the court stating that the relaxation of procedures for procuring weapons, and other defence-related materials, made by the NDA government in the wake of the Kargil war were not in violation of the financial rules of the government or the Defence Procurement Procedures of 1992. These were made to simplify the procedures and shorten the time frame for imports, keeping in mind the exigencies of the

---

[90]'What Barack Obama Says about Sonia Gandhi's "Beauty" in His Memoir "A Promised Land"', *Times Now*, 13 November 2020, https://tinyurl.com/2fn6d8y5. Accessed on 6 October 2023.

war situation. Fernandes immediately declared that he was being given a 'clean chit' by the UPA government.

All hell broke loose within the Congress and UPA. Pranab explained that it was not a 'clean chit'. The affidavit did not mention Fernandes or any other person. It simply stated that the validity or the legality of the modified procedures were not in question. It did not give any confirmation regarding whether these procedures were executed accurately or not. For that, the government was preparing to file a second affidavit (which it did subsequently) referring these cases to the Central Bureau of Investigation (CBI).

But Sonia was livid, and taking a cue from her some Congress leaders and ministers in the government attacked Pranab viciously. Rumours circulated in the media suggesting that he would be dropped from the Cabinet. The Left parties and other allies too were up-in-arms against him.

Pranab felt so harassed that he submitted his resignation to the PM. On 7 April, he wrote in his diary, 'Disgusted with this orchestrated campaign against me, I offered my resignation letter to PM. He however requested me with folded hands to withdraw the same.' Ten days later, on 18 April he wrote, 'Sonia Gandhi is still upset with me. I explained to her the whole sequence of events and their implication [...] I don't know for how long I will be in this ministry. However, I would not like to precipitate any crisis and because of that I did not press for acceptance of my resignation.'

But the storm blew over. Going by his diaries, things seemed to be back to normal within the next few days. He continued to be the defence minister for another one-and-a-half years.

ADVENTURES AWAY FROM HOME

Blissfully unaware (most of the time) of my father's travails, I was busy looking for opportunities to travel to exotic destinations during his tenure as the defence minister. As a result, I accompanied him to two incredible places that are not typically visited by tourists.

In August 2004, I accompanied my father to the Siachen Glacier, often termed as the 'highest battlefield in the world'. The glacier and its frontier posts are known for having the most extreme conditions in the world. Winter temperatures that can drop to below -60°C, low oxygen saturation levels (at merely 10 per cent of the levels in plains), snow storms, strong winds and avalanches, coupled with enemy shelling, truly push the boundaries of human courage and endurance.

We arrived at the Siachen base camp on a bright and sunny day, followed by a visit to Kumar Post. The special winter clothing that we were given and the warm, welcoming smiles of our soldiers helped ward off the cold. Now, the area between Siachen base camp (at 12,000 ft) and Kumar Post (at 15,000 ft) has been opened to trekkers. Back then, it was closed to civilians. Luckily, the army did not consider the Defence Minister's daughter a security threat and allowed me to accompany him. It was a once-in-a-lifetime opportunity and I could not have missed it. Today, sitting in the cosy comfort of my room, I can only salute the fortitude of our valiant soldiers and bow my head in gratitude at the immense sacrifices they make to keep us safe.

Another memorable visit was a trip to Antarctica. Pranab was to embark on an official tour to Chile in

October 2005. The Chilean government also extended an invitation to him to visit the country's research base in Antarctica during the trip. My father made the mistake of mentioning it to me. He did not like taking family members to official trips abroad. But as I heard this, I did not give him much choice. I joined him on the trip to Chile, and together we ventured to Antarctica on 29 October.

The evening prior, we travelled to Punta Arenas, one of the last large cities in the Southern Hemisphere. From there, we were scheduled to fly by a military aircraft provided by the Chilean government to King George Island, where the Chilean research centre was located. However, the following morning, we were informed that the trip had to be cancelled due to unfavourable weather conditions. This news brought about an hour of profound disappointment and despair. Yet, shortly after, we received word that the weather was improving and that we still might have a chance to proceed with our journey. I cannot recall my exact reaction to this news, but fortunately, it seemed to be in sync with others in our group. Pranab wrote in his diary, 'Munni went wild with excitement, so were others.' Though Pranab tried to act nonchalant, he too must have been equally thrilled as he wrote after the trip, 'It was a lifetime experience.'

King George Island is the largest island belonging to the group of South Shetland Islands in Antarctica. We were driven around in motorized sledges around the island. The scene was straight out of a National Geographic documentary. At one point, I got so excited that I just started running and rolling on the snow. Though my father was quite embarrassed by my behaviour, others laughed and some even joined me, perhaps to show diplomatic solidarity.

The Indian flag was hoisted at the Chilean base in Pranab's honour and he saluted the flag.

It was the farthest that we had travelled from home. The distance from there to New Delhi was 23,361 km, more than half the circumference of Earth, which is around 40,000 km. But though we were far, we were not cut off. To my great astonishment, I realized that our mobile phones had signals. I spoke to my mom. My dad spoke to her, as well as the PM and Sonia. Sadly, our Indian research centres in Antarctica have no such luxuries as those are situated far deeper in the polar region. There are no air strips and these stations can be reached only by ships. I remember Pranab interacting with our scientists based there through satellite phones, both as defence minister and later as president.

For me, the journey itself was as exciting (if not more) as the destination. Immediately after take-off from Punta Arenas, one of the crew members asked me if I would like to go to the cockpit. I jumped at the offer. The view from the cockpit was simply breathtaking. The sky was turned upside down, a vast shimmering veil of blue with icebergs floating around like clouds of varied shapes and sizes. Sensing my excitement, the pilot allowed me to remain in the cockpit throughout the duration of the flight, even at the time of landing. As we approached the landing, I could see nothing but a patch of land full of snow and ice. As the aircraft touched down and skidded across the icy ground at breakneck speed, before coming to a halt, I couldn't help but wonder if I would freeze to death before drowning, and how painful it would be if the aircraft plunged into the icy depths of the ocean. With my heart in my mouth, I feared that a journey to the 'end of the world' could probably become the end of my journey in this world.

But obviously, nothing untoward happened as I am still alive to tell the tale. After spending six hours in Antarctica, we were back to civilization with some extraordinary and delightful memories.

COALITIONS, COMPULSIONS AND COMPROMISES

Pranab's contributions in managing the UPA governments have been well recorded and duly recognized. Described by various epithets—Mr Indispensable, chief trouble shooter, the 'go-to' man of UPA, fire-fighter and more—Pranab's proficiency in governance and statecraft, as well as his decades of experience in politics were thoroughly tested throughout his tenure in both UPA governments.

The first UPA government in 2004 was formed with the outside support of the Left front, as mentioned earlier. Having a sizable number of 61 MPs, the Left exercised considerable influence and pressure on the government. Almost from the beginning, it was a turbulent relationship. While the Left supported social legislations and empowering Acts that were part of the CMP, they were opposed to the economic reform agenda of the Manmohan Singh government. Several government bills and initiatives like foreign direct investment (FDI) in retail, increasing FDI cap in telecommunication, insurance and civil aviation, Pension Fund Regulatory and Development Authority Bill, banking reforms and other issues faced stiff resistance from the Left. The government could push its way through in some cases, but had to shelve others.

There are many entries in Pranab's diaries of that period where he felt unhappy about the obstacles created by the Left in carrying out the government's reform agenda. While he understood the Left's 'ideological and political compulsions', he felt that by choosing to remain outside the government, they were indulging in the exercise of authority without any responsibility.

Other than economic reforms, another major point of contention with the Left was foreign policy. During UPA-I, India's bilateral ties with the US acquired new depth. As the EAM in the Narasimha Rao government, and as defence minister in UPA-I, Pranab felt the need to forge closer ties with the US in the post-Cold War world. While being a strong votary of maintaining India's traditional relationship with Russia, he felt that it was necessary to reduce India's dependence on Russia for its security requirements in the long run. He wrote in his book:

> The dismemberment of the erstwhile Soviet Union posed, in its wake, new problems. Many of the famed defence industries of the erstwhile super power were established in the Commonwealth of Independent States (CIS) countries. Consequently, not only were there enormous delays bedevilling the implementation of projects concluded with the former Soviet Union, but even servicing and sourcing of spare parts had also become very difficult [...] The time has come to engage with the US and I directed the [Defence] ministry to work towards building closer ties with the Pentagon.[91]

On 28 June 2005, Pranab and the then US Secretary of Defence Donald Rumsfeld signed the historic 'New Framework for India–US Defence Relations'—a roadmap

---

[91]Mukherjee, Pranab, *The Coalition Years: 1996-2012,* Rupa Publications, 2017, p. 91.

for establishing closer defence relations between the two nations in the coming decade.[92] Under this broad umbrella, the air forces of the two nations were to conduct a joint exercise at the Kalaikunda Air Base in West Bengal in November that year.

This triggered a major crisis which threatened the stability of the government. The joint exercise was to begin from 7 November. On 3 November, Pranab's diary entry began on an ominous note: 'There is a serious crisis.' Pranab received a call from Buddhadeb Bhattacharjee, the then CM of the Left-ruled West Bengal. He told Pranab that they would hold a massive demonstration against the joint exercise with the US which could turn violent. Additionally, he mentioned that he would not have the ability to maintain control if the situation escalated into violence.

Pranab firmly conveyed to Buddhadeb that the exercise could not be shifted or delayed since defence activities could not be influenced by political vagaries. He explained that these were routine exercises and, in fact, the fourth such exercise with the US. He also caustically reminded the CM that he should not forget that his Finance Minister would be visiting the US soon to invite potential investors to his state. But Buddhadeb remained adamant. Pranab immediately informed the PM and an urgent meeting was called. The PM himself spoke to Buddhadeb but without any result.

The following morning, another meeting was called at the PM's residence, which was attended by Sonia as well. Pranab explained the gravity of the situation. If the demonstration was to turn violent and some untoward

[92]Ibid. 93.

incidents were to occur against the defence forces, the central government would have no option but to dismiss the state government in West Bengal and impose President's Rule. In that eventuality, the Left would definitely withdraw support, and the central government, in all likelihood, would collapse. It was an extremely tricky situation.

Pranab wrote: 'PM expressed his disappointment with his talk with Buddhadeb and suggested that a line should be drawn beyond which we should not succumb to the pressures of Left.' After a long-drawn negotiation, finally a compromise formula was reached:

1. CPI (M) would hold a demonstration but would ensure that it is peaceful.
2. The demonstrators should not cross the barricade, which were to be placed 300 m away from the gate.
3. No one should carry food packets as that would attract the birds.
4. No slogans should be raised against the armed forces.

A crisis was averted. On 7 November, Pranab noted in his diary that everything went smoothly. He must have been smiling when he wrote, 'Some journalists told me that the demonstrators converted into spectators, often breaking into spontaneous applause causing lot of embarrassment to CPI(M) leaders.'

He concluded with relief and perhaps gratitude—'Buddhadeb babu kept his words.'

The stormy relationship between the Left and Congress ended in a much-publicized estrangement on the issue of the India–US Civil Nuclear Cooperation Agreement, known as the nuclear deal. Initiated by Dr Manmohan Singh and the then US President George W. Bush in July 2005, the nuclear deal involved a long and complicated process of tough negotiations not only between India and the US, but with the International Atomic Energy Agency (IAEA) on India-specific safeguards agreement and a special waiver also from the Nuclear Suppliers Group (NSG) to facilitate India's entry to the nuclear regime. It ended India's isolation in international trade in nuclear fuel and provided access to critical technology for civil nuclear programmes. The deal was signed on 10 October 2008 by Pranab, who was then the EAM, and by Condoleezza Rice, the then US secretary of state.

From its inception in July 2005 to its conclusion in October 2008, the deal had to pass through many twists and turns both internationally and at the domestic front. From the very beginning, the proposal was vehemently opposed by the Left. As the EAM, Pranab was the key negotiator with the US and other international agencies. At home, he was the primary negotiator with the Left on behalf of the government.

Pranab's diaries during this period contain such a wealth of information that one could possibly create a separate book dedicated to the nuclear deal, and the negotiations with the Left. Nevertheless, the situation gave him many sleepless nights.

The deal was concluded successfully but the Left withdrew its support to the government when the PM, during his visit to Japan, declared his government's intention to go to the IAEA for approval for the India-specific safeguards agreement in a statement. On 8 July, the Left withdrew support. On 10 July, Pranab offered his resignation from the Cabinet to the PM owning responsibility for the failure of talks with the Left leaders and their subsequent withdrawal of support. It was not accepted. Pranab wrote in his diary, 'PM did not even read the letter. He said, "This government would not run one month without your cooperation and guidance... But for your efforts the Left would have withdrawn support long ago. So please do not talk of it."'

Pranab and the government had to go through another acid test. The government moved a confidence motion in Parliament and won the trust vote with support of Mulayam Singh Yadav and his Samajwadi Party.

A PRIME MINISTER AND A GENTLEMAN

Pranab had a habit of offering resignations. In his diaries between 2004 to 2012, I read about at least a dozen occasions when he tendered his resignation, sometimes on seemingly trivial grounds. In 2008, Pranab had offered to resign and retire when the PM, in a core group meeting, proposed to lower the age profile of both the Cabinet and party organization. The offer of his resignation and retirement was not taken seriously. Pranab noted that Sonia had brushed it off. Though he did not elaborate in his diary, I felt that Pranab might have had taken it personally. It is possible that he felt frustrated due to the fact that around 25–26 years ago, he held the distinction of being the youngest member of Indira Gandhi's Cabinet and was also second in command. However, after all these years, he was *still* in the same position, despite being one of the senior-most members in the Cabinet (excluding the PM and Arjun Singh).

Many people have speculated that Pranab perhaps resented working under a person whom he had appointed as the Reserve Bank of India (RBI) governor way back in 1982, during his tenure as the finance minister. I don't think that was an issue. Pranab had once told me that in the Westminster system of governance, the PM is first among equals. Though the buck finally stops with the PM, the power and responsibility lie collectively with the Cabinet. He confided that he would have rather worked under Dr Singh than anyone else in the party. The simple reason for this was the exemplary courtesy shown by Dr Singh to Pranab, and the independence he was given to function throughout their long period of association. Pranab stated in his book, 'I say this out of personal experience of the Prime Ministers I have worked with—Indira Gandhi and Narasimha Rao—I got the maximum autonomy when I worked with Manmohan Singh.'[93]

The tone was set in the days of Narasimha Rao's tenure when Dr Singh was appointed as the finance minister and Pranab was the deputy chairperson of the Planning Commission. Dr Singh came to meet Pranab regarding some discussion on plan allocations. He told Pranab, 'You were my minister. So whatever you decide, I will agree.' Pranab further noted in his diary, 'What a gentleman he is.' Any discussion I had with my father about Dr Singh was either preceded or followed by the remark—'He is a true gentleman.'

It's not that everything Pranab said was accepted. In his diary entries from that period, he highlighted a Cabinet meeting in which he made three suggestions but the 'FM [finance minister] accepted only one'. Sensing that the FM had made up his mind about the other two, he did not

[93]Ibid. 78.

pursue the matter any further. Pranab adhered to his limits.

Contrary to what many people believe, Dr Singh was no weakling. He showed determination and nerves of steel when he insisted on going ahead with the nuclear deal despite strong opposition from one of the most important coalition partners, even with their eventual withdrawal of support. Going through Pranab's diaries and from whatever conversation I have had with him, I felt that while Dr Singh might not have been as aggressive as Pranab in voicing his opinions, he definitely had views of his own and pushed them through whenever necessary. I also read that Dr Singh shared with Pranab his unhappiness with some of his Cabinet colleagues, and occasionally even about the Congress President. Pranab's general advice to him was to discuss these issues with the persons concerned and the Congress President 'frankly and firmly'. On occasions, Dr Singh was even ready to quit and Sonia Gandhi had to pacify him.

As mentioned earlier, during the Vajpayee period, Dr Singh was nominated as the LoP in Rajya Sabha by Sonia Gandhi. Pranab was the chief whip. Pranab's earlier experience as the leader of the House in Rajya Sabha during the Indira Gandhi years, and his vast knowledge about parliamentary proceedings and rules came in handy. Going by Pranab's diaries of those years, it seems Dr Singh depended substantially on Pranab to discharge his parliamentary duties, and they worked effectively as a team.

During UPA-I and -II, Pranab shared a significant workload of the government by heading a large number of Group of Ministers (GOMs) and Empowered Group of Ministers (EGOMs)—an institutional mechanism within the Cabinet to facilitate quick decision-making and resolve contentious matters before they came to the

Cabinet. Pranab chaired 95 GOMs during UPA-I and -II and headed 24 out of 39 GOMs and EGOMs before he became president in 2012. The PM consulted him on all important issues. One Cabinet Minister of UPA government told me that the PM would often leave it to Pranab to conduct Cabinet meetings, while another said that his decision would generally be the last word.

Even Opposition leaders seem to understand and appreciate it. At the last session of Parliament of the fourteenth Lok Sabha (end of UPA-I), the then LoP in Lok Sabha L.K. Advani showered Pranab with praises, saying, 'Sometimes I think had Pranab not been there, what would happen to this government. Whenever there is a crisis, he is there. Twenty-five years ago, he presented the budget and did so again yesterday as it was a crisis situation… Ever since I was introduced to Pranab, I have always appreciated his ability, his strength and his capability to shoulder responsibility.'[94]

In the relationship between Pranab and Dr Singh, there were some personal touches too. On 15 August 2005, Pranab had to go to Sri Lanka to attend the funeral of Lakshman Kadirgamar, the then foreign minister of Sri Lanka who was assassinated by a suspected LTTE sniper. Being the defence minister of India, the threat perception against Pranab was very high. The PM specially called him and requested him to strictly follow the security advice in Colombo. Pranab wrote in his diary, 'I was touched by his concern.'

I myself was witness to his concern when Pranab met with a serious accident. On the night of 7 April 2007, on his way back from Murshidabad to Kolkata, a truck collided

---

[94]'Advani showers praise on Pranab', *The Times of India*, 18 February 2009, https://tinyurl.com/yv6j66ru. Accessed on 7 October 2023.

with Pranab's car. All the passengers and the driver of the car were injured. Pranab sustained a severe head injury. He was rushed to a local health centre where the doctor stitched up his scalp wound before shifting him to Kolkata. Next morning, he was brought to Delhi on a special air force aircraft. As I was waiting at the airport to receive my father, a visibly distraught PM walked in. He disregarded all protocols to make his way to the airport to see his injured colleague. It was pretty obvious that he was distressed. He kept fidgeting with his hands and continuously inquired about the latest update on my father's condition, though I am sure that as the PM he had more information than me on the subject. When the plane finally landed, he did not even wait for Pranab to be brought down from the plane. He went inside taking me along. Pranab had by then regained consciousness. Seeing the PM, he tried to get up and reassure him that he was perfectly fine and strong enough to undertake his upcoming visit to Saudi Arabia two days later. The PM told him gently but firmly that he was going nowhere other than the hospital, and had to remain there until he was given permission to leave by the doctors.

There have been attempts by some people to play up the differences between Pranab and Dr Singh. In the much talked about book *The Accidental Prime Minister*, Sanjaya Baru, media advisor to the PM in UPA-I, recounts some incidents that imply that Pranab deliberately tried to ignore or undermine the authority of the PM. He wrote:

> After returning from an important visit to Washington DC, Pranab chose not to brief the PM for three days. He had gone to see Sonia Gandhi but had not sought an appointment with Dr. Singh. On the third day, I asked

> Dr. Singh what had transpired at Pranab's meetings with President Bush and Condoleezza Rice. "I don't know" was his plaintive reply.[95]

I presume Baru was referring to Pranab's visit to Washington from 23 to 25 March 2008, during which he met President Bush and Secretary of State Rice. This was the only visit where Pranab did not meet the PM right after returning from abroad. But it did not mean that he did not brief the PM. On his way back from the US, Pranab halted for a day in London to meet the British Foreign Secretary. As I read in his diary, on the night of 26 March, Pranab spoke to the PM on the phone and briefed him in detail about his meetings with Bush and Rice, a fact that perhaps Baru was not aware of. If the PM informed Baru that he didn't know about what had happened, it is possible that he simply chose not to disclose the details of what transpired. Pranab returned to Delhi late on 27 March. On 28 March, he indeed went to meet Sonia as stated by Baru. But it was not to brief her about the US visit, but to attend a core group meeting. The core group meeting should have been attended by the PM too, as is customary. But I'm not sure if the PM attended, as Pranab's diary is silent about it. Something else occupied the space. At the meeting, Pranab lost his cool, and so did Sonia. They had a 'heated exchange of words' about certain impending issues related to the party, that Pranab believed were being excessively delayed in terms of decision-making. The very next morning, Pranab left for Kolkata and went to his constituency to attend some programmes which were

[95]Baru, Sanjaya, *The Accidental Prime Minister: The Making and Unmaking of Manmohan Singh*, Penguin Random House India, 2015, p. 174.

planned long back. He then returned only on 31 March. On 1 April, he met the PM.

Baru again claims that 'similarly Pranab would "forget" to brief the PM on his meetings with the Left'.[96] As Pranab was known for his prodigious memory and Baru could not have been unaware of that, he obviously tried to imply that this was done deliberately. Going by Pranab's diaries, this again seems to be false. If Pranab had even had an 'informal' conversation with Jyoti Basu or Buddhadeb Bhattacharjee during his visits to Kolkata, he would call the PM and Sonia, usually at night, to brief them. In his papers, I have found copies of written reports of his meetings with the Left, including one detailing an informal conversation with Buddhadeb that took place while he was waiting in an airport lounge.

Sadly, Pranab's relationship with the PM seemed to have taken a turn for the worse during UPA-II. On 8 July 2009, a depressed Pranab wrote, 'Some persons are spreading rumours that I am trying to overshadow the PM. What can I do if this kind of wrong, malicious campaign is being built against me? The same game is being played again and again since '80s. I've resigned to my fate.'

An early and visible manifestation of it was, perhaps, reflected in Pranab's exclusion from a high-powered lunch hosted by the PM in July 2009 for the visiting US Secretary of State, Hillary Clinton. As economic cooperation between the two countries was high on Hillary's agenda, the decision to not invite the then Finance Minister raised many eyebrows in Delhi's power corridors. Though Pranab did not document this event in his diaries back then, a month

---

[96]Ibid.

later, he mentioned another dinner hosted by the PM for the judges of High Courts and Supreme Court on 16 August for which only Pranab and the law minister were invited. Pranab noted, 'My invitation is perhaps to make up for the adverse comments voiced in media of my exclusion in PM's lunch for USA Secy of State Hillary Clinton.'

Earlier on 9 August, Pranab had attempted to comprehend the growing distance between him and PM and noted, 'It may be because of (1) my economic policy which he feels is left of the centre, and (2) his desire to give concessions to Pakistan which is again different from my policy.'

The latter likely refers to the joint statement made by PM Manmohan Singh and the PM of Pakistan Syed Yusuf Raza Gilani after their meeting on the sidelines of the Non-Aligned Movement (NAM) summit at the Egyptian resort of Sharm El Sheikh in July 2009—barely seven months after the 26/11 Mumbai terror attacks by terrorists from Pakistan.

After the Mumbai terror attacks, all structured dialogues with Pakistan were suspended. India was clear and firm in its stand that the composite dialogue process could not be resumed unless Pakistan cracks down against terrorism and terrorists operating from Pakistan. Pranab declared, 'If they don't act, then it will not be business as usual.' India shared evidence with Pakistan, as well as with other countries, that clearly linked elements in Pakistan to the Mumbai terror attacks. Due to India's efforts, the United Nations Security Council (UNSC) imposed sanctions on Jamaat-ud-Dawa (JuD), a front organization for Lashkar-e-Tayyaba (LeT) and some other individual entities based in Pakistan.[97] However, Pakistan's response was far from satisfactory, and it did not show any genuine attempt to address India's legitimate concerns.

During a time when the nation was still reeling from the Mumbai terror attacks and mourning the loss of its victims, the joint statement of the Indian and Pakistan PMs, which appeared to be favourably tilted towards Pakistan, rattled the entire nation.

There were primarily two problematic points in the statement. One was the resumption of the composite dialogue process, de-linking it from Pakistan's action on terror against India. Second was the unprecedented mention of Balochistan in a joint statement. Pranab wrote in his diary that the statement was a blunder. The government faced criticism not only from the Opposition parties (other than the Left), but from within the party itself. Sonia was extremely upset. In a meeting between the Congress President, Pranab, Ahmed Patel and A.K. Anthony, she suggested distancing of the party from the statement. Pranab noted that Patel went to the extent of wanting to curb the powers of the PM by ensuring pre-consultation with the Congress president. Pranab strongly opposed both the suggestions. 'I told them we can't denigrate the office of PM. Secondly, the govt [government] is headed by Congress. Distancing [by the party] on the floor [of Parliament] will only damage ourselves and help the Opposition,' he noted.

It seems that the PM did not consult his senior officers before issuing the statement. Pranab later learnt what

---

[97]Mukherjee, Pranab, *The Coalition Years: 1996-2012*, Rupa Publications, 2017, p. 125–26.

transpired on 21 July 2009. He wrote in his diary:

> Called Shankar [Shivshankar Menon] today. He told me what happened. This happened during hour long one to one meeting between PM and Gilani. In presence of Gilani, PM directed Shankar to draft the joint statement containing points of discussion including Balochistan and delinking Dialogue with action against terrorists. Later realizing the implication of it, he reiterated India's stated position in a press conference. However, irreparable damage has been done to national interest.

At a later period, Shivshankar Menon, in an interaction with MPs maintained that the drafting of the statement 'could have been better'.[98] He was doing his duty in maintaining confidentiality, and rightly so.

The intention behind Dr Singh's desire to extend an olive branch to Pakistan should not be questioned. Perhaps, it is the dream of every Indian PM to improve ties with Pakistan and find a permanent solution towards peace. Even his successor, PM Narendra Modi, made an attempt in December 2015 to create a better environment of trust through his 'surprise visit' to Lahore to meet his counterpart, Nawaz Sharif. Dr Singh, the economist-PM, realized that India's growth story could not reach its optimum without ensuring peace and prosperity in the entire region. But the timing of the Sharm El Sheikh statement was perhaps not right. It was just too soon after the Mumbai terror attacks, and the public sentiment at home was not yet conducive to restart the dialogue and

[98]'Newsmaker: Shiv Shankar Menon', *Business Standard,* 20 January 2013, https://tinyurl.com/ysd5pu7w. Accessed on 7 October 2023.

delink it with terror. Further, the mention of Balochistan should have been avoided. At home, this proved to be a political blunder, as the Opposition tried to create an image that the Congress was not serious in tackling cross-border terrorism.

Pranab's own stand on Pakistan was far stronger. While time and again he reiterated the need to maintain peace in the region and forge better ties with India's neighbours, including Pakistan, he was clear that Pakistan needed to reciprocate India's desire for peace through concrete actions and not mere words. He once tried to explain to me the complexities within Pakistan. There was one particular remark of his that has remained imprinted in my memory. He said that Pakistan is neither a 'normal democracy' where there's clear segregation of power and authority between institutions, nor a 'normal dictatorship' where all power is concentrated in the hands of one individual or institution. There, the civilian government, army, ISI, religious leaders and militants all have their own power, influence and support base. Within each, there are different factions. Whenever the India–Pakistan peace process seemed to have progressed a little—whether through the composite dialogue process or through back-channel diplomacy—some elements within Pakistan sabotaged it. To have a truly meaningful dialogue, Pakistan must clear its own internal mess. Comprehensive multilateral dialogue is the only way forward. But no one should expect a miracle. He concluded by saying that our leaders must understand this.

Besides policy differences, there seems to be a human angle too in the problems between the PM and Pranab. It has been suggested by some that the PM perhaps grew resentful towards Pranab during UPA-II. Pranab himself felt that some people, including a few of his Cabinet colleagues, tried to influence Dr Singh negatively towards him. On 1 December 2010, Pranab commented on 'lack of warmth' in his interactions with the PM. He wrote, 'What I do not understand the reason behind it. (sic) Do they sincerely believe that I am rival of Manmohan Singh? A few newspaper articles in my favour should not be taken as my plotting against anybody.' I don't exactly know if anything particular transpired that day, as there are no other details given in his diary, but Pranab was disturbed enough to talk about it with Sonia the very next day. He noted, 'I expressed my anguish and told her that from day one of UPA govt [that] I have expressed my unwillingness to remain in Cabinet. I feel I should quit now. Sonia ji told me that's out of question. There after we discussed J&K, Omar Abdullah, food security, Sharad Pawar, minimum wage for NREGA etc.'

As I went through Pranab's diaries, I discovered numerous instances of sparks flying, heated arguments and growing distances for a period. However, after a while, things seemed to be back to normal. With regard to his association with Dr Singh and Sonia, Pranab mentioned to me multiple times that it wasn't necessary for them to always be in agreement. He often said, 'You do not need to agree on everything every time.' During the course of working together for so many years under such high-pressure conditions, there were bound to be differences. There was nothing unusual about it. But differences do not mean conflict, he clarified. Most importantly, they knew how to handle the differences.

Pranab had genuine regard for Dr Singh and it seems

to have been reciprocated. Whatever the differences might have been, it is undeniable that both of them treated each other with utmost respect and dignity in public and in private. In January 2009, when Dr Singh was scheduled to undergo a bypass surgery, Pranab was officially given the responsibility of presiding over Cabinet meetings. He was given additional charge of the Ministry of Finance that was held by the PM himself, since the earlier Finance Minister P. Chidambaram was shifted to the Home Ministry following the resignation of Shivraj Patil after the Mumbai terror attacks. For a few months till the next government was formed after the general elections in mid-2009, Pranab simultaneously held two of the most important portfolios: Finance and External Affairs. He continued to hold the Finance Ministry in UPA-II till he became the president in 2012.

As president, Pranab thought about awarding the Bharat Ratna to Dr Singh. On 30 October 2013, he wrote in his diary:

> I discussed with Cabinet secretary the idea of conferring Bharat Ratna to PM Dr. Manmohan Singh. He is recognised all over the world as a great economist under whose guidance Indian economy introduced major reforms in 1991-96 as FM and in the last 9 years under his leadership, India's economy grew at a high rate of 7.9 pc pa during 2003-4 to 2012-13 despite major international financial crisis in 2008-9 and Euro Zone crisis in 2012-13 onwards. (sic) I asked Cabinet secretary to talk to Pulak Chatterjee to ascertain views of Sonia Gandhi and let me know.

However, there was no further reference of it in his diaries.

The next year, the Bharat Ratna was awarded to C.N.R. Rao and Sachin Tendulkar.

DOOMED TO IMPLODE

The UPA-II government was formed in 2009, after the results were announced on 16 May. However, the bonhomie that seemed to have existed between key players within the Congress during UPA-I appeared to be losing its sheen during UPA-II. Right after the swearing-in ceremony on 22 May, on 24 May Pranab wrote in his diary that Ahmed Patel had paid him a visit at night. He wrote, 'He told me that it [Cabinet formation] will take more time as PM and CP [Congress President] are not agreeing on many names but CP is not ready to concede to PM's choices. He also told me that number of ministers would be large.'

While it is the PM's prerogative to select his Cabinet, the PM always needs to operate within certain practical constrains when choosing his Cabinet—keeping caste, gender and regional factors in mind. In a coalition government, this task becomes even more complicated. While it's not surprising that Sonia, being the UPA chairperson and Congress president would have played a major role in Cabinet formation, its noteworthy that Dr Singh was asserting himself which perhaps he didn't do five years earlier.

It has been alleged that during UPA governments, the real centre of power was 10 Janpath. Going through Pranab's diaries, I felt that the answer was not that simple and straightforward. I did not get any impression that Sonia interfered in matters of government functioning, though she did keep track of the government's performance, especially on the promises made in the manifesto. There was nothing untoward in that. But she seemed to have been the decisive voice in appointing ministers from Congress and also people in key positions like governors. She consulted the PM, occasionally Pranab as well, on such matters. But the final decision seemed to be hers. In a political culture where getting appointed in a position of power seemed to have become the ultimate goal for a majority of politicians, the balance naturally tilted in favour of the person who was the decisive authority in such matters.

The UPA-II seemed to be imploding almost from the very beginning due to tensions between the Congress and its coalition partners and external allies. Despite the Congress getting a larger number of seats than in UPA-I, the coalition was on shaky ground from the very beginning. The withdrawal of support by the Left in UPA-I had its consequences for UPA-II. Baba once explained to me that UPA-I with support from 61 MPs from the Left was more stable than UPA-II which had a larger number of Congress MPs. During UPA-I, the Congress as a party and the government had to deal primarily with the Left as a bloc that spoke more or less in one voice, and was more predictable and upfront in their opposition to the government agenda (on ideological grounds). The CMP provided a roadmap in the government's dealings with the Left. In the absence of one solid bloc of external support, with which negotiation was easier, UPA-II had to deal with a number of multiple allies and external support of several political parties—each wanting to get its own pound of flesh—often leading to unreasonable demands and conflict of interests.

Within a year of forming the government, the

Women's Reservation Bill, a major agenda of the UPA government, could not be passed in the Lok Sabha due to stiff opposition from the SP–BSP–RJD trio, who were allies of the government. The overbearing attitude of some of the Cabinet ministers from coalition parties undermined the stature of the PM and the government. Mamata Banerjee created trouble almost from the very beginning. As the union railway minister, she announced 75 days productivity-linked bonus to railway workers without taking prior approval from the Cabinet. On 24 August 2009, Pranab wrote in his diary: 'Mamata came at 8 pm. I told her firmly she should attend Cabinet meetings and follow norms of the govt. She should have taken permission of Cabinet and finance before announcing 75 days bonus to railway workers.' Later in the year, on 17 December, he noted, 'Mamata created another problem. She wants to place on the table of the House a white paper on railway and a vision document. These documents haven't been seen by anybody—neither Cabinet nor PM. When I suggested to her to show it to PM, she grumbled and protested.'

Following the massive victory of the TMC in the 2011 West Bengal Assembly elections, Mamata resigned as union railway minister to become CM of West Bengal. She nominated Dinesh Trivedi, MP from her party, to succeed her in the ministry. In the 2012–13 railway Budget, Trivedi announced a major fare hike and other reforms in the railways. Mamata was enraged; Trivedi had to resign and the government had to roll back the fare hike.

There were more challenges for the government from another ally—the DMK. Faced with allegations of irregularities in the allocation of 2G spectrum, the then Union Minister of Communications and Information

Technology A. Raja was advised to resign in November 2010. DMK supremo M. Karunanidhi was not convinced, and had to be persuaded with much difficulty. In February 2011, A. Raja was arrested by the CBI. A month later, the DMK threatened to pull out of the UPA government, withdrawing its six Cabinet ministers and extending only issue-based support, purportedly on the issue of seat sharing with the Congress for the Assembly elections in Tamil Nadu in the same year. The relationship was further strained with the arrest of Kanimozhi, DMK MP and Karunanidhi's daughter, by the CBI in the 2G scam in May.

Another important ally, veteran politician Sharad Pawar too was unhappy with the government and complained of a lack of coordination with the alliance partners. The TMC and DMK eventually withdrew support, making the government even more unstable.

Pranab's diaries in the years of UPA-II often give a sense of despondency. Personally, he was getting tired both physically and mentally due to the overwhelming work demands and constant challenges encountered during the tenure of UPA-II. He frequently fell ill during this period, which the doctors attributed to lack of adequate sleep and rest. On 30 May 2010, Pranab noted, 'Now a days I am feeling too tired. Foreign and domestic travels are becoming too exacting. I do not know for how long I shall have to carry this burden.'

This became a recurring theme coupled with a sense of dejection, as reflected in his diary entries. As early as 19 September 2010, a year after the formation of the UPA-II government, Pranab noted in his diary, 'I am worried over the situation prevailing in the political arena. I do not know how to run a government where nobody takes decision and if somebody wants to do something, others resist and do not cooperate. There appears to be no cohesion in the functioning of the state.'

UPA-II was plagued with inner tensions and faced a number of crises. It was blamed for having 'policy paralysis'. The economic reforms that were expected to get through without Opposition from Left in UPA-I, were now stalled due to opposition from other allies. Pranab's much-desired GST (goods and services tax) Bill could not be pushed through due to stiff opposition from the BJP. On 17 August 2010, he wrote, 'At 1pm I met Sushma [Swaraj], Arun [Jaitley] and Yashwant Sinha. They agreed to support Civil Nuclear Liability Bill but told me that on GST, they would not support because of CBI case against Modi govt in Gujarat.'

ANTI-CORRUPTION AGITATION OR BIGGER GAME PLAN?

The raft of issues created by the allies was not the only challenge that the government faced. In the summer of 2011, UPA-II came up against some domestic headwinds in the form of the Gandhi-cap wearing veteran social activist, Anna Hazare. For a few months, he became the face of an anti-corruption agitation that dealt a serious blow to UPA-II. On 5 April 2011, Hazare sat on an indefinite fast at Jantar Mantar, New Delhi, demanding immediate enactment of the Jan Lokpal Bill that would facilitate setting up of an all-powerful anti-corruption ombudsman. The agitation attracted massive media attention, drawing a large number of people (especially the youth) to join the anti-corruption campaign. On 9 April, the UPA government declared setting up of a joint committee with representation from the government and from the Hazare team. From Pranab's diary entry on 8 April, I learnt that he did not want to be part of the committee and had expressed his reluctance to the PM, but he was overruled.

After his initial reluctance, Pranab felt that this could perhaps be a unique experiment of actively engaging with civil society to enact an important law. But he was soon disappointed. The joint committee held several meetings, but the talks failed. Pranab felt, whether rightly or wrongly, that the representatives from Hazare's side were not really interested in finding a solution or enacting the bill. They were insisting on pushing through their own version of the bill and were demanding impossible timelines.

In Pranab's view, involvement of civil society through suggestions, proposals and even agitations were welcome, but it cannot bypass duly-elected legislatures and legislative procedures by attempting to delegate legislative authority upon itself. This sentiment was reflected in an all-party meeting held in Parliament on 3 July in which representatives of 52 political parties were present, out of which 32 spoke. Pranab noted in his diary that in the meeting that lasted for three-and-a-half hours, he explained the outcome of the meetings of the joint committee; areas of divergence; and the views of the state governments and major political parties. He further noted that the representatives of various political parties raised a very pertinent question: Unlike the elected representatives who are accountable to the people, what is the accountability of the civil society and who are they accountable to? The meeting ended with a resolution that due process of legislation should be followed, and the government should prepare a draft and present it before Parliament. In December 2013, the Lokpal and Lokayuktas Bill, 2011, was passed in Parliament. In January 2014, Pranab, as president, gave assent to the bill.

During the time when the Anna Andolan was in progress, there was another development. Yoga Guru Baba Ramdev announced his plan to initiate another hunger strike demanding the return of black money, allegedly stashed away in overseas accounts. The media reported that four high-ranking Cabinet ministers, including Pranab, went to the airport to meet Ramdev. In an event organized by *The Indian Express,* held in October 2017, called 'Indian Express Adda', Pranab explained in detail what had transpired. It was not a government decision to send ministers to the airport to meet Ramdev. Pranab came up with the idea that he would personally approach Ramdev in an attempt to persuade him, and nip in the bud the possibility of another agitation. But then he explained that there was a problem of communication. 'He would not have understood my Hindi, and I would have not understood his English. So then how do we talk?' he asked, amid laughter from the audience. To circumvent the problem, Pranab asked Kapil Sibal (fluent in both the languages) to join him. He did not mention anything about why the other two joined. The PM was informed about this meeting. Pranab later acknowledged that this decision was a 'misjudgement' on his part.

One of the most visible faces and loudest voices in the Anna Andolan was Arvind Kejriwal, the current CM of Delhi. Riding on the popularity of the agitation, Kejriwal floated the Aam Aadmi Party (AAP) that went on to achieve spectacular success in winning three consecutive elections in Delhi. He fought his first two elections on the promise of introducing the Jan Lokpal Bill in Delhi that was supposed to be far stronger and more transparent than the Central Act passed by UPA-II in December 2013. Almost 10 years have passed since (the first government collapsed after 49 days), and Kejriwal continues to head the third consecutive AAP government in Delhi with negligible opposition. The Jan Lokpal Bill is still not legislated.

At the time of writing this book, Kejriwal's two ministers, including his former Deputy CM, are in police custody on serious allegations of corruption and money-laundering. Chief Minister Kejriwal's official residence has reportedly been 'renovated', at a whooping cost of approximately ₹53 crore, for which a special audit of CAG was to be conducted for scrutinizing administrative and financial irregularities. It is quite revealing, considering the fact that the 'Aam Aadmi' leader, Kejriwal gave an affidavit before fighting his first election in 2013 that he and his MLAs would not use government bungalows, security and cars if elected to power.

Reflecting on these agitations, it is natural to question the true intentions behind them and the outcomes they yielded. One tends to feel that the hidden agenda of these agitations was not really to fight corruption, but perhaps to destabilize a duly-elected government and wrongly defame the leadership of the ruling party. The link between the Anna Andolan and the RSS has now come out in the open. One of the most visible faces of the movement, prominent civil rights lawyer Prashant Bhushan said that the Anna Andolan was 'propped-up' by BJP–RSS to bring down the UPA government.[99] Hazare himself admitted that the

---

[99]'Once its Core Member, Prashant Bhushan Says IAC Propped up by RSS, BJP', *The Indian Express,* 15 September 2020, https://tinyurl.com/cuxecmcm. Accessed on 8 October 2023.

BJP had used him to win the 2014 Lok Sabha elections.[100] During an interaction with journalists in Kolkata in November 2011, RSS Chief Mohan Bhagwat reportedly said that the RSS had urged Anna Hazare to go on the anti-corruption crusade. He also reportedly claimed that they had similarly urged Baba Ramdev to start the anti-corruption movement. Bhagwat admitted that though the RSS was not officially involved, its activists were present in the Ramlila grounds.[101]

Whether the anti-corruption agitations were effective in terms of actually curbing corruption is questionable. Despite the Lokpal Act being passed in January 2014, it took the BJP government five years to appoint a Lokpal. It happened only in March 2019. About the return of black money, allegedly hoarded abroad, no concrete measures have been taken by the current government other than what had already been done by the previous government. There is no dearth of allegations of corruption against the current government, but the anti-corruption champions are simply missing. However, one thing can definitely be stated for certain. Two of the most immediate and most undisputable beneficiaries of the 'movement' were the BJP and Arvind Kejriwal.

In view of the policy paralysis—the inability of the UPA-II government to implement policies and the reform agenda due to opposition from alliance partners—and the

---

[100]'BJP Used me to Win 2014 Lok Sabha Elections, Says Anna Hazare During Hunger Strike', *Scroll.in*, 5 February 2019, https://tinyurl.com/2rcvpfyr. Accessed on 8 October 2023.

[101]'Anna and RSS Links Go Back a Long Way: RSS Chief', *Firstpost*, 10 November 2011, https://tinyurl.com/mu46mbzs. Accessed on 8 October 2023.

alleged scams, Pranab once mentioned to me that he had recommended early dissolution of the government, seeking a fresh mandate from the people. His argument was that even if they were to lose and were in the Opposition, it was better to be a strong Opposition rather than a weak government. However, it was not accepted by either the PM or the Congress President. Perhaps, it would have been better. Rather than waiting to reach its nadir—with all these allegations of scams, the Anna Andolan and countrywide agitation in which people seemed to have lost all faith in the Congress—an early dissolution might not have led to UPA-III government, but perhaps it could have provided the country with a more formidable Opposition than what it currently has.

BOUQUETS AND BRICKBATS

Pressure from coalition partners, alleged scams and policy paralysis were just some of the challenges that threatened to derail the UPA-II government. However, the greatest challenge that Pranab had to surmount emanated from his ministry—the Ministry of Finance—that he took over at an extremely difficult time. The world was facing an economic meltdown due to global recession. But Pranab was able to steer the economy through the global financial crisis and balance strong growth and fiscal responsibility. In 2010, Pranab was declared 'Finance Minister of the Year for Asia' by *Emerging Markets*—a daily newspaper of record for the World Bank and IMF—for his initiatives to bring fiscal transparency, fuel price reforms and inclusive growth strategy.[102] The award was based on nominations from public and private sector economists, analysts, bankers, investors and other experts. This was exactly 26 years after his stint as the finance minister, in a much-changed India post liberalization.

However, Pranab was severely criticized, and still is, for perhaps the most controversial decision that he took as the finance minister: the (in)famous Retrospective Tax. It was introduced in 2012, through an amendment to the Income Tax Act, 1961, that allowed Indian tax authorities to levy tax on offshore deals involving transfer of Indian assets with retrospective effect. It came in the wake of the Supreme Court judgment in favour of Vodafone, in an ongoing case between Vodafone and Indian tax authorities.

In 2007, a Hong Kong based company called Hutchison Telecommunications International sold its stake in Hutchison Essar Ltd (an Indian company) to Vodafone International Holdings (a company from the Netherlands). The deal was structured in such a manner that Vodafone did not buy Hutchison Essar directly, but bought the entire shares of Hutchison Essar held by CGP Investment (Holdings)—a company based in Cayman Islands, a tax haven. CGP Investment (Holdings) held 67 per cent shares of Hutchison Essar. As the case involved transfer of assets in India, the income tax issued a show cause notice to Vodafone in September 2007. Incidentally, Pranab was not the finance minister then.

The notice was challenged in the Bombay High Court which gave a verdict in favour of the revenue department.

---

[102]'Pranab "Best Finance Minister" in Asia', *The New Indian Express*, 11 October 2010, https://tinyurl.com/4mtxbjcm. Accessed on 7 October 2023.

The matter was taken to the Supreme Court, and in an interim order on 15 November 2010, the Supreme Court directed Vodafone International to pay ₹2,500 crore and provide a bank guarantee of ₹8,500 crore. However, it changed its decision and on 20 January 2012 directed the tax department to refund ₹2,500 crore with 4 per cent interest within two months.[103] Following this verdict, the Retrospective Tax Law was passed in 2012.

My father would quickly become impatient with me if he had to explain economic policies due to my limited understanding of the fundamentals. As a result, I never ventured to discuss this issue with him. So, I have given Pranab's rationale behind this decision in his own words, as I read in *The Coalition Years*:

> It [The Bombay High Court Verdict] laid down the legal position, following which, several other multinational corporations paid taxes leading to an increase in tax revenue [...] With the Supreme Court setting aside the judgement of the High Court, it created an unusual situation where the tax department would have to return several thousands of crores to several companies.[104]

About the concerns regarding FDI, he wrote:

> Since India offers a huge domestic market, low costs of operations and a cheap and skilled workforce, a direct tax policy that does not discriminate between domestic and foreign entities has very little role to play in attracting FDI.

---

[103]Mukherjee, Pranab, *The Coalition Years: 1996-2012*, Rupa Publications, 2017, p. 188.

[104]Ibid.

> As a matter of policy, the source country should protect its tax base by ensuring that those foreign investors who have earned through their investments in the source country should also pay taxes like any other domestic investor or resident taxpayer. Just because some foreign investors choose to structure their investments through tax havens, they should not, as a matter of policy, get away without paying any taxes.[105]

He concluded, 'As the finance minister, I was convinced of my duty to protect the interest of the country from revenue point of view.'[106] Notwithstanding Pranab's rationale, the retrospective tax faced widespread condemnation. I have heard countless discussions in social gatherings about the potential impact of retrospective taxation on FDI.

In this context, I am intrigued by the assertions of the Modi government regarding the inflow of FDI since they came to power in 2014. It is worth noting that the retrospective tax remained in effect until August 2021, after which it was scrapped when the government lost court battles against Vodafone and Cairn Energy in international tribunals. As per a statement made by Finance Minister Nirmala Sitharaman on 29 March 2022, FDI into the country was $500.5 billion during the Modi government's tenure, 65 per cent more as opposed to the UPA regime.[107] Unless this amount of $500.5 billion, or a major part of it, came during the seven-month period between scrapping of the retrospective tax and making this statement it may

---

[105]Ibid. 189.

[106]Ibid. 190.

[107]Dutta, Sharangee, 'India's FDI Inflow 65% More Under PM Modi Than in UPA Regime: Sitharaman in Rajya Sabha', *Hindustan Times*, 29 March 2022, https://tinyurl.com/5fdj4nmv. Accessed on 7 October 2023.

be reasonable to infer that there are additional factors, as outlined by Pranab, that determine the inflow of FDI.

The counter-argument could be that if the tax wasn't there, perhaps the quantum of FDI inflow would have been much higher. That raises an important question: Why did it take so long for the GoI to scrap the contentious tax? It did not need any major Constitutional Amendment. Everyone seemed to be against it. So, why did it get to a point in which the Indian government had to face the possibility of seizure of its assets in foreign lands, against the backdrop of the judgment in the Cairn Energy case by an international tribunal?

More importantly, when all the subsequent finance ministers, including Pranab's successor in UPA-II had openly expressed their criticism of retrospective tax, why did they continue to use those very provisions to persistently impose tax and penalties on various companies? It seems as much as ₹1.10 lakh crore of back taxes were sought from 17 entities using the 2012 legislation.[108]

Pranab demitted office as finance minister in June 2012. Instead of scrapping the controversial law, his successor slapped a tax demand of ₹14,200 crore or Vodafone in January 2013. In February 2016, the Finance Minister of the BJP government enhanced it to ₹22,100 crore and interest.[109] In the Cairn Energy case, it was slapped with an assessment of ₹10,247 crore in January 2014, when Pranab was nowhere in the picture. It could be argued that perhaps it would have been embarrassing for the UPA

---

[108]PTI, 'Govt Exorcises Retro Tax Ghost Brings Bill to Withdraw Tax Demand on Cairn Vodafone', *The Week*, 5 August 2021, https://tinyurl.com/4hma4hj9. Accessed on 7 October 2023.
[109]Ibid.

government to overturn a law enacted by one of its own ministers. However, the same argument did not apply to the BJP. I seriously wonder why the BJP government didn't simply repeal the law instead of relentlessly pursuing the cases, even in the international court of arbitration. One can safely assume that the government did not oppose Vodafone and Cairn Energy in the international tribunal for arbitration with an expectation of losing the cases. It's logical to think that the government hoped to win. Had it won, the government would have received both the credit and the revenue. However, in case of a loss, there is always the fall guy to pin the blame on.

People wiser than me have suggested that if any successive finance minister or the government would've done it, they would have been accused of cutting a deal with affected parties like Vodafone and Cairn. But who would have accused them? The principal opposition party, the Congress, including its former Finance Minister, had been quite openly critical of the retrospective tax. The reaction of the industry and the media to the introduction and subsequent removal of the retrospective tax was undeniably in favour of its withdrawal. The ordinary person on the street, perhaps, did not even know about the retrospective tax. It's highly unlikely that Anna Hazare and his team would have mounted another 'anti-corruption' agitation against the current government after the scrapping of the tax. Then who could have opposed it?

Pranab had to bite the bullet and take an extremely unpopular and controversial decision that he thought, rightly or wrongly, was in the interest of the country. Why couldn't his successors take a similar step of scrapping it immediately if they thought that it would have been in the interest of the nation, rather than waiting for eight years and facing a public humiliation internationally?

These are just a daughter's feeble attempts to make sense of a controversial decision taken by her father. I personally wish Pranab had not introduced the Amendment. It could have spared me numerous sarcastic comments in 'polite' circles, attributing the country's economic downfall to retrospective tax. Likewise, in the impolite realm of social media trolls, Pranab was branded a 'traitor' who deliberately ruined the economy. In Hindi, there is a saying, *'Na hota baans, na bajti bansuri!'* It's impossible for me to translate it in English, but the spirit of the proverb is—in the absence of the origin, there would not be any consequence. I wish Pranab had listened to his PM and not introduced the tax.

BONDS BEYOND BORDERS

Pranab's economic legacy may be marked by the controversial 'retrospective tax', but in the realm of diplomacy, there can be no dispute about the significant role his close personal connection with Bangladesh PM Sheikh Hasina played in forging closer ties between the two neighbours.

Such was the camaraderie between them that Sheikh Hasina would simply pick up the phone and talk to Pranab directly. Every time Pranab attempted to highlight her complete disregard for protocol, by mentioning that as the PM of one country she should not be contacting a minister in another country, Sheikh Hasina would retort in Bengali, '*Dada, raakhen aapnaar protocol* (Dada, keep your protocol to yourself)!'

The relationship between Sheikh Hasina and our family goes back a long way. In a larger sense, it is rooted in history. Pranab, being a Bengali from this side of the border (West Bengal) had an emotional connect with Bangladesh, erstwhile East Pakistan (or East Bengal, in the common parlance of Bengalis). Like most Bengalis born in pre-partitioned India, he nurtured a deep sense of nostalgia for the other side of the land that became separated from India solely on the grounds of religion, without any consideration of its shared ethnic, cultural and linguistic heritage. As mentioned earlier, he also had a family connect, as his wife Geeta came from Nadail.

The emergence of Bangladesh is a classic example of how a country cannot be held together solely on the basis of religion, ignoring language, ethnicity and other cultural complexities that form the core of a person's identity. The Pakistani government, which was dominated by leaders from West Pakistan, and was mostly under army dictatorship since its formation in 1947, totally refused sharing and devolution of political power and economic resources with the then East Pakistan. They tried to suppress the linguistic and ethnic identity of the Bengali population. Known as East Pakistan after Partition, the land erupted when in 1948 the Pakistan government declared Urdu as the sole national language in the entire country. After massive and protracted protests, the government banned all rallies and public meetings. Defiant students of Dhaka University and other activists organized a protest on 21 February 1952. When the police brutally killed the protesting students, it provoked widespread unrest throughout the area. The *Bhasha Andolan* served as the catalyst for the assertion of Bengali national identity as a political movement, laying the foundation for the later nationalist movement and Bangladesh's Liberation War.

Following the call for total liberation on 7 March 1971, by Bangabandhu Sheikh Mujibur Rahman, the ruthless Pakistani government unleashed unimaginable horrors of mass murders of students and intellectuals, rapes and other atrocities against the ordinary citizens residing in East Pakistan. Pranab, like all Bengalis, was following the developments with keen interest, and in his own words, 'was passionately concerned about the events that were unfolding there.'[110] In June 1971, he initiated discussions in the Rajya Sabha, categorically asking for according diplomatic recognition to the Government of Bangladesh in exile in Mujibnagar and giving them material help.[111] In September 1971, despite him being a relatively junior MP, Indira Gandhi sent Pranab as a member of the Indian Delegation to the Inter-Parliamentary Union in Paris. There, he and other delegates could present India's point of view to a large number of delegates from other countries, and urge them to intervene with their governments to speak out against the gross violation of human rights in East Pakistan. Incidentally, that was Pranab's first trip abroad. From there, he was sent to the UK and Federal Republic of Germany with the same purpose.

On 3 December 1971, Pakistan attacked India. India won a swift and decisive victory and Pakistan surrendered to the Indian army on 16 December 1971 at Dhaka. A new nation was born. Though I was quite young at that time, I still remember the celebratory atmosphere at home,

---

[110]Mukherjee, Pranab, *The Dramatic Decade: The Indira Gandhi Years*, Rupa Publications, 2014, p. 38.
[111]Ibid. 40.

marked by the sound of conch shells and distribution of sweets to visitors.

Four years later, on 15 August 1975, when India was celebrating its Independence Day, a shocking and shameful political assassination was added to the violent and bloody history of the subcontinent. The founding father and first PM (and later president) of the newly formed nation of Bangladesh, Sheikh Mujibur Rahman was brutally gunned down along with his entire family—that included his wife, two sons and their wives, and the youngest son Sheikh Russel, who was just a 10-year-old boy—by some personnel of the Bangladesh army. The only members of the Mujib family to survive were his two daughters, Sheikh Hasina Wazed and Sheikh Rehana, who were in Europe at the time of the assassination. In the aftermath of the assassination, Sheikh Hasina along with her husband M.A. Wazed Miah (a nuclear physicist), and her two little children Joy and Putul (nick names) took political asylum in India by the end of 1975.

Pranab was given the task of looking after Sheikh Hasina and her family. That was the beginning of a relationship that spanned over decades to come. Not only with Pranab, Sheikh Hasina also forged a strong bond with my mother—a bond which withstood the test of time and distance. They soon became a part of our family and would be there for all family occasions like birthdays, get-togethers and annual picnics. Apart from a select few family friends, no one knew her true identity. My mother would introduce her to strangers as her sister. I had no recollection of it. Sheikh Hasina personally shared this memory with me while reminiscing about her time with Ma, when I called on her during her visit to India as the PM of Bangladesh in

September 2022. It was a far cry from her days in exile here, but she did not forget anything. This also resolved a mystery for me. I used to wonder why she addressed my father as '*dada*' (elder brother) and my mother as '*didi*' (elder sister), and not '*boudi*'—the appropriate form of address for an elder brother's wife. As she was supposed to be my mother's sister for strangers, this subterfuge was perhaps adopted to ward off any unwanted attention and suspicion. Even after so many years, she became emotional talking about Ma. After returning to Bangladesh at the end of her exile, she would send exquisite Dhakai Jamdani sarees for Ma and for all the female members of the family. Ma would always reciprocate.

In 2011, I visited Dhaka for a dance performance. Hearing this, my mother insisted that I take sarees for Sheikh Hasina and others in the family. As it was not possible to simply walk into the PM's office with sarees in hand, I requested my father's office to talk to the appropriate authorities and get me an appointment to call on her. That very night, Pranab received a call from Sheikh Hasina on his mobile. She told him straight, 'What call on? Munni is going to stay with me.' As my visit coincided with the visit of our PM Dr Manmohan Singh to Bangladesh, Pranab attempted to discourage Sheikh Hasina by mentioning that she would have a busy schedule. But his arguments fell on deaf ears. So, I stayed with her. At night, after her official engagements, she came to my room to ensure that everything was okay. After chatting for a while, she insisted on tucking the mosquito net herself just as any ordinary, traditional *mashi-pishi* (aunts) would do. The only difference was that she was no ordinary *mashi-pishi*—she was the *prime minister* of a country.

The next day while having breakfast, she got an array of sarees and asked me to choose. So far so good! Once I made my choice, she gave me some money to go and do some shopping. This is a practice in traditional Bengali households that when children visited their relatives' house, the elders would give them some money to buy little trinkets. As a child, I used to look forward to it. But now the problem was that I was 45 years old. I became embarrassed and refused to take the money. Her eyes grew moist. She said, 'What are you saying? You are like my daughter. You were very young and probably don't remember my days in Delhi. Leave aside dada [my father], if didi wasn't there I would have gone mad. My entire family was killed. I was emotionally in ruins. I was in exile. Didi made us a part of your family. It was her love that sustained me during that difficult period of my life. Now you are doing formalities with me?' I quietly took the money.

Her fondness for my mother once created another major protocol issue for Pranab. During her state visit to India as PM of Bangladesh in January 2010, she insisted on coming to our residence to visit Ma. Pranab was the finance minister then. Owing to her health issues, it was not possible for my mother to meet Sheikh Hasina outside. Pranab again cited protocols. But for the visiting PM, protocol was hardly a deterrent. She informed Pranab that if protocol was such a concern for him, he could choose not to be present. It didn't matter to her, as she was determined to meet her Didi regardless. So, she and her sister Sheikh Rehana arrived. Naturally, Pranab was present, along with all of us, to welcome them. During the visit, my four-year-old niece Brishti created an awkward moment. In order to impress upon her the significance of the visitor's stature, her mother informed Brishti that a 'queen' from another country would be coming to see us. When they arrived, Brishti asked her mother where the queen was. Her mother discreetly pointed to Sheikh Hasina and whispered that she was the queen. A disappointed Brishti cried out at the top of her voice, 'She is not a queen. Where is her crown?' The uncomfortable silence was interrupted by Sheikh Hasina, who quickly understood the situation and laughed, saying that Brishti was absolutely right. In a democracy, there are no kings and queens. Brishti was comforted with a sweet treat.

Pranab wrote in his book, 'All my visits to Bangladesh (including the one after my presidency) during Sheikh Hasina's tenure were like a family reunion of sorts for me.'[112] While he argued that personal relationships are not significant in international relations—as leaders ultimately prioritize the interests of their own nations over relationships—personal equations between leaders can foster an environment of trust that can be advantageous for both countries involved. The relationship between Pranab and Sheikh Hasina is a shining example of that.

When my mother passed away in 2015, Sheikh Hasina and Sheikh Rehana flew to attend the funeral. She could not control her tears. Five years later, when Baba became gravely ill and slipped into a prolonged coma for three weeks before ultimately passing away, she called me every day. Her calls were not only to enquire about his well-being, which she must have been informed about through official channels, but also to offer me emotional support and fortitude.

After Pranab's passing, Bangladesh mourned the loss of a 'real friend' and observed one day of state mourning.

[112]Mukherjee, Pranab, *The Presidential Years: 2012–2017*, Rupa Publications, 2021, p. 119.

Sheikh Hasina expressed that her family had lost their 'guardian'. The relationship continues. Thanks to her, I still feel connected to the land where my mother was born.

TOWARDS RAISINA HILL

On 17 November 2011, after a one-to-one meeting with Sonia Gandhi, Pranab noted in his diary:

> In my discussions with her the following points emerged:
>
> 1. Rahul is not going to lead the govt; he may support her in building the party organization.
> 2. She would not quit as party president.
> 3. We should defer decision on Telangana.
> 4. She did not approve my decision to retire from public life and told me that if I am finding it too hectic to manage the constituency with my workload, I shall be brought to R.S. [Rajya Sabha] whenever I would so desire.
> 5. She wants me to continue as the Leader of the House and as minister—that means I am not in consideration for the office of the President.

Exactly seven months later, on 16 June 2012, Pranab was declared as the official candidate of the Congress and UPA for the Presidential election.

On 3 April 2012, Sonia showered Pranab with praises. 'She was very warm and positive. She said that I am aware of the heavy burden you are carrying, but I have no one like you with such vast experience in politics, economics and diplomacy and moreover, the respect you command with all parties is unique. It was high appreciation,' Pranab noted in his diary. As I read this, I immediately became apprehensive. Though Pranab himself never commented on it, after going through my father's diaries over the years, I noticed a pattern wherein 'high appreciation' and 'high praises' by Sonia was usually followed by withholding of something that Pranab desired.

However, as I already knew the final outcome, I was not unduly worried. And lo and behold! On 5 April, Ahmed Patel met Pranab. He was informed that Patel had raised the issue of Pranab's candidature for presidency with Sonia and indicated that he (Pranab) may get the support of Mulayam Singh and the Left, thus ensuring his victory. Pranab further wrote, 'Then she raised the usual question what will happen to the govt in his absence. [...] As per Ahmed, he suggested to her [that] let PM be elevated to President and he [Pranab] be made PM. She did not respond to that.'

Perhaps, this conversation with Ahmed Patel triggered in Pranab's mind the last ray of hope of becoming PM. Pranab himself candidly admitted it in his book that at the end of a meeting with Sonia on 2 June 2012: '[...] I returned with a vague impression that she might wish to consider Manmohan Singh as the UPA presidential nominee. I thought that if she selected Singh for the Presidential office, she may choose me as the Prime Minister.'[113] However, that was not to be.

Perhaps, there was some genuine apprehension regarding sparing Pranab from the government, given the

[113]Mukherjee, Pranab, *The Coalition Years: 1996-2012*, Rupa Publications, 2017, p. 208.

immense workload and responsibilities he was managing. On 2 June 2012, Pranab had a long meeting with Sonia to discuss various issues. He noted, 'She was very warm, receptive and appreciative. While talking about presidential nominee, she told me that you are the best choice but I shudder to think what would happen to running the government. I told her that I'm a party man, and whatever responsibility party gives me, I shall discharge that.'

It has been suggested to me by some people, including a former senior bureaucrat, that M. Hamid Ansari was Sonia's first choice. I can't ascertain the veracity of it, but from Pranab's diaries I learnt that Sonia was definitely trying to gauge Ansari's chances of winning and acceptability among coalition partners and other parties. UPA needed roughly 1 lakh votes more than it had to win the presidential election. Pranab stressed the importance of winning the presidential election, conveying to Ahmed Patel that he enjoyed broad acceptance to rally support, even from non-UPA parties. Finally, two factors tilted the decision in Pranab's favour: first, his winnability; and second, Mamata Banerjee. By opposing Pranab's candidature, more importantly the manner in which she did it, Mamata perhaps unwittingly helped seal the deal in his favour.

Like all major events in Pranab's political life, his nomination as a presidential candidate too was full of dramatic twists and turns. During the period of intense speculation regarding whether Pranab would be announced as the presidential candidate for the UPA, I recall asking him why he didn't approach Mamata and request her to propose his name to the Congress President. Baba replied that Mamata would be the one to oppose his name.

As it transpired, in a meeting with Sonia, Mamata reportedly rejected both Pranab and Ansari, as suggested by Sonia. Mamata said that she would be meeting Mulayam on this issue and would provide an update afterwards. However, instead of an update to Sonia after the meeting, Mamata and Mulayam gave a joint statement to the press and declared that their choices of presidential nominees were A.P.J. Abdul Kalam, Manmohan Singh and Somnath Chatterjee. Pranab later told me that perhaps Sonia felt it was a direct affront to her leadership as the UPA chairperson. Had Mamata discussed with her before going to the press directly, it might have been a different story. In his later years, Pranab would jokingly remark, 'Thank God Mamata opposed me. Else it might have been difficult.'

Pranab's name was declared after a Coordination Committee meeting with alliance partners (which Mamata did not attend) on 15 June. Within hours, Mulayam declared his support for Pranab. Pranab also got immediate declared support from BSP, Mulayam's arch-rival in UP. The announcement of Pranab's nomination for the presidency broke ranks within the Opposition NDA. Nitish Kumar's JD (U) in Bihar and Shiv Sena in Maharashtra, formal constituents of the NDA at that time, declared support for Pranab. Shiv Sena's support came as a surprise as it had been a traditional ally of the BJP since long. Pranab felt that Sharad Pawar was instrumental in influencing Bal Thackeray's support, and he advised Pranab to meet Thackeray during his upcoming visit to Mumbai on 13 July. Sonia Gandhi and Ahmed Patel were not comfortable about Pranab meeting Thackeray, considering his sectarian views in politics. However, Pranab made the decision to personally meet him for two specific reasons. Firstly, he believed that it would be highly impolite on his part to not acknowledge and express gratitude to Thackeray, considering the fact that Thackeray had publicly declared his support for Pranab without any prompting. Secondly, Pranab also took into account the already strained relationship between Pawar and the government. Recognizing that the government still had two more years to fulfil its obligations, Pranab deemed it politically prudent to avoid alienating Pawar by refusing to meet Thackeray.

In that meeting, Thackeray jokingly told him that it was but natural for the Maratha Tiger to support the Royal Bengal Tiger.[114] Much later, in November 2019 when the Congress–NCP alliance joined hands with the Shiv Sena to form the government in Maharashtra, I reminded Baba about Sonia's reservations about him meeting Thackeray during the presidential polls. He remarked, 'In politics, there are no permanent friends or permanent enemies.'

With support pouring in from various political parties, Pranab's victory was assured. Mamata held on for as long as she could. Some of her supporters unleashed personal attacks on Pranab using the most unsavoury, abusive language. Perhaps she was hoping that Pranab would react, and that would give her an excuse not to vote for him. But if nothing else, every political leader could learn patience and *vak-sanyam* (restrain in speech) from Pranab. He ignored the attacks and refrained from attempting to meet or contact her, as he was quite certain that regardless of her erratic nature, politically, she could not afford withholding her support for him given the prevailing sentiment in Bengal.

---

[114]Ibid. 220.

Pranab might not have been a mass leader, but on the announcement of his name as the presidential candidate—bringing with it the possibility of having a Bengali occupy the highest constitutional office in the country for the first time since Independence—the mood in Bengal was jubilant. As I learnt from Pranab's diary, many of Mamata's own party MPs and MLAs had called him personally to assure him of their support. As there is no whip in presidential voting, there was every possibility of cross-voting in TMC had Mamata not declared her support for Pranab. Finally, on 17 July, just two days before the presidential poll, Mamata declared her support for Pranab with a 'heavy heart'. A day before, she sent a message to Pranab's long-time associate Pradyut Guha, 'Tell dada not to worry about me.'

As the news of her support became public, Pranab called to thank her. She assured Pranab of her full support and told him that she would personally monitor the voting to ensure that not a single vote goes to waste. She kept her word. She also demanded that as president, Pranab should make his first trip to Bengal. It was not an imposition at all. For Pranab too, Bengal would have been his natural choice for his first visit outside the capital as the president of India.

At home, the mood was both euphoric and chaotic. As Pranab's name was declared as the presidential candidate, there was a flood of phone calls and visitors. That was also my first exposure to the media. Earlier, as a classical dancer, I had given some interviews to the press (mostly print media) discussing my dance productions. But this was an entirely different ball game. The media didn't just want a general reaction on my father's presidential nomination, but rather had some tricky questions too regarding

Mamata, and Pranab being offered the post of president as a 'consolation prize'. I decided to speak candidly. There was no other choice, as I was till then quite distant from politics. About Mamata, I said that I was genuinely surprised about her stand as I believed that she was very close to our family, also appealing to her to reconsider her decision. About the PM question, I said that for people who were devoted to their work, satisfaction was in the work itself and, eventually, the position or status becomes irrelevant. I also pointed out that to term the highest constitutional office of India as a 'consolation prize' was to denigrate the office. Despite his hectic schedule of campaigning, Pranab kept an eye on what his family members were telling the press. He told me later that my responses were absolutely right and 'politically correct'. I think this was the time he got an idea that initially startled me, but later directed the course of my life for the next few years.

Amid all this excitement, preparations for leaving Pranab's official house and moving to Rashtrapati Bhavan were on. As the presidential polls are through an electoral college of MPs and MLAs, and the members mostly vote on pre-decided party lines, the result in terms of winning or losing is pre-determined. Though I decided not to move to Rashtrapati Bhavan and continued staying at my cosy two-bedroom apartment in GK, I was fully involved in packing for my parents. Late one night, I walked into Baba's home office to take some instructions about packing his personal belongings. He was sitting at his desk writing his diary. As I entered the room, he looked at me and asked in Bengali, '*Lodbi* (Will you fight)?' I was taken aback, as I believed he was insinuating that I had fought with someone. I strongly objected, stating that I had not been involved in any kind of fight with anyone. He clarified, 'Would you like to contest the election from Jangipur?' I was shocked to say the least! Never in my life had I shown any interest in politics, and neither had my father said anything about it before. My response was an instant 'No way'. He did not say anything else.

But his question caught me off guard, prompting me to enquire the following day about why he had suddenly posed that question. I enquired about his opinion regarding my strengths and weaknesses, if I were to enter politics. The positives were very limited. He said, 'You like to read, have a good sense of history, could be logical and articulate when you want to. I think you will be a good parliamentarian.' The negatives were: impulsive, impatient, moody, lazy (I protested), short-tempered, adamant...the list went on and on. I got irritated and retorted that if he believed there were so many drawbacks, why had he asked me the question to begin with. He smiled and suggested that I calmly consider his proposal, and get back to him within the next few days. I told him categorically that I was not interested. I had a dance tour planned in five different countries in Europe, and I was not willing to give that up to fight an election. And with that, the conversation came to an end.

But I think, that day my father planted the seed of an idea in my head that fructified two years later when I decided to take the plunge and join politics.

On 25 June 2012, Pranab attended his last CWC meeting. It was a poignant moment. It was his childhood ambition to become a CWC member one day, having read about members during his school days. He became a member of CWC in 1978 and continued to be a part of it till June 2012, except for a period of four years. In total, he was associated with the CWC for 30 years. Pranab wrote in his diary that night:

> Today CWC met to give an emotional farewell. Soniaji said [that] Pranabji was the most effective and decisive member in formulating policies and taking decisions. A void will be created and we will feel his absence in CWC. PM, [Motilal] Voraji, [R.K.] Dhawan, Mohsinaji [Kidwai] became emotional. In my response, I said that this is both the proudest and saddest moment in my life. Proudest because the highest policy making body of this 127 year old party is recognizing the work of an ordinary Congressman; and saddest because I shall not be able to attend any party functions with which I was associated for decades.

The next day, Pranab resigned from the Cabinet.

A month later on 25 July 2012, after 43 years of being in politics, with some achievements and some controversies, some dreams achieved, some goals reached and some desires remaining unfulfilled, Pranab Mukherjee took oath as the 13th President of India.

chapter 8

Abode under the Dome

Rashtrapati Bhavan with all its grandeur can be quite intimidating. The main structure, spanning approximately five acres, is located within a vast estate of 330 acres. It boasts 340 rooms, 2.5 km of corridors and a sprawling 190-acre garden.[115] It is reportedly the largest residence for any head of state in the world.

After the swearing-in ceremony, the president and his/her family initially move into what is known as the Guest Wing. The H-shaped Rashtrapati Bhavan has the North (Family) Wing and the South (Guest) Wing joined by the 'State Corridor'. For protocol and security reasons, the president, after the swearing-in, cannot continue to live outside Rashtrapati Bhavan. Similarly, till the president-designate takes oath, the outgoing president (who is the president till the swearing-in) cannot stay outside. Consequently, the moving-in of the president-designate, and the moving-out of the outgoing president happen simultaneously. The new president and the family first move into the Guest Wing, for a couple of months, till the Family Wing gets cleaned and renovated to welcome the new president. The Guest Wing, which is far more resplendent

---

[115]'Rashtrapati Bhavan Main Building', *Rashtrapati Bhavan*, https://tinyurl.com/wkuf6d5h. Accessed on 16 October 2023.

than the Family Wing, was the family quarters of the British viceroys till independence. When the first Indian Governor General C. Rajagopalachari moved in to Rashtrapati Bhavan (or Government House, as it was called then) in 1948, he felt that the splendour and the luxury of the living quarters of the colonial rulers should be discarded in favour of a comparatively simple and modest accommodation. He moved to the other side of the corridor, to the current Family Wing, which is comparatively more modest, as it accommodated the viceroy's officers rather than the viceroy. The Guest Wing now hosts presidents and prime ministers of other nations invited by our president.

The rooms in Rashtrapati Bhavan, decorated with antique furniture and Persian carpets, are palatial with high ceilings and thick walls to keep out external noise. The presence of liveried staff carrying tea in embossed china on silver trays with silver cutlery, uniformed men from the three services, along with armed guards posted on the adjoining corridors within the family quarters, hardly create a welcoming atmosphere unless one is accustomed to such grandeur. In fact, the size of my bathroom at Rashtrapati Bhavan was large enough to accommodate half of my apartment in GK!

There is hardly any segregation between private and public spaces at Rashtrapati Bhavan. I learnt it the hard way on the very first morning of my stay.

After the swearing-in ceremony, I stayed at Rashtrapati Bhavan for a week to ensure that my parents were comfortably settled. Additionally, I was keen on experiencing the initial days alongside them. For us, it was a historic occasion. After all, we were till then only one of the 13 families since independence who had stayed there as the family of the president of India.[116] Considering that President Kalam was a bachelor, we were actually the twelfth.

My aunts and some other relatives from Bengal had come to attend the swearing-in ceremony. After enjoying a peaceful night's rest, largely due to the absence of external noise, I made my way to my aunts' room for a chit-chat. Since my room was adjacent to theirs, I decided to not bother putting on a different outfit and went in my nightgown. The nightgown in question was one of those classic, well-worn ones that have become so cosy over time that you simply can't bring yourself to get rid of it. As I came out of my room, right outside the door stood a tall gentleman in a crisp white naval uniform, giving instructions to a few liveried men. All heads turned towards me in unison. The gentleman in the uniform clicked his heels in typical military style and greeted me saying, 'Good morning, Ma'am. Hope you had a pleasant sleep.' The 'ma'am' in question simply muttered a response and hurried to her aunts' room to conceal both her embarrassment and the worn-out nightgown.

My aunts too had their moments! After the swearing-in ceremony, lunch was organized for the new president and his family in the state dining room with all the paraphernalia of a state banquet. One of my aunts, sitting next to me, whispered, 'What do you do with so many pieces of cutlery?' I told her to eat with her hand. I said I would do the same. But she was hesitant. She did not want to break the rules of 'etiquette' on the very first day of her brother's presidency and be condemned to the special 'hell'

---

[116]The first president of India, Rajendra Prasad, was elected twice

reserved for those lacking so-called 'social grace'! Not just her, I saw many at the table exchanging furtive glances. Noticing the tension and immediately realizing the cause of it, my father declared in a loud and clear voice: 'Eat with your hand.'

Later, in the privacy of her room, my aunt asked me, 'Munni, how will you live here?' I declared that I had no such intention. Then she asked, 'How will Dada live here?' I quipped, 'That's his problem, not mine.' But no matter how unfamiliar a situation might be, human beings have immense capacity to adapt and adjust to it. Very soon, clothed in my faded t-shirts and shorts (my at-home day wear), I was chasing my dogs in the long corridors of the Family Wing, much to the bewilderment of the armed guards posted there. And I brought two of my large coffee mugs from home. I didn't want to begin my day having tea in embossed china!

Pranab's first evening at Rashtrapati Bhavan was spent in the Dwarka suite, which was previously inhabited by British viceroys, with Lord Mountbatten being the last occupant. Being a history buff, it was an extraordinary moment for him. It symbolized not just how far he had come personally, but also how the son of a freedom fighter—jailed several times by the British—was now sleeping in the room once occupied by the chief of the colonial masters. For him, it symbolized the journey of a nation.

After his swearing-in, Pranab spent an entire evening with his family after many years. He wrote in his diary, 'After so many years I could enjoy the company of my family members and specially with my 3 sisters. (sic) It was really nice.' But the mood did not last even 24 hours. The next day, he was feeling 'a bit bored'. The day after, on 27 July, there was an outburst. He wrote, 'I don't know how am I going to adjust to this new life. There is no stress, no strain and in fact no activity. This is really painful.' This was despite the fact that there was some activity. The PM came to meet him in the morning and they had a 'long discussion'. There were also internal meetings and courtesy calls by several officers of Rashtrapati Bhavan.

Pranab obviously missed being occupied for 18 hours a day and having a crisis to resolve. But then he rationalized, 'What to do? One has to call it a day and hang his boots.' However, he was yet to hang his boots. Though retired from politics, Pranab became a proactive president. He quickly became busy in taking on various roles as the visitor of central universities and the supreme commander of the armed forces in his capacity as president, reviving many traditions of Rashtrapati Bhavan and introducing several new initiatives. One of his main objectives was to make Rashtrapati Bhavan more accessible to the people. Though nothing compared to his days in politics, he found himself quite occupied. He also had his fair share of 'stress and strain'.

There were several lessons for me as well. It was during this time that I learnt an interesting fact about the president's security. Despite being the supreme commander of the forces, the multi-layered security of the president of India is handled by the police, not the armed forces. In Delhi, the president's security is managed by the Delhi Police. When the president travels outside the state, it becomes the duty of the respective state police forces to ensure the president's security.

I asked my father why the responsibility for presidential security is not entrusted to the armed forces, given that the president is their supreme commander. He explained that the president is the head of a civilian state, and it is the responsibility of the civilian government to provide protection. The intention behind this action was not mere symbolism to make a point, but to ensure that the president, as the supreme commander, does not overstep his/her boundaries and assume unconstitutional powers with the support of the armed forces.

AROUND THE WORLD

In the very first year of his presidency, Pranab visited 23 states and union territories. As president, Pranab also had to undertake several trips to foreign countries to strengthen bilateral relationships. The president's international tours are decided by the government of the day. Being EAM twice, Pranab understood India's foreign policy well. I learnt from his diaries that he also made suggestions to the governments of the day regarding his presidential tours. Significantly, as president, he made his first foreign trip to Bangladesh. It was a historic visit considering that he was the first Indian president to visit Bangladesh since 1974. My mother accompanied him. Once his aircraft entered the Bangladesh airspace, it was escorted by aircrafts of Bangladesh Air Force till the Dhaka Airport where they were received warmly by PM Sheikh Hasina and her Cabinet.

Squadron Leader Abhinav Bhattacharya, ADC to the president, had accompanied Pranab. Abhinav later jokingly described the visit to me as a 'protocol nightmare'. A large number of local political leaders and other dignitaries wanted to meet him. Pranab gave instructions to accommodate as many as possible. Before each meeting, the ADCs were supposed to brief him about the visitor. However, they soon realized that it was not necessary. Pranab did not need any prompting from the ADCs to brief him about the visitors. He greeted each one of them by name, enquiring about their families with a familiarity that only comes with years of association. By protocol, the visitors were expected to maintain a certain physical distance from the president. No one was supposed to touch the president's feet. But each visitor, upon entering the room would shout 'dada' and plunge at his feet. 'Dada' too smilingly disregarded the protocols. Abhinav, who had been present since the previous president's tenure, claimed that he had never witnessed such a phenomenon before.

Though Pranab had visited Bangladesh many times before, he had never had the opportunity to visit my mother's birth place, Nadail. This time, a special programme was organized there in honour of the First Lady. They were given a unique reception. Pranab was greeted with all the traditional rituals associated with welcoming a newly-wed bridegroom visiting his in-laws place for the first time after marriage. On 5 March 2013, he wrote in his diary, 'After 56 years of marriage, I was made to feel like a newlywed bridegroom.'

During this visit to Bangladesh, Pranab was conferred the Bangladesh *Muktijuddho Sanmanona* (Liberation War award), the nation's second highest civilian award. He was also awarded an honorary doctorate degree at a special convocation in Dhaka University. Keeping aside the written speech, Pranab gave an extempore speech. It was a highly emotional speech in Bengali highlighting the shared history and cultural legacies of the two nations. This received a standing ovation from the audience.

In the early years of his presidency, I had the opportunity to accompany him on a few of these tours. However, with the exception of a single trip to China in 2016, I had to forgo all the other tours after I joined politics and contested the 2015 Assembly election from Delhi. The tours were extremely hectic, packed with consecutive official events, allowing only a brief window to return to the hotel and change clothes before the next programme. Pranab would not 'waste' even a minute during these tours, and would board the flight to get back home the minute the official engagements ended. Several journalists, who were part of the presidential delegation (or accompanied him on foreign tours even before he became the president), revealed that a select few among them would muster the courage to ask him if he could spare some time for sightseeing. Pranab would snap at them saying, 'I am not a tourist.'

Nevertheless, these tours gave me the extraordinary experience, honour and luxury of travelling with the presidential delegations as the president's daughter. As I was not expected to attend the official meetings, some sightseeing tours would be planned for me. These were pre-scheduled, strictly timed and replete with protocol and security paraphernalia. Nevertheless, I was in a much better situation compared to the other delegates. Some of them were simply required to attend the meetings without speaking a single word, as relayed to me by two young MPs who were part of one such tour.

Occasionally, visits to tourist places for the entire delegation would be organized by the host countries as part of the official programme. Despite claiming that he was 'not a tourist', Pranab enjoyed these tours, especially

Top: Baba and I interact with Bhutan's King Jigme Khesar Namgyel Wangchuck and Queen Jetsun Pema, during their state visit as the Chief Guest at the 64th Republic Day celebrations in January 2013.

Bottom: Pranab is made to feel like a newlywed bridegroom after five decades of marriage. He is welcomed with pomp and fervour at his wife's ancestral village Bhadrabila in Nadail district of Bangladesh during the presidential visit in March 2013. Geeta Mukherjee *(seated)* looks on.

Soaking in the Naga spirit: Pranab, as president, dressed in a tribal attire during his visit to Nagaland in May 2013. I am seen here with Governor Ashwani Kumar (second from left) and Chief Minister Neiphiu Rio (first from left)

Top: The First Lady celebrates her birthday—Geeta Mukherjee's birthday celebrations at Rashtrapati Bhavan in September 2013 with her granddaughter Brishti, son Indrajit and officers and staff

Bottom: Ceremonial reception at Rashtrapati Bhavan during state visit of Emperor Akihito and Empress Michiko of Japan in December 2013

Top: The MP from Varanasi, Prime Minister Narendra Modi, compliments our dance troupe for capturing the true spirit of Benaras in the dance performance at Rashtrapati Bhavan in 2014.

Bottom: I explain the beauty of the Indian Pashmina shawl to the President of Finland Sauli Niinistö and the First Lady during Pranab's state visit to Finland in October 2014. Baba listens intently.

Top: Reading briefs during tours with the President

Bottom: Candid conversation with Baba aboard the presidential aircraft, AI-1

Top: Jingle All the Way—meeting the 'official' Santa Claus at his hometown Rovaniemi in Finland, during the President's State Visit to Finland in October 2014

Bottom: Not just another fairy tale—Baba and I with His Majesty King Harald V and Queen Sonja, the King and Queen of Norway, during the President's State Visit to Norway in October 2014

Top: Happy Birthday, Mr President—Baba's birthday celebrations at Rashtrapati Bhavan in December 2016

Bottom: Bonds beyond borders—Accompanying the Prime Minister of Bangladesh, Sheikh Hasina, in Rashtrapati Bhavan during her state visit to India in April 2017.

Just another day in Rashtrapati Bhavan: *(From left to right)* Jugnu, Fuhrer and Rangeela in the lawns of the President's Estate

A voracious reader and astute academic surrounded by his books

'Call me Mukherjee Sir': Pranab interacts with children in Rashtrapati Bhavan

Looking forward to life's next season: Pranab at his post-retirement home, 10 Rajaji Marg, just before the end of his presidency in 2017

Staying active and productive after retirement: Pranab working on his computer.

Top: Pranab re-discovers his childhood with granddaughter Brishti, whom he fondly called Gurguri

Bottom: Former Prime Minister Dr Manmohan Singh and his wife, Mrs Gursharan Kaur, join Baba, Abhijit and me for lunch at 10 Rajaji Marg in 2018

Relationship beyond ideology: Prime Minister Narendra Modi visits us at 10 Rajaji Marg after the 2019 elections

An honour for India's people: Pranab wears the Bharat Ratna medal with pride at 10, Rajaji Marg in August 2019

When siblings bond: Pranab with his 3 younger sisters *(left to right)* Swagata, Jharna and Krishna, during their surprise visit to Delhi to celebrate Pranab's birthday in December 2019

when they involved visiting places of historical importance. He was mesmerized by his visit to Waterloo in Belgium—the famous battleground that turned the course of fortune for Napoleon Bonaparte and subsequently became an important landmark in European history. A fun trip was to Rovaniemi, the capital of Lapland in the north of Finland, which is the 'official' home town of Santa Claus. Another such trip was to Cappadocia in Turkey.

These tours gave me the rare opportunity to interact with some of the world leaders and their spouses. Often, I would have a 'one-to-one' meeting with the spouse of the head of the state of the host country. One of my most memorable meetings was with Queen Sonja of Norway. Not just a meeting, she personally took me for a tour to the splendid Opera House in Oslo, followed by a visit to the studio of a designer of Indian origin. For me, the kings and queens were characters from fairy-tales written by Grimm brothers and Hans Christian Andersen. However, thanks to being my father's daughter, I had the opportunity to meet and interact with these royal figures, not with a sense of awe but as a respected guest from a different country.

UNOFFICIAL 'OFFICIAL' HOSTESS

Due to my mother's ill health, I often had to step in as the 'hostess' for official functions and banquets when foreign heads of states visited with their spouses. Attending the banquets was a relatively simpler job. I received a briefing which included extensive background notes on the visiting dignitaries' country; profiles of the delegation members; bilateral relationship between the two countries; and concise notes on the main issues expected to be discussed during the visit. As each 'brief' was more like a volume of a hefty doctoral thesis, I decided to keep it simple. I read the profiles of the main guest and the spouse; a little bit about the country and bilateral relationship between the two countries; and thoroughly about their performing arts traditions, an area of my interest. With sufficient conversational material to last for a few hours, these interactions were usually smooth sailing.

Bigger events lasting a couple of days, like the Republic Day or foreign visits, needed more preparation. These would be really hectic, consisting of one official programme after another. My first such experience was for the Republic Day in 2013. The chief guest for that year was the young king of Bhutan, His Majesty Jigme Khesar Namgyel Wangchuck, and his beautiful queen, Her Majesty Jetsun Pema. As I knew them from before, it became quite an enjoyable experience. The young queen confided to me that it was her first state visit abroad following her marriage. She was happy that it was to India and felt at ease upon discovering that I would be her 'hostess' throughout the visit.

India's relationship with Bhutan was close to Pranab's heart. He shared a warm and personal friendship with the royal family, especially with the former king, His Majesty Jigme Singye Wangchuck, the father of the current king. Pranab first met him in the early 1990s during his first trip to Bhutan as deputy chairperson of the Planning Commission. He had great regard for the King who ushered in democracy in his country, voluntarily stepped down in favour of his son and mooted the concept of 'gross national happiness' (GNH), rather than GDP as a measure of the well-being of his citizens. When democracy was introduced in Bhutan, Pranab was closely involved at every stage of the transition and had the privilege of advising King Jigme Singye. In 2007, India and Bhutan signed the India–Bhutan Friendship Treaty. The King suggested that the then Crown Prince (the current king) sign it on behalf of Bhutan, and Pranab as the EAM should sign the treaty on behalf of India. Pranab, being a stickler for protocol, highlighted the fact that the Crown Prince held a higher position in the protocol ranking than him. The King laughed and said, 'Doesn't matter, our relationship is not only special but it is extraordinarily special.'[117]

I had the privilege of experiencing how 'extraordinarily special' this relationship was during my first trip to Bhutan in 2010. I was a personal guest of Pavan K. Varma, then our ambassador in Bhutan. Both Pavan and his graceful wife Renuka are very close friends. During that visit, I was invited for lunch by the former king, His Majesty Jigme Singye. He is married to four sisters, one of whom was out of the country during my visit. After a delicious lunch with him and his three queens, I bid them goodbye and we exited together. Outside the reception hall, there was an open landing from where one had to climb down a flight of stairs to reach the car. As it was drizzling, there were men waiting at the landing carrying open umbrellas. To my utter shock, the former king took an umbrella and held it over my head as I started walking down the stairs. There I was, with a former king holding an umbrella over my head, flanked by his three queens. One of them jokingly said, 'You never did

---

[117]Mukherjee, Pranab, *The Presidential Years: 2012-2017*, Rupa Publications, 2021, p. 47.

it for us!' His Majesty responded solemnly, 'I am doing it for her father. He is a true friend of Bhutan.' He didn't just hold the umbrella, but he also walked all the way to the car and opened the door for me.

Upon my return to Delhi, I reported this to my father, causing him to nearly lose his balance in disbelief. He exclaimed, 'Do you realize what an honour this is?' he asked. Of course I realized it. Regarding his relationship with the former king, Pranab wrote in his book, 'We could discuss a wide range of topics—political, economic etc. without the fear of being misunderstood.'[118] In the world of international diplomacy where every word is measured, such trust and understanding was indeed remarkable.

DESPAIR AND HOPE

Amid this whirlwind of diplomatic activity, there was trouble brewing at home for the government that Pranab had earlier been a minister of, and the party that he had served for more than four decades. Within the Congress, Rahul's influence was growing. Going by Pranab's diaries, there did not seem to be much interaction between him and Rahul during Pranab's UPA days. One of the early references in his diaries about Rahul was on 29 January 2009, in the context of a CWC meeting that had discussions on strategies for the upcoming Lok Sabha elections as one of the agendas. Pranab wrote, 'Rahul Gandhi spoke vehemently against coalition. I told him [that] he should elaborate his ideas and it should be logically put. He said that he'll discuss with me.'

---

[118]Ibid.

After that, there are few references in his diaries of Rahul visiting him at his residence. Pranab described him as 'very courteous' and 'full of questions', which he took as a sign of Rahul's desire to learn. But he felt that Rahul was 'yet to mature politically'. Rahul continued to meet Pranab at Rashtrapati Bhavan, though not very frequently. Pranab advised him to join the Cabinet and gain some first-hand experience in governance. Rahul obviously did not heed the advice, as we all know. During one of these visits on 25 March 2013, Pranab noted, 'He has interest in diverse range of subjects but moves very quickly from one subject to another. I don't know how much he listened and absorbed.' On 15 July 2013, Rahul came for lunch. As per Pranab's diary, Rahul spelt out in detail his plans for revamping the organization. Though Pranab did not write anything about those plans, he was appreciative and noted that Rahul 'appeared confident of meeting the challenges'. But had Pranab known what Rahul was about to do two months later (perhaps, Rahul himself didn't know it then), he would have very strongly advised Rahul against it.

On 27 September 2013, Rahul Gandhi walked into a press conference held by former Cabinet minister and the party's Communication Department Chief Ajay Maken and vehemently trashed a proposed government ordinance calling it complete nonsense, adding that it should be torn up. Infamously known as 'Save the Convicted' ordinance in popular parlance, it came in the wake of a Supreme Court judgment that ruled immediate disqualification of a legislator if convicted in a criminal offence (with a jail sentence of two years or more). The ordinance aimed to bypass the Supreme Court order of immediate disqualification, and proposed instead that the convicted legislator may continue as a member while an appeal in a higher court was pending. In the meantime, the voting rights and the salary of the member would be withheld. A bill was earlier introduced in Parliament, in the Monsoon Session of 2013, and sent to a parliamentary standing committee for scrutiny. The move to promulgate the ordinance was seen by many as a means to protect Lalu Prasad Yadav, a long-term ally of the Congress, who was accused in the fodder scam and was awaiting verdict on 30 September. The ordinance was cleared by the Cabinet a week before and was sent to the President for his assent.

Pranab himself was against the ordinance. A day before Rahul's public outburst, he had summoned the then Home Minister, Law Minister and Parliamentary Affairs Minister. During the meeting, he questioned the urgency behind the promulgation of the ordinance. Going by his diaries, I learnt that he had informally advised some of his former colleagues in the party to not take the ordinance route. He felt that bypassing Parliament on such an important issue was not correct. He also felt that amid growing public anger towards criminalization of politics, bringing such an ordinance without wider political consensus would not be politically wise and would have negative consequences for the Congress and the government. So, in principle, he agreed with Rahul. But he was aghast at the manner in which Rahul acted. I was the one who first broke the news to him. After a long time, I saw my father getting so angry! His face became red and he shouted, 'Who does he [Rahul] think he is? He is not a member of the Cabinet. Who is he to publicly trash a decision of Cabinet? The Prime Minister is abroad. Does he even realize the implication of his actions and the effect it will have on Prime Minister and the government? What right does he have to humiliate the PM like this?'

That night, he wrote in his diary, 'Rahul Gandhi gate-crashed a press conference by Ajay Maken and described the decision of Cabinet as "nonsense". This is totally uncalled for. He has all the arrogance of his Gandhi–Nehru lineage without their political acumen.' He continued to write that his office got a call from Kapil Sibal, and he himself got a call from Ahmed Patel requesting him not to take any action on the ordinance. He also wondered how Rahul's actions would impact the coalition partners.

Much later, after I had joined politics, during a discussion with my father about the reasons behind the Congress party's poor performance in the 2014 elections, he told me that, among other reasons, Rahul's outburst was the final nail in the coffin for the Congress. 'The party's vice-president had shown such disdain for his own government publicly. Why should people vote for you again?' he asked. Later, a senior Congress leader told me that Rahul had tried his best within the party to not promulgate the ordinance, but no one had listened. When I reported this to my father, he sharply remarked that despite his many years in politics and his influential position within the party, if Rahul couldn't persuade his colleagues without resorting to theatrics, then maybe politics wasn't his calling. I think his faith in Rahul was shaken after this incident.

Even before the election results were announced, it was clear that the 10-year rule of the UPA government was coming to an end. The mood in the Congress was gloomy. Several leaders of the party and the UPA came to meet Pranab before the elections. All the predictions pointed towards a victory for the BJP/NDA, yet none had anticipated such a washout for Congress. Finally, when the results were declared on 16 May 2014, the Congress had fallen to an all-time low with just 44 seats, while the BJP on its own got an absolute majority winning 282 seats.

That day, Pranab wrote in his diary, 'We shall have to see how this new man [Modi] emerges. Stability of the govt. is assured, but what about social cohesion? I am really worried.'

The next day, PM Dr Manmohan Singh handed over his resignation and that of the Cabinet to him. It was a poignant moment for Pranab. He noted, 'I thanked him for his contributions as FM and PM for steady economic development of the country. He also thanked me for helping him in running the government for eight years. Our official association for more than 30 years comes to an end today. Farewells are always sad.' After the meeting, Pranab broke all protocols to see off Dr Singh to his car. Another moving entry from that time was about his meeting with Sonia, just a few days before, on 13 May. Pranab noted, 'She was looking sad and tired... Before leaving, she told me, "Pranabji, I am missing your presence every day since the last two years and I shall be missing you more now." I was simply touched.'

Rahul visited Pranab after this disastrous defeat. Pranab found it surprising that 'he [Rahul] gave his views on the election performance of the party in a most detached way, from a distance as an outsider as if he was not the face of the campaign and the main campaigner of the party'. Pranab further wrote, 'Perhaps his distance from the party and a lack of killer instinct could be reasons for his failure to enthuse the party workers to fight the election which BJP got from Narendra Modi.'

The reports he got from his former colleagues in the

Congress were not very encouraging. He noted that some leaders 'poured venom' against Rahul and many senior leaders complained that Rahul was not meeting them. Pranab felt that some of the comments made by Rahul reflected his political immaturity. He was also disappointed by Rahul's frequent disappearing acts. Pranab believed that serious politics is a 24x7, 365-day job. He personally did not believe in taking time off, and diligently attended all official and party events. He felt that Rahul's frequent breaks, particularly during a crucial period for the party, were causing him to lose the perception battle. Rahul was conspicuously absent during the flag-raising ceremony at the AICC on the party's 130th Foundation Day on 28 December 2014, barely six months after the party's devastating loss in the general elections. Pranab noted in his diary, 'Rahul was not present at the AICC function. I don't know the reason but many such incidents happened. As he got everything so easily, he does not value it. Soniaji is bent upon making her son the successor but the young man's lack of charisma and political understanding is creating a problem. Can he revive Congress? Can he inspire people? I do not know.'

Pranab was also critical of the coterie around Rahul, possibly based on feedback received from senior party leaders. He advised Rahul to include both new and old leaders in his team. In this context, there was once a funny incident. One morning, during Pranab's usual morning walk in the Mughal Gardens (now Amrit Udyan), Rahul came to see him. Pranab disliked any interruptions during his morning walks and puja. Nevertheless, he decided to meet him. It turned out that Rahul was actually scheduled to meet Pranab later in the evening, but his [Rahul's] office mistakenly informed him that the meeting was in the morning. I came to know about the incident from one of the ADCs. When I asked my father, he commented sardonically, 'If Rahul's office can't differentiate between "a.m." and "p.m.", how do they hope to run the PMO one day?'

However, he thought that perhaps Rahul could still get his act together. He noted in his diary that Rahul was making good interventions in Parliament on the Land Acquisition, Rehabilitation and Resettlement (Amendment) Bill. On 2 March 2016, he noted, 'Rahul made a good speech today in parliament. Good if he learns. It's his 12th year in Lok Sabha, but better late than never.'

Ahead of the 2019 Lok Sabha elections, there was a sense of anticipation within the Congress, and even in some sections of the media, that the party would perform significantly better than in 2014 and pose a formidable challenge to the BJP. During a conversation with my father, he said that he would acknowledge 'the emergence of Rahul Gandhi as a leader if the Congress party wins 88 seats'. The reason behind this number remains unclear to me, perhaps it was a doubling of their existing count of 44 seats. I got angry and accused my father of being cynical. Unfortunately, he was correct. Congress could win only 52 seats. After the elections, when Rahul resigned as the Congress president and insisted on having a 'non-Gandhi' as the party president, I asked Baba's views on it. He responded with a counter-question, 'How much autonomy or authority would a "non-Gandhi" president have?' I questioned why he was considering such a scenario. He snapped at me, 'Don't teach me Congress politics.'

Though Pranab was critical of Rahul and seemed to

have lost faith in his ability to revive the Congress, one thing is undeniable. Had Pranab been alive today, he would have definitely appreciated Rahul's dedication, tenacity and the outreach during the Bharat Jodo Yatra. This 145-day Yatra, spanning over 4,000 km, has arguably positioned Rahul as a highly credible face of the political narrative countering bigotry.

THE PM AND THE PRESIDENT: A SUCCESSFUL DYNAMIC

On 26 May 2014, Pranab administered the oath of office and secrecy to the 15th Prime Minister of India, Narendra Damodardas Modi, along with 45 members of the council of ministers. The grand ceremony was held in the early evening in the open forecourt of Rashtrapati Bhavan.

Despite the scorching heat, Pranab felt a sense of relief. He wrote in his diary:

> It was a grand show but I was nervous on two counts. First, if it rains, there would be total chaos, and till yesterday there was rain and thunderstorm. Secondly, from the security angle, the entire political establishment of the country along with high security risks foreign dignitaries were present. Though all agencies were involved in making arrangements, ultimate responsibility was with the President's office as it was the venue and the cards were issued by us. Thank God, everything went smoothly.

The ceremony was a grand success. Yet, at a personal level, Pranab felt dejected by the disastrous performance of Congress. In his diary, he further noted:

> I performed my duties of administering the oath and talking to people but with a heavy heart. I am no longer associated with any political party, but how can I forget that I was associated with Congress for more than 40 years? Before me, my father was an active member of Congress for 30-40 years. What enormous abjection in 129-year-old grand party (sic) which brought freedom to this country and laid the basic foundation of a modern state.

Leaving aside his personal sadness, Pranab, the president, was relieved that the electorate had given a decisive mandate to a single party to form the government. After 1984, no political party had been able to attain an absolute majority in the Lok Sabha in the 30 years and seven elections that followed. Being an active participant in Indian politics for decades, Pranab believed that in situations of fractured mandates leading to coalitions, governments are frequently constrained by their coalition partners resulting in policy paralysis and conflicting interests within the government. He firmly believed that such coalitions cannot serve as a substitute for a strong government at the centre. On 23 May 2014, Pranab noted in his diary:

> After 30 years, single party majority rule at centre with Modi getting 282 seats along with well-crafted pre-poll alliances has provided him with sufficient elbow room even to deal with dissent in his own party. Even if he takes them [alliance partners] into govt., he would not be held hostage to whimsical opportunistic partners. He can show them the door without risking the continuation of his govt.

Perhaps, this reflected his own frustrations of dealing with coalition partners when he was in government.

I always wondered about Pranab's relationship with PM Modi. Despite belonging to two very different political ideologies, and with both being strong personalities, they seemed to get along famously. One of the reasons was perhaps Pranab's interpretation of the role of President and the institutional relationship between the president and the executive. I got further insight on this after reading his diaries.

Modi's first meeting with Pranab as president is recorded in Pranab's diary. Modi was the CM of Gujarat then. In an interesting entry on 18 August 2012, Pranab noted:

> Narendra Modi [CM Gujarat] came to see me. He is a bitter critic of Congress and the govt. but seems to have a strange soft corner for me. In the meetings of CMs/NDC, I sharply reacted to his comments, and he also retorted back sharply. But whenever he meets me personally, he always touches my feet and tells me that it gives him pleasure to do so. I don't know the reason for it.

Perhaps, one of the reasons could be that Pranab knew how to give credit where it was due.

In his diary entry of 6 February 2010, when Pranab was the finance minister, he mentioned that he 'had a spat' with Modi at the Chief Ministers' Conference on price rise. Then on 2 March 2011, Pranab noted, 'Gujarat CM Narendra Modi submitted the report of Consumer Affairs sub group of CMs meeting on price rise in Feb 2010. The report is quite interesting and professional. I must call and congratulate him.' I don't know whether Pranab called Modi, but later he wrote in his book:

> Narendra Modi, the then chief minister of Gujarat, was extremely critical of Sonia Gandhi and the Right to Food Bill [at the CM's conference] ...However, Modi's outburst provided the basis for the Bill. He headed one of the several sub-committees instituted to look into the issue. The comprehensive report prepared by him, which was purely administrative in content and without any political bias, laid the foundation for the Bill.[119]

At a later point, PM Modi personally told me about his practice of touching Pranab's feet. He shared that he had known Pranab for a long time, even before he became the CM of Gujarat. Modi would frequently visit Delhi for organizational duties and would stay in the North/South Avenue area. He would occasionally meet Pranab during his morning walks. Pranab always spoke kindly to him, and Modi would always show respect by touching his feet.

On 18 August 2012, CM Modi extended an invitation to Pranab, requesting his presence at the Vibrant Gujarat Summit to be held in January 2013. Pranab pointed out to him about the upcoming elections in Gujarat and the possibility of a change in government. Modi was quite confident of victory. Regarding this meeting, one of the ADCs—who was waiting outside the president's office to escort the CM to his car—told me an interesting anecdote. Supposedly Modi emerged from Pranab's office muttering

---

[119]Mukherjee, Pranab, *The Coalition Years: 1996-2012*, Rupa Publications, 2017, p. 170.

to himself, *'Kya bhavya vaktitwa hai* (What a towering personality).'

After the declaration of the 2014 Lok Sabha elections, the BJP and other NDA leaders, led by the then BJP President Rajnath Singh, met Pranab to hand over a letter and a resolution of the BJP Parliamentary Party electing Narendra Modi as its leader and requested the President to invite him to form the government. The PM-designate held a private meeting with Pranab later that same day. Pranab noted in his diary, 'Modi touched my feet and said, "Dada, you guide and advise me as your younger brother." I assured him of my fullest cooperation.' Pranab further noted, 'His idea of inviting the SAARC heads of state and the governments for the swearing-in is quite novel. I advised him to ensure tight security.'

Much later, I came to learn more about the meeting directly from the PM. By his own admission, PM Modi was a little nervous when he went to meet Pranab. The latter put Modi at ease and told him candidly, 'We belong to two different political ideologies. People have given you the mandate to rule. Governance is the domain of the Cabinet headed by the prime minister. That's your job. I will not interfere. If you need any advice on constitutional matters, I will definitely help you.' Modi told me, 'It was a very big thing for Dada to say.' From the conversation, it seems that there was an openness and honesty in their interaction from the very beginning.

Pranab then asked Modi about his analysis of the election. Modi responded that after three decades, a political party had achieved an absolute majority. Pranab then asked him, 'What else?' When Modi didn't answer, Pranab told him that the 2014 election was unique in the history of Lok Sabha elections, as it featured a declared new face as the prime ministerial candidate. Pranab emphasized that people had not only voted for Modi's party, but also for him as the PM. While narrating this incident to me, Modi explained that the 2019 election was different, as it was assumed that he would continue as the PM.

He further added, 'I never thought of it that way till Dada pointed it out.' Perhaps Modi was being modest, but then modesty is usually not one of his greatest virtues.

In Pranab's papers, I found a typed note without any signature. Written in bullet points, it seemed to present a few observations on the first Cabinet meeting of the Narendra Modi government held on 27 May. It made certain interesting points:

> Hon'ble PM was in total command and control right from the first meeting of Cabinet held on 27th May 2014. He had complete clarity of thought and purpose, and he is highly focused. He means business as far as good governance is concerned. He emphasized repeatedly on good governance and delivery within available finance. He mentioned that finance is never a bottleneck and stressed on innovative thinking. Hon'ble PM reminded his Cabinet colleagues that as the election was over, the politics is now past and we have to separate politics from administrative decisions and governance issues.

The note continued to state that only 5–6 veterans like Rajnath Singh, Sushma Swaraj, Arun Jaitley, Venkaiah Naidu and Ram Vilas Paswan spoke, 'but every time they looked at Hon'ble PM for direction'. It further noted, 'The first impression what one gets was most of the

Cabinet members are not very knowledgeable and did not have clarity on issues. (sic)' In the note, there were three points regarding the President:

- When the discussion on ordinance was going on especially on the Polavaram Project, the sense one got was that Hon'ble PM and his senior colleagues were not taking the President for granted and therefore planned to bring the amendment in the Parliament.
- From the discussions of the Hon'ble PM and his senior Cabinet colleagues, it was seen that all of them have great respect for the Hon'ble President.
- Issues about the forthcoming address of the Hon'ble President to the Parliament were also discussed. Though there will be some criticism about the policies etc. of the previous government, Hon'ble PM directed that Hon'ble President must not be embarrassed. So criticism will not be emphatic.

The presidential addresses to the Joint Sessions of Parliament are drafted by the Cabinet. The president's job is to just read it out. I learnt from Pranab's diary entry on 6 June 2014 that when he read the first draft of the address that came from the PMO, Pranab asked his office to contact the PMO suggesting certain changes. As per his diary, the PMO initially showed reluctance towards the proposed modifications. Pranab then asked his office to request the PM to meet him in the evening. He was informed that the PM would visit him at 7.30 p.m. By 6.00 p.m. the PMO sent a revised draft in which most of Pranab's concerns were addressed. When the PM arrived for their meeting, Pranab suggested some further changes, which the PM readily accepted. Pranab further noted in his diary:

> We had discussions on various issues. He told me that he valued my advice and I told him that he will get my full cooperation. It is quite clear that:
>
> 1. he has clarity in his thoughts and has a professional approach to statecraft
> 2. he feels the pulse of the people very strongly
> 3. he wants to learn and does not pretend that he is 'Mr. Know all'
> 4. As a hardcore RSS man, he is fiercely patriotic and nationalist.

Regarding the second point, Baba mentioned to me multiple times that, in his opinion, Narendra Modi is the only PM after Indira Gandhi, who has the ability to feel the pulse of the people so acutely and accurately. On 23 October 2014, he noted in his diary, 'PM's decision to spend Diwali with jawans at Siachen and flood affected people at Srinagar speaks of his political sense which was not visible in any other PM except Indira Gandhi.'

As I read Pranab's first address to the Joint Session of Parliament of the sixteenth Lok Sabha, there was hardly any criticism of the policies of the previous government. Rather, its focus was on the future; a strong and positive policy statement of the plans and vision of the new government. As I researched the Polavaram Project, a multi-purpose irrigation project in Andhra Pradesh, I learnt that the legislation for the project was cleared by Parliament through the Andhra Pradesh Reorganisation (Amendment) Bill.[120]

---

[120]'Polavaram Project Gets Parliament's Nod', *The Times of India*, 15 July 2014, https://tinyurl.com/tcznfkcj. Accessed on 22 March 2023.

So, it seems that though belonging to two vastly different ideological backgrounds, from the very beginning, the President and the PM made genuine efforts to work as a team.

PM MODI, AS I KNOW HIM

Soon after Narendra Modi became the PM, I think I inadvertently put him in a bit of an uncomfortable situation by inviting him to attend one of my dance programmes. Pranab had started a monthly cultural programme called 'Indra Dhanush' at the Rashtrapati Bhavan auditorium, where renowned artists from across India were invited to perform. Siddharth Sharma, the internal financial advisor at Rashtrapati Bhavan, was a multi-tasker and looked after the Indra Dhanush programme as well. Since the beginning, he had been asking me to perform there. I requested him to directly approach my father regarding the matter, as any such proposal when put forward by me would have been summarily dismissed.

Siddharth also faced difficulties in convincing Pranab to give me permission to perform at the Rashtrapati Bhavan. Pranab firmly stated that the programme was reserved for the most renowned artists in India, and I did not fall into that category. Siddharth stood his ground and emphasized that although I may not be among India's most esteemed artists, I am Pranab's daughter and a talented dancer. 'All members of Rashtrapati Bhavan were keen to watch her performance and it was a popular demand,' Siddharth asserted. Eventually, Pranab relented and granted permission. All these discussions took place somewhere in early August 2014, and the programme was scheduled for the following month.

I decided to present a new production of mine, centred around the theme of Benaras (Varanasi), which had its first showing in February 2014. On 15 August, at the Rashtrapati Bhavan 'At Home' programme, I impulsively decided to invite the PM for the show. To my delight, he kindly accepted the invitation and agreed to attend. My father was furious with me later on because he believed that I had put the PM in an 'awkward situation'. He argued that the PM had countless responsibilities to handle and shouldn't have to attend a cultural event. I countered by pointing out that the PM was also the MP from Varanasi (Benaras). Therefore, I didn't see any harm in inviting him to a dance production that was specifically created to showcase the timeless spirit and cultural ethos of Benaras. Moreover, the PM had agreed to come. So, I argued, asking my father why he was making such a big deal out of it.

As I shared the news with my dancers, they became ecstatic. It was the first time I witnessed the immense popularity of Narendra Modi among young people. These girls, in their late 20s and early 30s, had been working with me for a while and were not particularly interested in politics. Prior to every election, I would urge them to vote for the Congress, and they would enthusiastically agree. I asked them if their enthusiasm was for the 'prime minister' in general or specifically for Narendra Modi. They all screamed in unison, 'Didi, it's Modi.'

Their excitement was only matched by their determination to deliver a flawless performance. The regular 2-hour rehearsal schedules easily turned into 4–5-hour sessions, not because I asked them to, but because each of them wanted to give their best and wouldn't stop until they were satisfied.

It was one of those shows that every performer dreams of! There were no last-minute glitches, no costume mishaps, no missed music or light cues. The coordination and precision were impeccable, filled with an energy that comes only with inner motivation.

Baba was duly impressed. He noted in his diary that night, 'Munni's program was simply brilliant. Through perfect choreography and performance of the dancers, with audio-visual projections, the spirit of Varanasi was truly captured. Everybody was impressed.' The PM also complimented me on 'capturing the true spirit of Benaras'.

My own interaction with the PM has been very limited, but always pleasant. Whenever we met at the Rashtrapati Bhavan programmes and banquets, he always spoke kindly to me. In April 2017, the very next day after the Delhi Corporation election results were declared, there was a banquet at Rashtrapati Bhavan. Despite massive anti-incumbency, the BJP had managed to win the election for the third term. At the banquet, I jokingly told the PM, 'Sir, you must teach me how to win elections.' He responded with a light-hearted laugh and invited me to meet him at some point in the future. To my astonishment, as he was leaving the banquet he mentioned it again that I should meet him soon.

A few days later, I made a request for a meeting with his office, although I didn't have high hopes of actually getting it. Surprisingly, I was granted an appointment within a week. Needless to say, I was extremely nervous! I turned to my father for advice on what to discuss with the PM of our country. He reassured me that it would be a brief courtesy call, lasting no more than five minutes. He suggested that I seek the PM's guidance and blessings.

The meeting lasted nearly 20–25 minutes. He put me completely at ease and never made me feel that I was talking to the PM of the country. About my query on how to become a 'successful politician', he pointed out that I have the best teacher at home, so why do I need to go elsewhere? I countered by mentioning that whenever I sought my father's insight on any matter, he would first recommend reading five books before engaging in further conversation. Hearing this, the PM had a hearty laugh. He advised me to concentrate on working in the organization.

When I asked about their agenda of a 'Congress Mukt Bharat', he shared an interesting anecdote from his early days. As a young RSS worker, he visited Guruji's (M.S. Golwalkar) residence. It was in 1969, just days after the first split of the Congress. As per him, Guruji was extremely upset about the split and reportedly told all present that a split in the Congress was not good for the country, as the nation needed a strong Congress. The PM went on to highlight how, in the early years of independent India, when the Congress was at its peak, there was no significant Opposition at the Centre. Now that the BJP is in power, he acknowledged the need for a strong Opposition, but stated that it is not the BJP's responsibility to put Congress's house in order.

Even after Pranab retired from presidency, I had a few one-on-one meetings with the PM. He always made time for me. During all of my meetings with him, particularly when I was involved in politics, I would raise a plethora of issues including attitude towards minorities, Women's Reservation Bill, criminalization of Triple Talaq and many others. He always gave politically-correct answers, which was expected considering he is perhaps one of the most astute politicians in India today. Although I didn't necessarily agree with everything he said, I refrained from engaging in heated arguments with him because I understood that he didn't grant me an audience due to my status as a prominent politician or journalist, but simply because I am my father's daughter. I had to maintain a level of decorum while politely expressing my disagreements. But what I found most remarkable was that he was never evasive, and never became dismissive or angry with me for asking these questions and voicing my opinion. When I reported these meetings to my father, he would often humorously comment on the PM seemingly having 'infinite patience'.

After Pranab demitted office as president, PM Modi visited him a few times. At Rashtrapati Bhavan, I never had the opportunity to observe Pranab and the PM together, except during official banquets. Now, I could see their interaction from close quarters. Although I wouldn't be present while they conversed, I would enter the room intermittently to offer tea and snacks. Undoubtedly, there existed a strong personal chemistry between the two leaders. The relaxed body language and the sound of laughter conveyed the same.

After each visit, I would ask my father about the nature of their discussions. Each time, his response was the same—'a political adda'. This was confirmed by his diaries. Unlike their meetings at Rashtrapati Bhavan, where the PM would brief the President on specific issues, these interactions appeared to be more like informal conversations in typical adda style. It goes without saying that their topics of discussion revolved around politics.

COPYBOOK PRESIDENCY

Pranab was extremely conscious of the limitations of his power as president, and equally cautious not to overstep his boundaries. Whenever he found himself uncertain or in need of guidance, he would seek advice from legal experts, including the attorney general, and abide by it. In his papers, I found a note of advice on whether the president can send messages to Parliament with regard to a pending bill or any other matter. As per the note, the president has the right to send messages to Parliament under Article 86(2) of the Constitution. However, with the 42nd Amendment of the Constitution in 1976, it became mandatory for the president to act on the advice of the council of ministers for the exercise of his/her functions. Given this context, the approval of the Cabinet is necessary even for messages to be sent to Parliament. The note further elaborated on this point by quoting constitutional experts like D.D. Basu and M.P. Jain. Basu clearly stated that the president 'would not give any address or message except on ministerial advice'. Jain stated that any other view would not be tenable 'as the action of the President to approach parliament over the head of prime minister is bound to create a constitutional crisis'.

As an experienced politician and a member of the Cabinet for many years under different PMs and presidents, Pranab was of the firm opinion that governance and administrative decisions are the responsibility and domain of the PM and the Cabinet as they were given a mandate by the voters. According to Pranab, the president's office should refrain from interfering in these matters. As he wrote in his book:

> I knew that my active political role had come to an end and that I would have to conduct myself as a constitutional head and not interfere unnecessarily in the domain of the executive. I had done enough of executive work for decades and now it was time to step back and adhere to the constitutional role that a president is expected to perform.[121]

Way back in 2007, there's an interesting entry in his diary on 27 June which discusses a core group meeting of Congress regarding the presidential election campaign of Pratibha Patil. One of the members suggested that Patil should engage with the public by discussing current events with the media, similar to how the BJP candidate Bhairon Singh Shekhawat was doing. Pranab pointed out that presidents are not elected by the people. He observed that discussions on current issues by presidential candidates were irrelevant in the Indian system, as it was not a presidential form of government. Furthermore, he emphasized that presidential elections were not fought on the basis of these issues. The limited electorate for presidential elections consists of MPs and MLAs who vote along party lines. 'If Presidents think that they have won the election through people's mandate, why should they listen to the PM? And in that process, the entire constitutional scheme would be frustrated,' he noted.

I found other diary entries during his tenure as the EAM that further substantiate his views. Pranab noted that

---

[121]Mukherjee, Pranab, *The Presidential Years: 2012-2017*, Rupa Publications, 2021, p. 174.

Dr Christy Fernandez, principal secretary to President Pratibha Patil, had written to the then Foreign Secretary Shivshankar Menon informing him of the President's desire to explore certain issues falling within the scope of the MEA. On Pranab's directions, Menon conveyed to Fernandez that in line with past protocol and the constitutional position, it would be most suitable for discussions regarding matters like this, as well as general policy briefings for the President, to take place during meetings between the PM and the President or the Minister and the President.

Another entry, during the same period, related to the presidential briefing by the Home Secretary and two senior officers of the MEA prior to President Patil's visit to a border state in May 2008. During the briefing, Secretary to the President mentioned that he had already asked a senior military officer a day before to inform his counterpart in the neighbouring country about the President's visit, and to ensure that no untoward incident takes place. Pranab noted that Menon wrote to him stating that all the three officers present at the briefing felt that it was wrong, for the Secretary to the President to deal with operational matters or to give instructions to the Army in this manner. Even Menon agreed with them. I also learnt that Pranab wrote to the PM about these occurrences, as well as a few others, raising his concern. He noted:

> Recurrence of such incidences can only lead to the creation of dual authority and erosion of well-established practices associated with the two highest offices of our parliamentary system. Unless we immediately put a stop to such incidences, it will do irreversible damage to

> our established system of devolution of power between the real executive authority and nominal executive authority.

Given Pranab's views on the matter, when he became the president, he accepted that he was only the 'nominal executive authority'. He was also extremely careful not to exceed his authority by interfering in the functioning or decisions of the elected government of the day, especially when it was led by a political party that had been the main Opposition during his time in government.

However, it would be wrong to say that he was just a mute spectator, or served as a 'rubber stamp' president. While being careful not to overstep what he believed were his constitutional limitations, he voiced his concerns and sought clarifications whenever he deemed it appropriate. But he did it behind closed doors. During his tenure, the imposition of President's Rule in Arunachal Pradesh and Uttarakhand became contentious issues. Both the states were then ruled by Congress governments and the moves to topple the duly elected governments by the BJP government were highly criticized. In both cases, the crisis was initiated by rebel MLAs of the Congress.

Arunachal Pradesh

In Arunachal Pradesh, a constitutional crisis arose when in November 2015, 21 Congress MLAs opposed to then CM Nabam Tuki, skipped a CLP meeting and challenged Tuki's leadership. On 9 December, they met Governor J.P. Rajkhowa and complained that the Speaker was trying to get them disqualified. In a bizarre move, the Governor then decided to advance the Assembly session by a month from 14 January 2016 to 16 December 2015 without consultation with the CM and his Cabinet. He also fixed the agenda of the House to consider a motion to remove the Speaker. In retaliation, the government locked the Assembly premises. Subsequently, on 16 and 17 December, the move to impeach the Speaker; passing of a no-confidence motion against the current government; and electing a rebel Congress MLA Kalikho Pul as the leader of the legislative party were held in a 'makeshift' Assembly premises in a community hall and a hotel. The same day, the Speaker issued notice to disqualify 14 Congress MLAs, whereas the Deputy Speaker quashed them.

Both the parties moved Court. On 5 January 2016, Gauhati High Court stayed the disqualification of 14 Congress MLAs. On 15 January, the Supreme Court referred all the petitions to a five-member Constitution bench which was to also examine the discretionary powers of the Governor. In the meanwhile, the Governor sent a report recommending imposition of President's Rule due to breakdown of constitutional machinery.

The proposal to impose President's Rule reached Pranab on 24 January 2016. That night, Pranab wrote in his diary:

> It is total chaos in Arunachal. Apart from the loss of majority MLAs support, locking up of Assembly premises, seizure of governor house and the role of governor Rajkhowa in favour of BJP have complicated the issue. (sic) The matter is being heard in constitutional bench now. The six months intervening period between the last day of the last session and the date of the next session is over, adding to the complication.

During a meeting with a Congress delegation on the Arunachal issue, Pranab raised the issue of not reconvening the next session. In response, he was informed by the senior leaders that since the matter was sub judice, there was no need to reconvene. Pranab expressed his dissatisfaction to Home Minister Rajnath Singh regarding the Governor's actions of convening the Assembly without consulting the Cabinet and holding sessions outside the Assembly premises. During their discussion, Pranab also questioned the legitimacy of these actions. In his book he wrote, 'I was expecting, as others were, of some interim order, but when it did not come, I had to act... Before signing the presidential proclamation, I had consulted legal experts.'[122]

In February 2016, President's Rule was lifted in Arunachal. On 17 February, Pranab wrote in his diary, 'The matter is taking a queer turn as governor, backed by union govt. assumed power which is not vested in him and now trying to install a govt by appointing a new CM by moving a motion on the floor of the House.' Pranab was definitely not happy with the Governor and questioned the government about the timing of lifting the President's Rule. On 19 November 2016, Principal Secretary to PM and Arun Jaitley came to meet him twice: at 11.00 a.m. and again at 2.15 p.m. Pranab wrote in his diary:

> I raised 3 questions:
>
> 1. Urgency of revoking proclamation now when time to GOI is available up to 24th March either to revoke or getting parliament approval.

[122] Mukherjee, Pranab, *The Presidential Years: 2012–2017*, Rupa Publications, 2021, p. 56.

2. What would be implication of judgement of SC setting aside the orders of governor from 14th Dec to 26th January?
3. What would be the impact of recalcitrant governor?

Govt. response was through FM that let the political process in A.P. start with the installation of a popular govt. The constitutional procedures and practice will be followed. Judgement of S.C. will be implemented by letter and spirit.

Following the revoking of President's Rule, rebel Congress leader Kalikho Pul formed the government with other rebel leaders within Congress and the support of the BJP. In July 2016, the Supreme Court ordered the restoration of the Nabam Tuki-led Congress government in Arunachal Pradesh. It unanimously indicted Governor Rajkhowa's decision to advance the Assembly session as unconstitutional.

However, it was too late for Tuki. He resigned before the floor test, realizing that he did not have the numbers. Governor Rajkhowa was forced to resign.

Uttarakhand

The crisis in Uttarakhand was precipitated by a controversy over the passing of the Appropriation Bill in the Uttarakhand Assembly on 18 March 2016. According to a report sent by the then Governor of Uttarakhand K.K. Paul to the President (with a copy to the Home Ministry), the Speaker did not allow any division of votes as demanded by the Opposition, and declared the Bill as passed before adjourning the House.[123] Sixty-eight members were present in the House, out of which 26 were from the BJP and nine rebel MLAs from Congress.

As the failure to pass a finance bill amounts to no confidence against the government, it was imperative to clear any doubt over it. Accordingly, the Governor directed the then CM Harish Rawat to conduct a vote of confidence on the floor of the House, no later than 28 March. Rawat agreed to it and the date was fixed for 28 March, as the Speaker had reconvened the House that day. Two days prior to the voting, the Speaker disqualified the nine Congress rebel MLAs for anti-party activities. Just a day prior to the floor test, on 27 March, the Centre imposed President's Rule in Uttarakhand.

Apparently, the decision taken by the central government was based on purported attempts by Rawat to engage in horse trading, as alleged by rebel Congress leaders in a 'sting operation', and the Governor's apprehension over possible pandemonium during the floor test.[124] In the multiple reports sent by the Governor to the President, there was no recommendation for imposition of President's Rule. Pranab wrote in his book:

> Here, it was not the governor's report but the recommendation of the union government on which I had to act. I accepted the recommendation of the home minister for imposition of the President's Rule, because, according to the Constitution, the president

---

[123]Tripathi, Rahul, 'President's Rule Imposed in Uttarakhand After Governor's Report', *The Economic Times*, 28 March 2016, https://tinyurl.com/cem89m4j. Accessed on 12 October 2023.
[124]Ibid.

> has to act on the basis of the report of the governor of a state, or otherwise. The term 'otherwise' could mean any other relevant authority of the government. In the case at hand, it was the union home minister.[125]

On 28 March, a day after the imposition of President's Rule, he wrote in his diary, 'On President's Rule in Uttarakhand, I find myself guilty but I could not do anything as Constitution has not given the president any discretionary power.' I asked my father the same question that was raised by the leaders in Opposition. They pointed out that he had the option to return the file for reconsideration. But as per him, that would not have solved the problem because the president has the power to return a file to the Cabinet only once. If the Cabinet returns the file without any change, the president is bound to act as per the decision of the Cabinet. He told me that returning the file would not have served any purpose other than making an empty statement and 'to make headlines' for being an 'activist president'.[126]

However, Pranab did not sign on the dotted lines without raising questions and advising the government against the imposition of President's Rule. On 26 March, at 11.00 p.m., Arun Jaitley and Principal Secretary to PM Nripendra Misra visited him. Pranab enquired why there was such a rush to declare President's Rule, merely 36 hours before the floor test. He further observed, 'Budget has been passed by voice vote as per Speaker's observation who is the competent authority. Why are you precipitating

---

[125]Mukherjee, Pranab, *The Presidential Years: 2012–2017*, Rupa Publications, 2021, p. 57.

[126]Ibid. 58.

a crisis?' He also asked whether they were relying on the word 'otherwise' in Article 356, in the absence of specific recommendation of the governor of the state to impose President's Rule. He was told about the alleged horse trading attempts by Rawat. As per Pranab's diary, he instructed his office to put down the observations in an official note.

Immediately after the imposition of President's Rule, Rawat challenged it in Nainital High Court. On 29 March, the High Court ordered a floor test on 31 March. It also allowed the disqualified MLAs to participate in the floor test. This order was challenged by the Centre at the double bench level of Nainital High Court, which quashed the proclamation and did not grant a stay. The Centre then moved the Supreme Court the next day and got a stay, restoring status quo as on the day of the proclamation. On 6 May, the Supreme Court passed an unprecedented order prescribing a court-monitored floor test to ascertain the strength of the Harish Rawat government on 10 May. As per the order, President's Rule was to be suspended for two hours for the floor test to be conducted.

On 6 May, Pranab called the Attorney General Mukul Rohatgi and Nripendra Misra seeking an explanation regarding the implications of the Supreme Court order. In Pranab's papers, I could not find a copy of the minutes of the meeting for 26 March, but found a copy of the same for the meeting on 6 May. It noted, 'The President reiterated that had his viewpoint expressed on 26th March 2016, to wait for another 36 hours and allow floor test in Assembly been taken note of before taking the decision in the Cabinet, this mess could have been avoided.'

Pranab wrote in his diary that night, 'From what they told me, it appeared that GOI will accept the result of the floor test and revoke President's Rule. I told Mishra (sic) that had he conveyed my advice to PM properly, perhaps this embarrassment to the govt could have been avoided.'

Harish Rawat won the floor test and formed his government. The whole Uttarakhand episode rattled Pranab. On 16 April, while interacting with eminent judges during a judges' retreat in Bhopal, he asked them, 'President takes oath to preserve, protect and defend the Constitution. How could this be implemented when president has to act according to decisions of Cabinet ? Can the president in India exercise his power independent of Cabinet ? Please advise.'

Pranab was now learning to see issues from a different perspective than his earlier role of being a member in the Cabinet. But whatever the advice might have been, Pranab did not change his views about the role of the president. On 21 July 2017, with just four days left to his presidency, Pranab noted in his diary:

> Since last five years, every day I was confronted with this question. I asked myself what should I do? Shall I become an 'activist' president capturing the headlines in newspapers? Then I remembered that headlines in newspapers remain alive for 24 hours and on TV for one and a half hour. So let me follow the spirit of parliamentary democracy. Policies and orders to execute them are the job of the PM.

Pranab, by his own belief and choice, wanted to be and remained a copybook president.

WITHOUT FEAR OR FAVOUR

Pranab's desire to be a copybook president does not mean that he observed events passively. He was a president who spoke his mind. Not only in Republic Day or Independence Day speeches, it was evident in many other speeches that he delivered through other platforms.

The president addresses the nation on the eve of Independence Day and Republic Day. As usual, Pranab did his homework and read the speeches of his predecessors to get a 'grasp of the exercise'.[127] He worked meticulously on these speeches, carefully selecting subjects that mirrored his concerns about present-day matters.

His speech on the eve of Republic Day in 2014 created some controversy. The contentious issues were two points in the speech. The first one was his statement that 'populist anarchy cannot be a substitute for governance'.[128] It perhaps came in the context of a strange and unprecedented crisis created by the then newly elected CM of Delhi, Arvind Kejriwal. Five days before Republic Day, he, his ministers and MLAs sat on a 'dharna' outside Rail Bhavan in New Delhi, even as preparations for Republic Day celebrations were on in full swing. His demand was immediate suspension of five police officers who refused to arrest some foreign citizens as per orders of Somnath Bharti, the then law minister of Delhi in the AAP government. A few days earlier, Bharti had conducted a 'midnight raid' with his supporters on the residence of few

---

[127]Ibid. 32.

[128]'Address by the President of India, Shri Pranab Mukherjee on the Eve of Republic Day of India 2014', *PresidentofIndia.gov*, https://tinyurl.com/mrxp2w27. Accessed on 12 October 2023.

foreign nationals from African countries, on the allegations of running a drug and prostitution racket. Four women complained that they were beaten up by the mob and were forced to submit urine samples (that later tested negative for drugs). The police refused to arrest the women on the ground that there was no warrant. The 'raid' itself was illegal and unauthorized, as it was conducted by Bharti and his supporters and not by the police. The then Law Minister of Delhi showed utter disdain for the law of the land and its due procedures by taking law in his own hands. Along with his supporters, he acted in a most shameful and unlawful manner with women from a foreign land. Instead of condemning his minister, Kejriwal decided to sit on 10-day dharna, not agreeing to wait for the results of a police inquiry ordered by the Home Ministry and proclaimed himself to be an 'anarchist'. He created an unprecedented crisis, in which a CM was trying to create a potentially disruptive situation at the time of the Republic Day celebrations—a source of immense pride for every Indian.

Pranab was greatly disturbed by the unfolding events. On 20 January 2014, he wrote in his diary:

> I feel very disturbed over the happenings in Delhi. CM Kejriwal and his band of followers have made the government, rule of law, civil administration a joke. He declared himself to be an anarchist. I don't understand what type of behaviour it is. If he is an anarchist, then why he is in government? Governance and anarchism do not go together. I called home minister Shinde and LG of Delhi Najeeb Jung and asked them how are they going to handle the situation.

Finally, Kejriwal called off his dharna by having the two police officers placed on leave. This served as a way for him to save face. This kind of politics by an elected government and a CM was anathema to Pranab. Hence, he chose to mention the term 'anarchy' during his speech.

The other point was his advice to the electorate to vote for a 'stable government'. He said, 'This year, we will witness the 16th General Election to our Lok Sabha. A fractured government, hostage to whimsical opportunists, is always an unhappy eventuality. In 2014, it could be catastrophic. Each one of us is a voter; each one of us has a deep responsibility; we cannot let India down. It is time for introspection and action.'[129]

Pranab wrote in his diary on 27 January 2014, 'My address to the nation on the eve of the Republic Day has triggered off a controversy. Some are appreciating it as timely, statesman like, appropriate, first-ever from a president; others are critical as highly political, harmful advocacy against regional parties, anti-Congress, pro-Congress, anti-AAP, non-conventional etc.'

Pranab himself wrote in his book that his message was a bit political, but felt that it was his duty as the first citizen of the country to advise the electorate to vote for political stability and not for a fragile coalition.[130]

In addition to the content of the speech, Pranab had to make other preparations too. As the presidential addresses to the nation were pre-recorded in a makeshift studio at Rashtrapati Bhavan, Pranab was advised to wear 'screen-friendly' colours—a tough choice between black,

---

[129]Ibid.

[130]Mukherjee, Pranab, *The Presidential Years: 2012–2017*, Rupa Publications, 2021, p. 29.

grey and dull brown. Another problem for him was to read by looking at the teleprompter. Pranab was used to giving extempore speeches. On international forums like UNGA and others, he would rely on prepared texts and deliver his speeches directly from them. The glare of the teleprompter screen, along with the harsh studio lights, hurt his eyes. However, when he reviewed the recordings of his speeches, he stumbled upon a surprising revelation. Much to his dismay, he noticed that he had unintentionally made 'funny faces' while speaking. He chastised himself harshly and resolved to rectify this issue without delay.

Pranab took the opportunity to share his views on burning issues of the day through various programmes that he attended, whether it was about crime against women or an increasingly polarized society. In the context of increased polarization and violence, he spoke about India's core civilizational values of pluralism and tolerance. This was one of the recurring themes in his speeches. In the context of Parliament logjams, he advised the government to carry along Opposition and appealed to the Opposition to not disrupt Parliament. He spoke against bypassing Parliament's authority by repeated promulgation of ordinances. He spoke against violence and discrimination against marginalized sections of the society. With the skills he had developed over decades as a politician, he managed to convey his views strongly without any direct criticism of the government or reference to any particular incident. Most importantly, he expressed his views without violating the dignity of his office. He wrote in his diaries that some of his speeches 'might raise eyebrows', but then came to the conclusion that he cannot remain a 'mute spectator'. Clearly, he was not.

ℴ

During his presidency, Pranab had to witness and was greatly disturbed by the systematic undermining of the legacies of earlier PMs, especially from the Gandhi–Nehru family, by the current government. On the 15 August 2014 'At Home' programme at Rashtrapati Bhavan, PM Modi had informed Pranab of his government's decision to not organize any birth or death anniversaries of leaders—except for Mahatma Gandhi—including the anniversaries of former PMs. As per Pranab's diary, Modi had further informed Pranab that this decision was taken by the Vajpayee government but it was not operationalized. He added that respective memorial trusts and societies would be encouraged to organize these programmes.

As per his usual practice, on 20 August 2014, Pranab went to Veer Bhumi to pay his respect to the former PM Rajiv Gandhi on his birth anniversary. On 21 August, Pranab noted in his diary that no minister was present at the function to commemorate the birth anniversary. He further wrote, 'Certain questions come out of this decision. Who will bear the cost of maintenance of these Samadhis? The land belongs to the government. Can the private societies be given the responsibility to maintain it?' He raised the same question to Home Minister Rajnath Singh, who visited him the next day. Pranab noted, 'He [Rajnath Singh] told me that no decision [about maintenance] has been taken as yet, but he agreed with me that while the anniversaries may be observed by the respective trusts or societies, the Samadhis should be maintained by the government.' Going by his diaries, Pranab seemed to have raised this question with the PM himself on 11 October 2014, and noted, 'PM agreed to instruct the competent authorities to maintain Samadhis at the cost of the government but the function has to be done by the respective trusts.'

On the death anniversary of Indira Gandhi on 31 October, Pranab wrote:

> For the first time in thirty years, there is no government program for Indira Gandhi. Modi Govt's program of 'De-Nehrufication' has begun. If they think they can erase Nehru-Indira-Rajiv from history, they are mistaken. All 3 have earned their places in history—Nehru as the architect of modern, secular, democratic India, Indira as the liberator of Bangladesh and as a crusader against terrorism and Rajiv as the architect of CIT revolution in India. Observation of Sardar Patel's birthday as 'Unity Day' is a welcome move, but for that to ignore others is not a healthy move.

In the context of Indira Gandhi's centenary year celebration, Pranab felt that it was totally wrong to ignore the contributions of these two great leaders (Pt Nehru and Indira) who were also the longest serving PMs of India. He noted, 'In democracy such impropriety reflects the meanness of the ruling party.'

Pranab was especially disturbed by the government's attempt to ignore Pt Nehru. I read in his diary that he had advised the PM to acknowledge Nehru's contributions. He noted, 'Thereafter he agreed to work out some programs for schools to mark his birthday, 14th November, and there should be efforts to inculcate scientific temperament in the students.' But as far as I know, no such programme was initiated by the government.

Though Pranab was critical about the government for failing to do its duty towards its predecessors, he did not spare the Congress either. On 14 November 2015, while lamenting about the current government's attitude to Pt Nehru, he observed that the Rajiv–Sonia regime has been guilty of perpetuating the Gandhi–Nehru legacy, while ignoring other PMs such as Lal Bahadur Shastri and P.V. Narasimha Rao, who were from the Congress. Once, Pranab sarcastically mentioned to me that Sonia and her children believe that apart from their own family, no other leader has made any contributions to the Congress or the nation.

As president, Pranab would always offer floral tribute to past leaders on their birth and death anniversaries. He also initiated the practice of inviting previous presidents' families to observe their anniversaries at Rashtrapati Bhavan. But this practice seems to have been discontinued now.

On the evening of 8 November 2016, PM Modi, through a televised address to the nation announced demonetization of ₹1,000 and ₹500 denominations of currency notes valued at approximately ₹14 lakh crore. At the stroke of midnight on 9 November, 86 per cent of Indian currency in circulation got invalidated. The stated objectives for demonetization were to flush out black money, to remove counterfeit currency and to stop terror funding.

Pranab became aware of the decision at the same time as the rest of India. Following the announcement, the PM came to meet the President to brief him. The PM requested Pranab's endorsement of the decision, to which Pranab agreed and expressed his support through a tweet. However, he raised certain concerns with the PM regarding the availability of adequate currency notes for exchange and its impact on the economy.

Pranab shared with a trusted colleague that upon hearing the announcement, his immediate concern was for the fate of millions of people across India. He was worried about the small grocery shop owners, landless labourers, farmers with small landholdings and fishermen in his village, as well as in countless other villages across the country. Additionally, he thought about the daily-wage labourers; the urban poor; women who had diligently saved meagre amounts over the years; and the owners and employees of micro- and small-scale industries. After all, 93 per cent of India's total workforce worked in the unorganized sector[131], while millions of people in distant rural hamlets had no access to any banking facilities.

The days following the announcement of demonetization were utter chaos. In urban centres, even in big cosmopolitan cities like Delhi with banks and ATMs in every locality, the long winding queues of people waiting to withdraw their hard-earned money is still etched deeply in people's memories. Inadequacy of smaller denomination notes coupled with the government's frequent, ever-changing announcement of regulations did nothing to ease the burden of the common man.

One of Pranab's greatest fears of this sudden demonetization was that it would undermine the trust people had in the currency and the banking system. In the 1970s, when Pranab was the revenue minister in Indira Gandhi's Cabinet, he had sent a note to her suggesting demonetization. Indira did not accept his suggestion on the grounds that it would shake people's faith in the

[131]'Unorganized Worker', *Ministry of Labour and Employment, Government of India,* https://tinyurl.com/ywr7fkfk. Accessed on 12 October 2023.

banking system, as all currency notes issued by the Reserve Bank of India represent the commitment of a sovereign government.[132]

In his diary, Pranab remembered an interesting advice given to him by Indira. He noted, 'When I was FM, while replying to a question whether Govt. is thinking of demonetisation—my reply was emphatic "NO". She told me, "Do not be so emphatic in parliament. Who knows you may be compelled to do so in future?' Three days after demonetization, on 11 December 2016, he noted in his diary, 'As a consequence of the crisis, gold price has reached to 55,000/- rupees per 10gm from Rs. 30,000/-. I am afraid that the price difference between Indian gold and international gold will be an incentive for smuggling activities in gold. In mid-seventies, I had to deal with this problem with a heavy hand.'

It is evident from Pranab's frequent diary entries that he was deeply concerned about the impact of demonetization and the way it was being handled. On 18 November 2016, Pranab called the PM. He wrote:

> I raised my concerns about
>
> 1. change of decision altering amount to be withdrawn within a week
> 2. about peoples' faith in the credibility of the currency system
> 3. to ensure that there is no problem for harvesting and marketing of Kharif crops
> 4. to ensure that the farmers realise price of their products of Kharif crops

---

[132]Mukherjee, Pranab, *The Presidential Years: 2012–2017,* Rupa Publications, 2021, pp. 157–58.

5. there should be adequate supply of valid currencies to ensure that Mandis and wholesale markets and retailers of perishable food items should not suffer because of lack of availability of valid currency notes
6. to ensure adequate supply of money to rural economy for sowing season of Rabi crops.

> He assured me that the system will be stabilized within next couple of weeks.

On 25 November, he noted, 'I am afraid that demonetization will have tremendous adverse impact on the economic growth of India.' On 7 December, a month after demonetization, he wrote, 'There is no ease of peoples' troubles. Acute shortage of currency notes is felt by everybody. Truly, it's a monumental mismanagement.'

On 21 December, the PM came to meet him again. Pranab noted:

> This is the third visit since he announced demonetization. I discussed with him on the issues of keeping people's confidence intact on the currency system, and govt. banking system should not be shaken as the stakes are too high. I told him that frequent change of rules does not inspire confidence in the minds of common people, so it should be avoided. Govt should assure Indian people that govt is fully aware and sensitive to the needs of the people and will take all necessary actions. I advised him to make a broadcast to the nation on measures being taken by the govt and also to assuage their fear that nobody's legitimate dues will be forfeited. It was a fruitful discussion.

Former PM Dr Manmohan Singh stated in his Parliament speech that demonetization would negatively impact GDP growth by 2 per cent, which proved to be true in the subsequent months. In response to those who argued that demonetization would have long-term benefits, he quoted the famous economist John Keynes that 'in the long run we are all dead'.

Pranab concluded in his book that the stated goals of the government for announcing demonetization were not met.[133]

❧

Unlike with demonetization, Pranab wholeheartedly welcomed a major and transformative economic measure that culminated during the Modi government—the introduction of the GST.

The idea of GST had a long journey of over a decade under several governments, and it was very close to Pranab's heart. As finance minister from 2009 till he demitted office in 2012, he worked relentlessly to develop consensus around the GST. It was then opposed by the BJP-ruled states. In 29 months, Pranab held around 20 meetings with different stakeholders that included state finance ministers, members of the empowered panel and full panel and CMs of states.[134] He introduced the Constitution (115th Amendment) Bill, 2011 in the Lok Sabha in March 2011, which was then referred to the Parliamentary Standing Committee on Finance. The Committee submitted its report in August 2013. It lapsed with the dissolution of the fifteenth Lok Sabha.

---

[133]Ibid. 159.

[134]Ibid. 162.

In December 2014, Finance Minister Arun Jaitley introduced the Constitution (122nd Amendment) Bill, 2014, in the Lok Sabha. In August 2016, the Bill was passed with amendments in both Rajya Sabha and Lok Sabha. After several complicated legislations, administrative procedures and ratification by states, the four GST Bills were passed as Money Bills in the Lok Sabha on 29 March 2017 and in the Rajya Sabha on 6 April 2017.[135]

On the morning of 30 March 2017, Pranab received an unexpected call from the PM. Pranab noted in his diary, 'He told me that last night as he witnessed passage of the GST Bill, he thought of me. [He said] "You took the initiative to pass this law but could not do so. Today when the bill is passed, I wanted to speak to you and offer this Act to you." I profusely thanked him as this is really a rare gesture of parliamentary courtesy.'

The government decided to launch GST on the midnight of 30 June 2017 by calling a ceremonial Joint Session at the Central Hall of Parliament. On 5 June, Jaitley came to meet Pranab and requested him to launch GST along with the PM. He mentioned that the PM desired so, considering Pranab's relentless efforts towards establishing the tax reform. Pranab again felt that it was a truly kind gesture. The PM didn't need to include him in the inauguration, since it was a government event, and in less than a month, Pranab would be demitting office as the president. But PM Modi thought that it was a 'historical coincidence' that Pranab as the president gave his assent to the Bill, hence he must be present.

---

[135]Sachdev, Alisha, 'One Year of GST: A Timeline of Events Which Led to the Country's Biggest Tax Reform', *Hindustan Times*, 1 July 2018, https://tinyurl.com/5dyavupr. Accessed on 12 October 2023.

In his speech at the launch of GST, Pranab outlined the 14-year-old journey of the initiative and said that it was a 'tribute to the maturity and wisdom of India's democracy'. He said, 'This consensus took not only time but also effort to build. The effort came from persons across the political spectrum who set aside narrow partisan considerations and put the nation's interests first.'[136]

The Congress along with few other political parties decided to boycott the midnight session to roll out GST. Pranab felt that it showed a lack of maturity of the Congress leadership. He also perhaps could not fully fathom the rapidly changing style of political discourse. One day in all seriousness, he asked me that why we (Congress) were terming GST as 'Gabbar Singh Tax'? I explained to him about the famous movie *Sholay* and its iconic villain, Gabbar Singh. I also informed him, as per the pointers given to us as party spokespersons, that the GST was extortionist in nature; it was unleashed on people without adequate preparation; and that it would negatively impact business and economy. The conversation further evolved as such:

Pranab: But GST was a Congress agenda. I myself tried hard to push it, but couldn't get it through due to political reasons.

Me: Why was it rolled out without adequate preparations, and why so many slabs and make it so complicated?'

Pranab: Any major change in tax regime would have some teething problems. When we introduced

[136]PTI, 'GST a Disruptive Change and Tribute to India's Democracy: Pranab Mukherjee', *The Times of India*, 1 July 2017, https://tinyurl.com/3cmjhxek. Accessed on 12 October 2023.

VAT, there were problems in the beginning, but it smoothened out. If you have objections about multiple slabs or any other issues, you must raise it. But to call GST 'Gabbar Singh Tax'? Ridiculous!

[He crinkled his nose in disgust.]

Me: Baba, it's catchy! See, even you are talking about it.

Pranab: Serious debates cannot be replaced by catchy slogans. People might remember your slogans, but will not pay attention to your arguments. You are simply trivializing the issue.

Recognizing his growing irritation, I quickly withdrew from the situation. After all, it was not a TV debate where you could drown your opponent's voice by simply having superior lung power. I had no hope of winning a debate with my father on GST, despite the pointers given by my party. Therefore, I thought that it was wiser to not push it further.

Pranab's presidency became controversial due to a large number of mercy petitions that were rejected by him, many of which were pending from earlier years, including those of Ajmal Kasab, Afzal Guru and Yakub Menon. However, he granted mercy and commuted the death sentence of four convicts involved in the Bara massacre in Bihar.

Based on the information found in Pranab's diary, as well as his book, I came to learn that in November 2012, he had sent seven petitions including that of Afzal Guru for a review to the then Home Minister Sushilkumar Shinde.[137] The file came back reiterating the recommendation of rejection.

While deciding on mercy petitions, Pranab read the case histories and judgments from trial court onwards. He used three broad guidelines in his decision-making process: the cases must fall in the 'rarest of rare' cases involving ferocity and cruelty; the death sentence from trial court onwards till the final verdict of Supreme Court should be unanimous; and the government should have recommended rejection of mercy.

I asked my father how he felt after rejecting mercy petitions. He replied that he felt terrible. He could not sleep for nights. He added that except for crimes against the nation, death sentences should be replaced by life imprisonments. I then asked him, 'What about the convicts in the Nirbhaya case?' Looking at my face, he hastily replied, 'That's a rarest of rare case.'

The human rights activists and various reports state that the death penalty does not deter crimes against women but surety and speedy dispensation of justice does. However, my personal opinion is that people who are capable of committing such heinous crimes and inflicting such brutal tortures on another human being do not deserve a second chance in life.

HIS LAST GOODBYE

During my father's presidency, we had to face one of the most traumatic events in our family: the death of my mother on 18 August 2015.

---

[137]Mukherjee, Pranab, *The Presidential Years: 2012–2017*, Rupa Publications, 2021, p. 77.

My mother had been at the centre of our family life. She provided Pranab an emotional anchor and was the glue that kept our extended family connected. At that point, she had not been keeping well for a long time. After finishing his puja every morning, Pranab would come to her room, place his hand on her head and do *japa*—offering silent prayers for her wellbeing. It was a daily ritual for him. That was the only overt gesture of affection towards his wife that I have seen in my entire life.

In his diaries, year after year, on the occasion of their anniversary on 13 July, Pranab repeatedly penned the story of their love and marriage, emphasizing that it was the best decision of his life. For me, she was one of the two persons I took for granted, the other one being my father. Like in most mother-daughter relationships, I fought with her relentlessly and got annoyed by her endless questions about my wellbeing, including whether I had eaten my greens or not. However, she was the focal point of my existence; something that I realized only after she departed from our lives.

My mother suffered a heart attack on 7 July 2015. She was immediately rushed to the hospital, but by the time she reached, she was already in a deep coma from which she never recovered. Pranab was in Odisha. He had left that morning, and had planned to return that same evening. My mother had urged him to stay an extra day in Puri so that he could visit the Jagannath temple and witness the Navakalevara festival (a ritualistic recreation of the idols of the deities taking place after 19 years). That morning was the last time that Pranab saw his wife in a conscious state.

After receiving the news, he flew back to Delhi late at night. Even though the doctors perhaps knew that there was no hope of her recovery, they provided the typical response that it was difficult to say anything before 72 hours. We hoped and prayed for a miracle, but sadly, it was not meant to be.

On the morning of 18 August, Pranab received news that the end was nearing. He rushed to the hospital carrying Srimad Bhagavad Gita. I was on my way from my residence, but by the time I arrived, she had already departed. I saw my father sitting at Ma's bedside with a stunned look on his face. His mind could not comprehend what had just happened. Later, he told me he was sitting by her side reciting the Gita. By the time he reached the fourth chapter, the doctors told him it was over. He told me that she went very peacefully, her pulse gradually declining till it stopped.

Numerous visitors began arriving. The following day, Ma was cremated with full honours befitting her status as the first lady. Vice President, PM and many senior members of the Cabinet, Dr Manmohan Singh, Sonia Gandhi, Mamata Banerjee, L.K. Advani, other Congress leaders and political leaders from other parties, family and friends attended the funeral. The PM of Bangladesh Sheikh Hasina and her sister Sheikh Rehana flew in to bid farewell to their beloved 'didi'.

After the cremation, Pranab immediately got back to work. He had a few official engagements that very day which he attended. Starting from the following day, he resumed his regular work routine. However, it was evident that he was going through the motions with a feeling of numbness. Pranab was not one to openly display his emotions, and unlike us, he didn't have anyone to share it with. The only hint of his inner turmoil was when he would frequently visit his wife's now empty room and simply stand there. We were instructed to leave her things exactly as they were placed while she was alive—her hairbrush on the dressing table and her spectacles on the bedside table. Only two years later, when he moved out of Rashtrapati Bhavan, were her things packed.

Two weeks after Ma's demise, Pranab's demeanour underwent a slight change. On 4 September, after a span of 47 years, Pranab assumed the role of a teacher, albeit for a couple of hours. He took a political science class for students of Class XI and XII at the Delhi-government run Dr Rajendra Prasad Navodaya Vidyalaya, situated within the Rashtrapati Bhavan complex. The CM of Delhi Arvind Kejriwal and the then Deputy CM Manish Sisodia had requested Pranab to conduct a class for students in the school to commemorate Teachers' Day. Though Teachers' Day is traditionally celebrated on 5 September each year, it had to be moved forward by a day due to the coinciding celebration of Janmashtami on that same date.

From his diary, it seems that due to his 'teaching assignment' and interaction with students, Pranab felt a bit lighter and was in a better mood for the first time since Ma's passing. He taught students about India's political history, the development of parliamentary democracy and the multi-party system. He continued to take 'class' for students on the occasion of Teachers' Day for the remainder of his presidency.

Pranab loved teaching and he loved children. At Rashtrapati Bhavan, children from various schools would come to meet him on festive occasions. Pranab thoroughly enjoyed interacting with them. He shared an amusing incident that took place once on Raksha Bandhan. As per regular practice, children would come to the president and tie a *rakhi* to him. The president then offered them candies kept on a large plate. One year, children from a particular school came dressed as freedom fighters. A 5–6-year-old girl dressed as Rani of Jhansi took some time selecting her candies. 'Tantia Tope', who was standing behind her, got impatient and gave her a push. True to her name, the Rani of Jhansi turned around and pushed Tope. A full-scale war was about to breakout but the teachers intervened and the 'warriors' were separated. Tope was pacified with a select choice of candies. Pranab loved to tell us such stories of his interaction with children.

RETREATS, RECORDS AND REPORT CARDS

No recounting of Pranab's life as president would be complete without a mention of the presidential retreats. The president has two residences other than Rashtrapati Bhavan: one in Mashobra near Shimla, and the other is Rashtrapati Nilayam in Hyderabad. As the president of India represents the Indian State, his/her yearly sojourn at these two retreats—one in the North and the other in the South—represents the office of the president as a symbol of unity and integrity of India.

Pranab would spend two weeks in winter at Rashtrapati Nilayam and about 5–6 days at Mashobra. It was not because of any preference for the southern states but simply because Pranab, perhaps, got a little bored at Mashobra. Making his base at Nilayam in Hyderabad, Pranab travelled to all the southern states to attend official programmes, meeting political leaders, academicians and dignitaries from the region. He was deprived of this opportunity in Mashobra, owing to its comparative inaccessibility other than via road transportation. There too, local dignitaries called on him. However, for Pranab, moving out of the retreat meant blocking off traffic in the narrow hilly roads and creating inconvenience for the people, something he wanted to avoid at any cost. Situated amid beautiful green forests and offering breathtaking views of snow-capped mountains, the presidential retreat at Mashobra was an ideal place for relaxing. However, Pranab found no solace in relaxation. Working less than 12 hours a day would only cause him stress and depression.

I always accompanied my father to Mashobra and simply loved it. Being a mountain person, I would spend my days hiking through the forests and the hills, and the evenings with Baba. During this time, he made an effort to watch a few movies. He was never a movie buff, and could probably count on his fingers the number of movies he had watched throughout his entire life. There is a story of how he reacted to a special screening of the famous Aamir Khan starrer *Rang De Basanti* when Pranab was the defence minister. In the movie, the defence minister is accused of major corruption for buying low-quality components for fighter planes resulting in the tragic death of a fighter pilot, who was the fiancé of one of the protagonists. As the plot unfolds, the defence minister is assassinated for his sins. The censor board wanted to ascertain the views of the Defence Ministry and arranged a special screening for the then Defence Minister. Pranab left the theatre during the interval, declaring that his job was to defend the country and not to give censor certificates to films. If the censor board did not have any problem, neither would he. The film was released and became a superhit.

In the evenings at Mashobra, Pranab began to watch a few old Bengali films. However, these movies were viewed in instalments, with only half an hour being dedicated to them each day. They would be resumed again the following day. At Rashtrapati Bhavan, there were special screenings of some films. Two of them found mention in Pranab's diaries indicating that he enjoyed them. One was the Amitabh Bachchan and Deepika Padukone starrer *Piku* (I think he enjoyed the father-daughter relationship portrayed in the film) and the other one was *Lincoln* directed by Steven Spielberg.

On assuming office, Pranab's foremost desire was to bring the office of the president closer to people and make Rashtrapati Bhavan more accessible to the public. He wanted 'de-mystification' of Rashtrapati Bhavan and democratization of the office of the president. Pranab believed that every public office, including the highest constitutional office of the country, needs to have a certain degree of accountability. At the end of every year of his presidency, he decided to bring out an annual 'report card' to put on record various activities of the president and initiatives taken by him during the year.

Soon after assuming office, he initiated a new set of protocols to discontinue addressing the president as 'His Excellency' and replace it with 'Hon'ble President'. In Hindi, instead of *'Mahamahim'*, it would simply be *'Rashtrapati Mahoday'*. 'His Excellency' would continue to be used for interaction with foreign dignitaries, as per international norms.

Being an avid book lover, one of his first tasks was to renovate the Rashtrapati Bhavan library. Designed by the architect of Rashtrapati Bhavan, Edwin Lutyens, the library contained some rare books which were restored with the support of experts from the Indira Gandhi National Centre for the Arts (IGNCA). An audio-visual section was added with speeches from Lord Mountbatten, C. Rajagopalachari, Dr Rajendra Prasad and other prominent leaders. A process of digitalization of the books, and making them accessible to research scholars and the common public through the Rashtrapati Bhavan archives was started. He also established the Pranab Mukherjee Public Library by renovating a dilapidated building marked for demolition for the Rashtrapati Bhavan residents. During Pranab's tenure, 23 publications were brought out documenting different facets of the Rashtrapati Bhavan, including details of its artworks, gardens and even the kitchen that served hundreds of dignitaries and heads of states.

Pranab believed in preserving heritage. He revived the tradition of using the horse-drawn 'state buggy' to attend ceremonial state functions like addressing Joint Sessions of Parliament and attending the 'Beating Retreat' ceremony. The buggy belonged to the British viceroys. During Partition, both India and Pakistan claimed it, and India reportedly won it through a toss. Yet another significant initiative was the establishment of a modern, state-of-the-art museum. Other than displaying historical objects from different presidential eras, a large number of artefacts belonging to the time of British viceroys, including some original furniture designed by Lutyens, were restored. One day, Pranab excitedly informed me that Edwina Mountbatten's bed had been uncovered from the heap of broken furniture dumped in Rashtrapati Bhavan's huge basement godown and was sent for restoration. I expressed my desire to sleep on it for a night once it was restored.

However, when I finally remembered to ask about it again, it had already been restored and sent to the museum. The desk at Pranab's office in the Family Wing belonged to the first President of India Dr Rajendra Prasad. Pranab was extremely proud of using that desk and would mention it to every visitor who happened to meet him there. Pranab understood the value of historical legacies. He once told me that his table at the Finance Ministry, during his first stint as the finance minister in the early 1980s, was historic. Since independence, all the finance ministers prepared Budgets sitting at that table. He was dismayed to find that the table was missing during his second stint as finance minister in 2009. He tried to trace it but could not. Given this mindset, Rashtrapati Bhavan simply fascinated him as every corner of it had tales from history. Pranab also took the initiative to catalogue all artworks—photographs, heritage furniture and digitalized old and rare photographs—for Rashtrapati Bhavan archives.

The president's movements within the city necessitate blocking off roads, resulting in huge traffic jams. Pranab decided to hold as many programmes as possible within Rashtrapati Bhavan itself to avoid causing inconvenience to people.

Before Pranab's presidency, only the Mughal Gardens was open to the public. Pranab wanted to share the legacy of Rashtrapati Bhavan with common citizens and opened the main building and its state rooms to the public as well. Anyone could make an online booking and visit the premises on a guided tour conducted by specially-trained guides. He also kept a track of the number of visitors.

Pranab initiated artists' and writers' residency programmes. Eminent artists, writers and scholars were now invited by the President to come and spend a week at Rashtrapati Bhavan and use the time and space for creative inspiration. Thanks to this initiative, I met one of my all-time favourite writers, Amitav Ghosh and his wife Deborah. They have become good friends since then. Pranab initiated internship programmes for young students to gain first-hand experience of the functioning of Rashtrapati Bhavan.

Rashtrapati Bhavan had a large auditorium, but it was in a pretty dilapidated condition. Pranab got it renovated and started a monthly cultural programme called the Indra Dhanush, inviting leading performing artists from all over India to showcase the great cultural diversity of the land. One of the most memorable functions conducted as part of the Indra Dhanush was a performance by the 108-year-old Indian classical vocalist, Ustad Abdul Rashid Khan. The wheelchair bound Ustad could not move on his own. But when he started singing, he simply mesmerized the audience not just by his total mastery over the art, but with the power of his voice and the breath control that would perhaps put a 20-year-old to shame. The performance received a standing ovation from an overwhelmed audience, which included the President.

Rashtrapati Bhavan took the initiative to start Smartgram projects in five villages in Haryana. Pranab also tried to make the president's house more eco-friendly by harnessing solar power, rainwater harvesting, waste management and recycling of waste water. He took initiatives for the residents and staff of Rashtrapati Bhavan, establishing recreational centres for the children and elderly.

Pranab was not a tech-savvy person. But he understood the need and influence of social media to reach out to people. Just a couple of weeks before demitting office, on 3 July 2017, he proudly noted in his diary:

> The official website [of Rashtrapati Bhavan] since its launch in August 2012 has received 49.19 cr hits, the You Tube site on RB has around 35.15 lakh views and over 20470 subscribers. Twitter and face book (sic) are used for livestreaming of events. The total number of likes on the face book page is over 4.8 millions and the cumulative reach of the posts is 15.20 cr. So far over 30 lakhs people have visited RB and since the opening of the Garage museum, thirty thousand people visited it in one year. All these have been done in last five years.

OFFICIALLY RETIRED

As Pranab's term neared its conclusion, there were speculations about potential candidates for the upcoming presidential election. One gentleman, who claimed to be close to PM Modi, informed me that the PM had supposedly told him that Pranab would be given a second term. I excitedly shared this with my father. He snapped at me, saying, 'You are in politics now. Try to develop some political sense. For the first time in history, BJP [with NDA] has the numbers to choose their own candidate. Why should they choose a Congress man?' I feebly tried to hold my ground saying that he shared an excellent rapport with the PM. Pranab clarified that personal relationships did not influence political decisions. 'If you are to remain in politics, you must understand this,' he advised.

From his diary, I learnt that CPI (M) leader Brinda Karat had expressed a similar sentiment when she met

Pranab on 17 May 2017. He told her, 'Why would they [BJP] support one who does not belong to them? Courtesy extended to me as President should not be misread as personal but institutional.'

Pranab was under no illusion of a second term. On 25 February, Sarsanghchalak of the RSS, Mohan Bhagwat, came to meet him. 'He invited me to visit RSS HQ at Nagpur after demitting office,' Pranab noted in his diary the same day. Before that, on 29 January after the Beating Retreat ceremony, he wrote in his diary, 'This was my last state function as President. I do not have any expectations or regret as nobody except an extraordinary man Dr. Rajendra Prasad, the first President of India, got a second term.'

Finally, it was time for farewells. On 22 July, PM Modi hosted a dinner in Pranab's honour at the Hyderabad House, where the heads of government typically hold their official banquets. In this context, Pranab recorded a light-hearted banter in his diary, 'PM asked me, "Rashtrapatiji, after how many years are you coming to Hyderabad House?" I replied, "After 5 years." Someone quipped, "That's a long time." I said, "Yes! I bet none of the persons assembled here have more familiarity with Hyderabad House than me, not even Advaniji, as I used to attend lunch and dinners hosted here since 1973."'

In a rare gesture, the Supreme Court hosted a farewell lunch for him. Pranab, as president, made it a practice to interact with the judges of the Supreme Court and High Courts regularly, inviting them individually with their spouses to have tea/lunch with him at Rashtrapati Bhavan. Pranab noted in his diary on 24 July, 'I was told that when CJI proposed it [the farewell lunch] in an informal meeting of the judges, they unanimously endorsed it. CJI profusely praised my conduct as President mentioning that the judges unanimously decided to declare that the President discharged his responsibility with dignity, aptness and unparallel sense of patriotism. I was overwhelmed.'

On 23 July, the Parliament of India gave him a farewell. It was truly an emotional moment for him. That night, he told me with a tinge of sadness that he would never be able to visit Parliament again.

On 24 July, Pranab hosted his last banquet as president for the PM and his council of ministers. On his last night at Rashtrapati Bhavan, Pranab noted in his diary, 'I became a member of parliament in 1969. I was MP for 37 years, minister for 22 years and President of the country for 5 years. I bow my head to almighty for his blessings on me.'

chapter 9

And Silently the Dusk Descends

Retirement can be a mixed experience for people. While some enjoy the newfound freedom, others may struggle to adapt. My father belonged to the latter group. As someone who had always been a workaholic, the prospect of suddenly having no work depressed him. Once I said to him, 'Baba, why can't you just relax?' He snapped, 'Relax and do what?' 'Read, write, go for holidays,' I said. He retorted, 'Work or no work, I always read. I'm writing the last volume of my autobiography. But that's not sufficient. I need something more productive to do.' I gave up!

After a couple of months of forced relaxation, Pranab got reasonably busy. He was invited to speak on various occasions including university convocations, seminars, memorial lectures, book releases and others. He addressed 25 events in 2018 and 38 events in 2019. Being a thorough person, he liked to work meticulously on his speeches. He also toured quite a bit for various programmes (no holidays though). Despite being less frequent and in fewer numbers compared to his earlier days, there continued to be a steady stream of visitors to his place—political leaders from various parties, former bureaucrats and ambassadors, senior journalists and personal guests. If, despite all of this, someone continued to complain that there was 'not enough work', then it was clear that there was no chance of finding any cure for the man!

In his personal life, Pranab was a man of very few needs. Other than books, he didn't have much interest in anything else. He liked to listen to Rabindra Sangeet. But with the gradual loss of hearing due to age, that too became infrequent. He didn't like wearing the hearing aid, except when meeting people. He was a frugal eater and disliked eating out. He didn't like travelling, except for work. Those too would be whirlwind tours. He was a strict teetotaller, never having tasted alcohol in his life. In his younger days, he used to smoke cigar and later changed to pipe. But he quit that too somewhere in the 1990s. He never had the time or the inclination to socialize and was totally out of the Lutyens' zone party circuit. He had very few personal friends and many of them had passed away. He had lost his wife. Given these circumstances, there was not much choice other than to fill his lonely days with work.

His days started with a morning walk. Over the years, he methodically noted in his diary how many kilometres he walked every day, and at what speed, by calculating the time. Another daily ritual was his puja. Pranab was a deeply religious person. After his retirement, he would spend at least two hours every day doing puja to his heart's content. He used to regularly recite Durga Saptashati, known in Bengali as Chandi-paath. He could recite it from memory. During the annual Durga Puja in our ancestral home, Pranab's recitation of Chandi-paath was always a treat to hear. My entire family is religious, me being the only exception. Pranab was not only religious, but observed all rituals as per the Hindu calendar. But neither he nor anyone else in my family ever tried to impose their faith on me. It was quite common that after observing a fast for the day for some religious occasion, my father would have fruits at night (Ma could never keep fasts), and sitting right next to him I would eat my fish curry and rice. In these times of religious dogmatism, I can only be grateful to my parents for their tolerance and acceptance, which they not only preached but also actively demonstrated in everyday life.

After Pranab's retirement, I moved in with him. Running a household was definitely not one of Pranab's many accomplishments. I don't think he ever entered the kitchen in his life. In Ma's absence, I had to be there with him not just to give him company, but to save him the ordeal of ordering groceries or deciding the menu for the day. I am sure he would have been totally lost! After many years, I finally had the opportunity to reside in the same house as my father. While my days were occupied with my 'political' work, I made sure to have dinner with him and spend quality time with him afterwards. It was during this time that I gained invaluable insights into his political journey.

Pranab's home after retirement was 10 Rajaji Marg in New Delhi. It is one of the rare two-storey bungalows in Lutyens' Delhi. A portion of it was turned into Pranab's office, where his secretarial staff would sit. After his daily morning ritual of morning walk and puja, Pranab would get dressed in his bandhgala suit and head to his office, where he would spend a few hours. He would repeat this routine in the evening as well. This was his ritual every day, except for Sundays. I asked him why he felt the need to dress formally each day for his 'office', even when there were no visitors or pending files. He responded gravely that it was crucial to maintain discipline.

In the early evenings, Pranab would sit in a covered veranda and watch my three dogs play in the back lawn while having his tea. During dinner time, he would report their activities to me. Everyone in our family, including our domestic help, are avid animal lovers. There were a couple of stray cats living in the house before we moved in. Our cook started feeding them. Slowly their numbers increased and then they were joined by stray dogs. They would come twice a day during feeding time, some loitering around in the compound throughout the day, resting under the shady trees or in the sun, depending on the weather. Once, one of the guards hit a dog. My niece Brishti complained to her grandfather, and the guard was severely reprimanded. During the Covid-induced lockdown, feeding them became a regular exercise with at least a dozen cats and around 20–25 dogs getting fed every day. Pranab, in his usual methodical manner, kept a daily track of it. After he passed away and I had to vacate the house, one of my major concerns revolved around who would feed the animals. Luckily, a friend of mine staying nearby, who is an ardent animal lover herself and feeds and takes care of stray dogs in her area, took on the responsibility.

One of the problems with the house was that it was infested with monkeys. There were at least 40–50 monkeys roaming around in the neighbourhood and our house. They created utter nuisance, breaking flower pots and ruining our efforts to grow vegetables. During the mango season, they would pluck raw mangoes from the trees and throw them around half-eaten. But no one could do anything about it. Pranab's logic was simple. He would say that we (human beings) have increasingly occupied their natural habitat, now we have to learn to share space with them. Once I complained to him about the monkeys plucking vegetables and the unripe mangoes. He retorted, 'They can't buy vegetables and fruits from the market like you. So, what will they eat?' An impeccably sound argument that I could not ignore.

In his post-retirement life, one of the most cherished and eagerly awaited visits was that of his granddaughter, Brishti (daughter of my younger brother, Indrajit). Brishti would visit with her parents during the weekends and stay over. Pranab fondly called her 'Gurguri' and looked forward to spending time with her. She was the only one in the family who dared to, and to some extent managed to, 'discipline' Pranab. She had framed '10 golden rules' that Pranab was supposed to strictly follow. The rules included regular eating hours and not continuing sitting in his office after 9.00 p.m. During her visits, she would walk into his office exactly at 9.00 p.m. and in true dictatorial fashion, would force Pranab to leave whatever he was doing (usually writing his diaries) and compel him go for his evening shower and then have his dinner on time. Once she confiscated Pranab's diary and locked it in her cupboard, refusing to give the key to anybody. It is said that people rediscover their childhood with their grandchildren. It was a pleasure to see an octogenarian squabbling with his granddaughter like a child. After Pranab's passing, I discovered a cache of handwritten scribbles, drawings and at least a dozen different versions of the '10 Golden Rules' by Gurguri tucked in between the pages of her grandfather's diaries.

HIS WISDOM AND HIS LEGACY

During my stay with my father, he would ask me every night about my political engagements for the following day. If there were no programmes, he would still insist that I go to the Delhi Pradesh Congress Committee (DPCC) office and sit there. Unless I had some specific programme at the DPCC, I preferred to meet people at home rather than at the party office. Pranab strongly objected to it. Once he told me irately that even if I didn't have any work, I should just go and sit at the room at DPCC that was allocated to me. I asked him, 'And do what?' He snapped, 'Stare at the walls, but for god's sake, go!' This was not for maintaining privacy at home, which he never did, but because he believed that party offices should be utilized for more political activities. As per him, a crowded party office creates a positive atmosphere where people/workers are able to just walk in and meet others without appointment.

He naturally kept a track of my political life, but refrained from giving unsolicited advice (other than visiting the party office every day). He expected me to find my own way and create my own space. I decided to join politics in 2014 after the general election results were declared. I thought that being a Congress person, I should come forward and work for the party. As mentioned earlier, after the announcement of his name as the presidential candidate, Baba enquired if I would be interested in running for his seat in Jangipur, which I had then declined. But when I ultimately decided to take the plunge, he was not very encouraging. He rightly fathomed that I was taking an impulsive decision and would not be able to sustain it. He told me categorically that I was joining at a very difficult time, and emphasized the importance of being absolutely certain because 'politics is a lifelong commitment'. I vigorously argued my case, telling him that I was dead serious. He then advised that I should go to West Bengal and establish my base there. However, I disagreed with that idea as well. I wanted to remain in Delhi, as I considered it my home and did not like the idea of being uprooted.

I contested the Assembly elections in Delhi in 2015 and, like every other Congress candidate, lost badly. I was then appointed chief spokesperson and head of the Communication Department in Delhi by then Delhi Congress President, Ajay Maken. Later, I was appointed by the AICC, first as a national media panellist, then as a national spokesperson and then as Delhi Pradesh Mahila Congress president.

During Pranab's time in office, I heard an amusing anecdote from Venu Rajamony who served as the president's press secretary. I was sent to Thiruvananthapuram for a press conference by the AICC to highlight the failures of the Modi government, on completion of its first year. I was expected to speak on the economy. Somehow, everyone in the Congress (at least in the media department) assumed that being my father's daughter, I understood economics well. No one listened to my protestations and I was asked to do the presser on it (my first one out of town). Despite the extensive notes given to me by the media department, I was nervous. I think my father was more nervous than me. He apparently asked Venu to monitor the progress of the event and inform him about its outcome. Venu, who hailed from Kerala, knew the media well. After the press conference, he reported to the President that it went well, and despite some heckling by a journalist, I held my ground and stuck to my figures. Venu later told me that on hearing this, the President was visibly relieved.

In his diaries, Pranab recorded his observations about me at various points of time. One such observation was: 'Munni speaks well in [press conferences] PCs but loses her temper in TV debates. She must control this.' He told me this a few times, but who remembers a father's advice amid a heated shouting match!

My father bequeathed to me a gift of remarkable import, the value of which I could fully appreciate only after he left us—his diaries. Even if he was extremely busy and couldn't write for a day or more, he would consolidate all the entries later on, based on the events and observations of each specific day. This habit also helped him refresh his memories.

His diaries have been the subject of much interest among journalists. For any journalist, observer or student of Indian politics, these diaries would be like a treasure trove. They not only chart the growth of a young politician—from a first-time MP in 1969 to being elected to the highest constitutional office in the country and serving as the 13th President of India—but also record the ups and downs, twists and turns of the exciting world of Indian politics from the perspective of an insider for nearly 50 years.

Pranab's habit of writing in a diary was rooted in a historical event, albeit a bloody one. In 1946, he arrived in Kolkata for the first time to attend the wedding of his eldest brother, Amiya. The date was 16 August 1946, a day (in) famous in history as the Direct Action Day. It was the day the All India Muslim League gave a call for taking 'direct action' for a separate Muslim state, after the withdrawal of the British from India. What followed was one of the bloodiest histories of riots in Bengal, especially in Kolkata. Somehow, the wedding took place, but the groom's family (that included my father) were stranded in Kolkata and were unable to return to their village until the situation calmed down. To confine a naughty and restless 11-year-old within the safety of a house was not an easy task. Someone came up with an innovative idea and presented young Pranab with a notebook with an instruction that he should write down his observations in it on a daily basis. That was the beginning. Since then, Pranab had been hooked to writing diaries. He left behind a total of 51 volumes.

The early diaries did not survive the ravages of time. The earliest one I saw was of 1973. As mentioned earlier, some of his later diaries got destroyed in the flooding of our basement in the GK house in Delhi somewhere in the mid-1980s. There are 8 missing volumes from 1978 to 1985. Pranab was terribly upset and thought of giving up writing. He continued writing only because Narasimha Rao urged him to do so, emphasizing that these writings could serve as a valuable record of the country's political history.

Over the years, his morning walks, puja and the habit of writing diaries at night were the three regular pivotal points in his life. If he missed out on any of these, especially the first two, he would be in a foul mood. Perhaps, these activities gave him a sense of regularity and points of orientation in an exceedingly unpredictable and ever-changing world of politics.

Pranab was a methodical man. He liked to be precise, especially about facts and figures. Whenever he travelled out of town, he had the habit of recording the distance he covered in kilometres for that day, along with the mode of transportation used. For example, on 28 January 1973, he travelled by train from Delhi to Kolkata. On top of the page, he wrote, 'By rail 1445 kms (Delhi-Howrah).' At the end of the month, he would note the total kilometres travelled. In January 1973, he travelled 'by train-7705 Km, by road-1550 km, by air-1445 km'. In 2012, for example, after noting down air travels for each month, at the end of that year, he summed up that he had travelled 177,578 km. Had he been with Indira Gandhi on her historic journey to Belchi, he would have probably added two more entries to his list: 'on tractor—X km, on elephant—Y km!' For most of the years, he wrote one page per day, but in his later years, especially after retirement, he wrote at length about his observations on various current events.

Being a history buff, Pranab developed the habit of documenting the pertinent historical background of an institution whenever he attended an event at that location. From an entry of 15 July 2011, when he attended the closing ceremony to commemorate 150 years of Income Tax, I learnt the history of it. Pranab noted:

> In 1860, just after 2 years of the Queen's proclamation of assuming the administration of India from East India Company, an officer of East India Company James Wilson introduced this Act in the council of Governor General to realise the cost of suppressing the First War of Independence in 1857. The realization from this tax in the first year was one crore 83 lakhs.

On 26 November 2011, Pranab had gone to Mumbai to attend a programme at the 'New' Customs House. Pranab noted, 'Though it's called new custom house, it was constructed in 1918 and for four years till 1922, it was used as the hospital for soldiers injured in the war. In the British days, Imperial Police Service and Imperial Custom Service were closely linked as officers from IPS used to be appointed to Imperial Custom Service.' There are many such mentions.

I heard two interesting anecdotes illustrating Pranab's love for history. The first was shared by journalist Jyoti Malhotra, who accompanied Pranab during his visit as EAM to Pakistan in January 2007. In Pranab's honour, his counterpart had hosted an evening of ghazals by the famous singer Farida Khanum. During the entire evening, while Farida enthralled the audience with her performance, Pranab reportedly remained seated with an expressionless, impassive face which sharply contrasted with the exuberant '*wah wahs*' and '*kya baats*' from the rest of the audience. The next day, Pranab and the other delegates were taken to Taxila, that was once a famous centre of learning in ancient India. According to Malhotra, Pranab was totally transformed and was fully engaged. He confidently led the delegates through the ruins, regaling them with tales from the site's history and related anecdotes. Pranab's interests were very clearly defined.

Sitaram Yechury, who accompanied the presidential delegation to Bangladesh with Pranab, shared another interesting anecdote. They were taken to Shilaidaha Kuthibari, a country house made by Dwarkanath Tagore, and famously associated with Rabindranath Tagore. Earlier a part of the zamindari estate of the Tagore family, it used to be a favourite place of Rabindranath Tagore. It served as a creative haven where he spent a significant amount of time, penning some of his most notable works. It now hosts the Tagore Memorial Museum. According to Yechury, brushing aside the museum officers who were there to show them around, Pranab became the official guide telling them all about Tagore's time and the works produced there. The delegates and the local officers were not only amused by the enthusiasm of the President, but also marvelled at his knowledge.

When Pranab got elected from his first Lok Sabha constituency, Jangipur, he discovered that a large number of students from his constituency and the district were enrolling at Aligarh Muslim University (AMU) for their studies. Many more wanted to go but could not, due to the distance and lack of resources. Pranab took the initiative to set up an AMU Centre in his constituency, for which the Left-front government allotted land in 2010. The first courses started in 2011. The campus was formally inaugurated by Pranab in February 2014 when he was the president. In his speech, Pranab gave a justification using history for setting up this campus centre. He said that one of the members of the Nawab family of Murshidabad, Nawab Shamsul Jahan Begum, had earlier donated ₹1 lakh to expand the Muhammadan Anglo Oriental College (MAO College). AMU was repaying this debt by establishing it's Centre here. He stated in his speech that the people of Murshidabad have a historic connect and claim to AMU.[138] Pranab's speeches and diaries are full of many such anecdotes from history.

My father made me the custodian of his diaries, but on the condition that these may be read and published only

---

[138]Lahiri, Gautam, *Pranab Mukherjee: Rajneeti-r bhetor Bahir Vol. 2*, Al-Hamra Prakashani, Dhaka, 2023, pp. 43–44.

posthumously, that too only if I think it is appropriate to do so. I had been in possession of his diaries ever since he shifted to Rashtrapati Bhavan (to prevent them from getting lost during the move). However, I refrained from succumbing to the temptation to read them, as doing so would have constituted a breach of trust. I wish I had not been so scrupulous, and had read them while he was still there to explain things. If nothing else, it would have saved me endless hours of research. The diaries cannot be published in their entirety due to their excessive length. Moreover, certain confidential details within the diaries should remain undisclosed to the public at this time. Pranab always maintained that certain secrets should go with him, and upon reading the diaries, I am inclined to concur with his viewpoint.

UPHOLDING DEMOCRATIC ETHOS

On 7 June 2018, Pranab visited the RSS headquarters in Nagpur to deliver the valedictory address to cadres at the conclusion of a three-year training camp for Swayamsevaks. He was invited to speak on the concepts of nation, nationalism and patriotism. When the RSS made an announcement in the media towards the end of May, it triggered off a huge controversy and greatly displeased the Congress leadership. Pranab was under tremendous pressure both from outside and within our family to withdraw his acceptance. Many of his former colleagues, both privately and publicly, advised him not to go. At home, my elder brother and I were unhappy with our father's decision and urged him to withdraw his acceptance. I was particularly belligerent and engaged in heated altercations with him on this. I received a call from Ahmed Patel requesting me to try to persuade my father not to go for the event. But I did not need a call from him or anyone else in order to do so. I was fully involved in Congress politics by then, and felt that by going to the RSS headquarters he was 'betraying' the party.

The atmosphere at home during those few days was gloomy. I was constantly raving and ranting. Pranab, on the other hand, did not utter a word and maintained a stoic silence. Only once he became irritated with me when I repeated a commonly heard argument in the Congress/ Left circles at the time, suggesting that his visit would give 'legitimacy' to the the RSS. Pranab retorted saying that who was he to give legitimacy to the RSS? He said that the people of India had given legitimacy to RSS and shown their acceptance by choosing an RSS Pracharak as the PM of India with a decisive mandate. 'You may choose to ignore it at your own peril,' he said. It was clear that he was firm in his decision to honour his acceptance and would not change his mind. Given the tense situation at home, I decided to retreat to the hills for a few days to cool down and to escape the media attention.

The day before his scheduled speech in Nagpur, rumours began circulating that I was allegedly joining the BJP. At the time, I was staying at a retreat in a forested area where the mobile signal inside the room was weak. When I stepped outside my room after taking an afternoon nap, I saw a flood of messages and missed call alerts on my phone. Even before I could realize what was happening, I received a call from Ajay Maken, the then DPCC President and my boss. I learnt from Maken that news channels were broadcasting a story about me joining the BJP. He called me to verify the truth. After listening to my vehement denials and angry outbursts, he asked me to calm down. Knowing my propensity to tweet on impulse, he advised me against posting anything or speaking to the media. He assured me that he would tweet my denial. However, I was seething with anger by then, especially with my father and could not restrain myself. Though I was certain that Pranab would not and could not endorse the RSS worldview, I felt that his acceptance of the RSS invitation had given rise to this kind of speculation, and that there would be more such instances. I tweeted exactly that. Later, I learnt that there was another rumour doing the rounds that I was asked by the Congress high command (through Maken) to tweet against my father. I would like to put it on record that it was not so. On the contrary, Maken advised me not to tweet or give any statement. Also, I believe that no matter what, both Sonia and Rahul are gracious people who would never ask a daughter to say anything against her father publicly. Doing so was totally my decision. If anyone else had asked me to do it, I would have resigned from the party then and there.

The next morning, I received a call from a journalist friend. She told me bluntly that I was overreacting. 'At least wait for his speech,' she said. 'Your father is no longer a young man. He must already be under tremendous pressure. Why are you adding to it?' she asked. That phone call made me feel guilty. I knew how tensed my father was before I left home. I was particularly concerned about his choice of attire. Considering the scorching heat and the outdoor venue of the event, I wished I had advised him to wear a dhoti-kurta instead of his usual bandhgala. It would have been more appropriate for the sweltering weather.

After venting through my tweet, my anger had subsided. So, I decided to call my father and make my peace. I was relieved to hear that he had already decided, on his own, to wear a dhoti-kurta. Later, I read in some article about how Pranab purportedly made a 'statement' by wearing an Indian outfit in contrast to the RSS members wearing khaki trousers and shirts. I never bothered to find out from my father whether his choice of outfit was due to the weather, or for the purpose of making a deliberate statement.

Pranab's speech at the event was widely publicized and telecast live by almost all major news channels. The speech is in public domain and has been dissected by many political pundits. He noted how Indian nationalism, unlike the emergence of European nation-states, was not based on monochromatic identity of one language, one religion, one ethnicity; but on values of pluralism, tolerance and accommodation of diversity enshrined in our Constitution, and which reflect our core civilizational values.

Pranab said:

> The construct of Indian nationalism is 'Constitutional Patriotism', which consists of an appreciation of our inherited and shared diversity... The soul of India resides in pluralism and tolerance. This plurality of our society has come through assimilation of ideas over centuries. Secularism and inclusion are a matter of faith for us. It is our composite culture which makes us into one nation.[139]

---

[139]'Full Text of Pranab Mukherjee's Speech to RSS Workers In Nagpur', *NDTV*, 8 June 2018, https://tinyurl.com/5xen99xu. Accessed on 16 October 2023.

After Pranab's speech, the Congress responded by saying that he had 'shown the mirror of truth to the RSS'.[140] Looking back at this entire episode, I think the Congress had jumped the gun. Rather than publicly expressing its concerns about Pranab's visit to the RSS, it should have waited for his speech. Pranab always believed in the importance of dialogue in a democracy. He also believed that in the current situation, the RSS cannot be ignored considering a large number of people in India chose to vote for an RSS man as the PM. One cannot simply ignore people's mandate. Pranab was acting as per his beliefs. He might have made the Congress high command unhappy, but he definitely did not betray the Congress values.

Ironically, Pranab used the RSS platform to expound the core values of the Congress ideology of pluralism, diversity, tolerance and constitutionalism. He once jokingly told journalist Sonia Singh that he wanted to go to the 'tiger's den' and witness it first-hand. It is one thing to preach to a friendly and sympathetic audience, but one needs a different kind of courage to venture into the 'tiger's den' and quote its bête noire Pt Nehru from there.

During this controversy, I learnt that Pranab had once suggested banning the RSS during an earlier AICC session. If so, then the credit goes to the RSS for inviting a person who once advocated its banning. Perhaps, the current brigade of Congress leaders should learn to be more tolerant and accommodate diversity of opinions. As for my reaction, I think I behaved atrociously with my father for a few days prior to the event. I had my 'I-told-you-so' moment

---

[140]'Pranab Mukherjee Showed RSS The Mirror of Truth: Congress', *Outlook*, 8 June 2018, https://tinyurl.com/ty2wr4bu. Accessed on 16 October 2023.

the very next day after the speech, when a morphed picture of Pranab doing RSS salute appeared on social media. Nevertheless, on later reflection, I think my behaviour reflected immaturity, bordering on stupidity.

Pranab's affiliation with Congress, both in terms of his family background and choice of political party, did not come in conflict with his respect for freedom fighters or ideologues who operated outside the Congress fold during pre-Independence days. These included those espousing very different ideologies from the Congress. As per Pranab, that did not make them any less patriots. He believed that it was important to view political figures and ideologues within the specific context and circumstances of the era in which they were active. He had great regard for M.N. Roy, one of the founding fathers of the Communist movement in India, as well as for Dr Syama Prasad Mookerjee, the Right-wing leader and president of the Hindu Mahasabha who went on to establish the BJS. I remember Baba telling me that Dr Mookerjee, along with the stalwart Congress leader from Bengal Dr Bidhan Chandra Roy, played a major role in ensuring a favourable deal for Bengal in the eastern border of India during Partition.

Pranab was sad about the blatant attempt of what he termed as 'de-Nehrufication' of the current goverment. He was also unhappy with the constant 'Savarkar-bashing' done by Rahul Gandhi. One of the most controversial Right-wing figures in India, Vinayak Damodar Savarkar, has been subjected to a series of disparaging comments by the Congress scion. In my presence, Pranab told one of the young Congress leaders that this approach was incorrect and entirely unnecessary. He also mentioned the physical torture that Savarkar endured while imprisoned in the

Cellular Jail in Port Blair, and insisted that under such extreme duress, if someone wrote mercy petitions, Pranab could not term him a 'traitor'.

As I went through Pranab's diaries, I learnt about his disagreement of views on Savarkar with Sonia. In February 2003, during the Vajpayee government, a portrait of Savarkar was unveiled by the then President A.P.J. Abdul Kalam at the Central Hall of Parliament. The Congress boycotted the function. The decision of installing the portrait was taken in a Parliamentary Committee meeting in which two Congress members, Shivraj Patil and Pranab, were present. Another illustrious member was Somnath Chatterjee from the CPI (M). The decision to install the portrait was unanimous. Later, Chatterjee, perhaps due to the pressure from his party, said that it was wrong on his part to agree.

Pranab wrote in his diary, on 25 February 2003, that in a Political Affairs Committee (PAC) meeting, Sonia was angry with Pranab for agreeing to put Savarkar's portrait in the Central Hall, as he had filed mercy petitions and bond of loyalty to British. Pranab told her, 'That doesn't reduce his sacrifice and patriotism.' Pranab noted, 'I told firmly that I agreed in the meeting [of the Parliamentary Committee] to the proposal as I consider him a patriot, whatever be his views in the later years.' He further added in his diary, 'People have become so small. How can one forget the sufferings Savarkar brothers had to undergo in cellular jail?' He told Sonia that he would not attend the function as the party had decided to boycott it, but it was wrong.

On 3 September 2004, Pranab again wrote about his disagreement with Sonia regarding Savarkar. This time it was in the context of the decision of Mani Shankar Aiyar to remove a plaque with a quote of Savarkar at the Swatantra Jyot memorial at Cellular Jail. Pranab felt it was wrong. Indira's government had issued a stamp on Savarkar in 1966. In 1980, Indira wrote to Pandit Bakhle, secretary of Swatantrayaveer Savarkar Rashtriya Smarak, 'Veer Savarkar's daring defiance of the British Government has its own importance in the annals of our Freedom movement. I wish success to the plans to celebrate the birth centenary of the remarkable son of India.'[141] Pranab's diary entry ended on a cautionary note, 'We are making a mistake. We are going to pay for it in future.'

While the Modi government's attitude towards the three previous PMs from the Gandhi family is totally condemnable, Rahul too seems to be playing the game with similar disgusting rules. With his series of venomous comments against Savarkar, Rahul has reduced the political narrative of the grand old party to the level of a social media troll. Both sides seem to be operating from a position of wilful ignorance and deliberate malice.

I remember having an interesting discussion with my father about the prevailing nature of political discourse in the country that lacks dignity and courtesy towards political opponents. The discussion started with the deteriorating standards of TV debates, and went on to touch upon broader issues of independence of media and other institutions. My argument was based on 'whataboutery'—if 'they' do it, why can't 'we'! I asked him that despite being in power for so many years, why couldn't we (Congress) capture the media and other institutions? His response

---

[141]'Indira Gandhi's Letter on Savarkar puts Congress in a Tight Spot', *The Economic Times*, 16 December 2019, https://tinyurl.com/ms45jy9r. Accessed on 16 October 2023.

was instantaneous and emphatic: 'Thank God we didn't do it. Else democracy would not have survived in India.' He said that both Right and Left parties and governments tend to do it, as both are inclined towards authoritarianism. He emphasized that it was the Congress that established parliamentary democracy in India and was responsible for its survival despite all odds. He felt that a greater responsibility lies upon the Congress to uphold and adhere to the ethos of parliamentary democracy than any other political party in India. 'You [Congress] cannot fight your own agenda and diminish your own legacy,' he concluded.

CONGRESS-MUKT BHARAT: ONLY A PIPE DREAM?

In his post-retirement days, I frequently asked my father about the revival of the Congress. His consistent response was that the Congress must and will revive. On one occasion, he got irritated with me and said, 'The task of reviving Congress is not your responsibility. Leave it to Congress president and other senior leaders of the party. You concentrate on the task assigned to you by the party.'

On 24 May 2014, just a few days after the Lok Sabha election results were declared, Pranab noted in his diary:

> Blame-game in Congress/UPA is going on as usual. It is not unexpected. A major debacle like this has its impact. But the shameless manner the cronies of Rahul Gandhi are behaving would further damage the party. But all is not lost and if genuine corrective measures are taken, Congress can revive. The restoration of internal democracy in party, decentralization of authority in AICC, PCC, DCC and BCCs are needed.

> Committees should be constituted as per rules and norms. Membership from booth is to be reintroduced. Even if there be some fake/bogus membership, it would be much better than no membership or ad hocism. Congress leadership must allow grassroot support to grow under the local leaders from Anchal/Block/Taluka level to DCC and PCC. If this happens, there will be no need to raise slogans like 'Priyanka Lao-Congress bachao'.

My father never had in-depth discussions with me regarding the prospects of the Congress, apart from a few casual remarks made in unguarded moments. He perhaps thought it was better not to dishearten me, as I was a Congress worker. In his diaries, he never provided a comprehensive analysis at any point in time.

But going over his diaries over the years, especially during the later years, I tried to gauge his thoughts. There's a telling observation as early as December 1975 in the context of the AICC session in Chandigarh. Pranab noted:

> What was noticeable in this session that there was no dissenting voice... Within Congress, there has always been a diversity of opinions due to which a consensus within Congress could broadly be considered as a national consensus on issues. One of the reasons why no national opposition or alternative to Congress could emerge was the ubiquity of Congress... I do not understand the reason for this [lack of dissent/ diversity of opinions] and I don't know if it's good for democracy.

It took Pranab more than 40 years to admit to himself that, perhaps, all was not well with his mentor Indira Gandhi.

In his post-retirement diaries, there are references to Indira's 'feet of clay'. He thought that the two splits in the Congress in 1969 and 1977 had weakened the organization. A personality cult and a cult around the Gandhi–Nehru family started developing during Indira's time. Perhaps, due to her own insecurities, Indira wanted to be in total control of the organization. In 1974, the party constitution was amended to give more power to the Congress president, even allowing her to remove elected CWC members. She systematically decimated all regional stalwarts and centralized power within the organization to herself. She unabashedly promoted her sons, first Sanjay, then Rajiv after Sanjay's death. Indira encouraged factionalism within the party and ensured that no one faction/leader became powerful enough to challenge her. The elections within the party were replaced by the 'nomination' culture, with the Congress leaders authorizing the Congress president to nominate not only the CWC members but even CLP leaders and CMs in states.

Indira was the main 'vote-catcher' for the Congress, and had the charisma and political acumen to carry it through. Her spectacular victory in 1980, after the 1977 electoral debacle, reinforced her own and the Gandhi–Nehru family's dominance within the party. This concentration of power and the cult around the family within the Congress led to sycophancy and a belief that only a member of the Gandhi–Nehru family could lead the party and lead it to victory. In an entry on 18 December 1998, in the context of a special AICC session held in Talkatora Stadium in Delhi, Pranab noted sarcastically, 'The whole session was "Sonia-Vandana". Nobody can beat Congressmen/women in sycophancy. Except me, everyone took her name at least half a dozen times in a speech of five minutes.'

Pranab himself was guilty of this 'sycophancy' to the extent that he too came to believe and accept the inevitability of a Gandhi–Nehru family member to lead the Congress. That's why he chose to play an active role in making Sonia the Congress president, replacing Sitaram Kesri. In his later-day reflections, he thought that Sonia's desire to form coalition governments with support from regional parties had further weakened the organization. Rather than strengthening the organization, the focus was to form the government, even at the cost of sacrificing the interests of the local state units to the compulsions of a coalition government at the centre. I remember hearing a fleeting conversation between him and Sonia during one of her visits after his retirement. As I entered the room to serve tea, I heard Pranab saying, 'I still stand by the Pachmarhi resolution.' At the Pachmarhi session of the Congress in 1998, the party resolved to go on its own and not cede space to regional parties by forming coalitions. It was reversed in 2003 in Shimla, where a resolution was passed making way for collaboration with other parties to form governments.

On 3 February 2016, Pranab wrote:

> A large number of people are leaving Congress. They are frustrated and it seems that even in the near future, there is no prospect of its revival. This is haunting a large number of Congress leaders and workers. Coalition politics with a strong desire of Gandhi-Nehru family, to which Congress has mortgaged itself, to keep power to itself has led to this situation (sic).

On 6 June 2016, at the presidential retreat of Mashobra, Pranab noted:

> In this solitude, one thought for the last few days constantly haunting me now what is the future of Congress? (sic) Would it revive like it did under leadership of Indira Gandhi or would it be like an opportunistic, capricious and fragile coalition govt headed by Congress? Or would the Congress simply disintegrate, and outfits like TMC and NCP having some elements of Congress ideology replace it? I do not have any answer. It is difficult for me to believe a 'Congress Mukt Bharat'. Congress is a national movement—its liberalism, firm commitment to parliamentary democracy and secular approach are at the core of India's nationhood. Can BJP transform itself into Congress ideological mould and expand without RSS support? Future of India is at stake and the stake is too high.

Before the general elections in 2019, Mamata Banerjee floated a concept of united Opposition with one candidate from a united Opposition contesting against the BJP in a given constituency. Pranab wrote:

> Mamata Banerjee is speaking about putting one candidate against BJP in all constituencies. Now the question is which parties will form the Federal Front? All the regional parties like SP/BSP, TMC, TRS, TDP, BJD etc? Where does Congress fit in this framework? Can it liquidate itself by conceding to regional parties in state after state? Has the relevance of Congress in the national politics of the party is gone forever? (sic) Is Congress in a permanent state of decline or is it

> reversable? It is theoretically possible to have third front but without Congress it will be impotent. Regional parties at the cost of a national party?

He firmly believed that a combination of regional parties at the Centre cannot be a substitute for a national party. As per him, a government formed through such arrangements would be extremely fragile. Further, no regional party would have a national outlook. According to him, this could be detrimental to India's interests in the long run, especially in areas like foreign policy, which might get subverted to the interests of local domestic politics. He illustrated this to me once, using the examples of Mamata Banerjee's opposition to the Teesta Water Sharing Treaty with Bangladesh, and of Tamil parties' domestic political compulsions influencing India's policy towards Sri Lanka.

On 28 July 2020, just a month before his passing, Pranab wrote in his diary:

> By making Congress a preserved playground for Gandhi-Nehru family, Congress lost its democratic character which impacted the polity of the country. After independence, if 5 family members of the same family controlled the Congress presidency for 37 years, it speaks of the worst form of hegemony. The family today is no longer providing vitality to the organisation but eating away its strength. Sonia Gandhi and Rahul since 2004 have lost base it acquired even partially by Soniaji in 2001-2003. They are just interested in somehow to form government at centre under Congress with other regional parties.

Pranab continued:

> Sometimes I think how far I am and people like me are responsible for this decline? (sic) Did the blind loyalty of people like me to Indira Gandhi in the 70s and 80s, and later to Sonia Gandhi greatly responsible for mortgaging the party to the family? (sic) Are we not accountable for stopping the democratic process of choosing the leader through election by the party members? People like us are responsible for allowing Congress to disintegrate and become a family fiefdom.

Pranab's day of reckoning was finally here.

It was during this time that I began contemplating leaving politics. The thought arose after the Congress party's disastrous defeat in the Delhi Assembly elections in February 2020. We not only failed to win a single seat for the second time, but our vote share had also fallen to a pathetic 4.26 per cent. I was depressed not merely because of the defeat, but also for what I perceived as lack of fighting spirit and an indifferent attitude of the party's leadership—including the top echelons of the party—towards the election.

With much trepidation, I asked my father during one of our dinner-time conversations, 'Baba, would you feel very bad if I quit politics?' Pat came the reply, 'When did you do politics that you would quit?' Normally, I would've reacted to such a dismissive attitude, but I chose to overlook it as my purpose was solved and I felt relieved. I also reassured him that I did not have any intention of joining any other political party. He quoted a Sanskrit phrase, '*Swadharme Nidhanam Shreyah* [It is better to perish in your own dharma]. Always remember that Congress is your

Swadharma.'[142] Congress is still my 'Swadharma' and I still, ideologically, belong to the Congress. But that Congress, perhaps, now exists only in the pages of history.

BHARAT RATNA: AN HONOUR FOR INDIA'S PEOPLE

In the early evening of 25 January 2019, I was sitting with my father in his study having a leisurely chat. Upon returning to my room, I noticed that my mobile phone, which I had left behind, had multiple missed calls. As I picked up my phone, I received a call from journalist Siddharth Sharma of ANI. He enquired whether 'Pranab da' was getting the Bharat Ratna. I was about to dismiss it as a rumour, but then remembered the other missed calls. I told Siddharth that I would get back to him.

I returned to Baba's study where he sat quietly reading a book. I asked him straight, 'Baba, are you getting Bharat Ratna?' He replied nonchalantly, 'Have they announced it officially?' 'What do you mean? You knew about it and didn't tell me?' I asked. He said, 'PM called me a little while ago and told me about it.' 'Why didn't you tell me? I was sitting with you till five minutes back. PM must have called you before that?' I raved. My father replied, 'One should wait for the official announcement first. That's the protocol.' I stomped my foot and slammed the door as I stormed out of his room in sheer exasperation.

It was one of the best moments for our family. After Pranab's presidency, I never thought that there would be another high moment of that magnitude in his life. But despite the joy, I missed my mother terribly. Had she been

[142]In this context, a closer meaning of *swadharma* would perhaps be 'to be true to your own nature'.

there, the moment would have been absolutely perfect. As the news spread, calls and visitors started pouring in. For the next few days, there was an atmosphere of celebration at home. Over our dining-table conversations, I learnt from Pranab that Dr Bidhan Chandra Roy, an eminent physician and former CM of West Bengal, was the first Bengali to be awarded the Bharat Ratna in 1961. Another Bengali woman, Aruna Asaf Ali (born Aruna Ganguly) was awarded the Bharat Ratna in 1997. A prominent freedom fighter, she hoisted the Indian National flag during the Quit India movement in Gowalia Tank maidan, Mumbai. She was the first mayor of Delhi, and incidentally the first DPCC president. Pranab recounted that when Morarji Desai became PM, he decided to do away with Padma awards, including Bharat Ratna. When Indira became PM in 1980, she wanted to start it again. But as she took oath on 14 January, there was no time to finalize the recipients of the Padma awards, which are typically announced on the eve of Republic Day. As a result, she decided to confer the Bharat Ratna instead. Pranab suggested the name of Mother Teresa, to which Indira readily agreed.

As president, Pranab had conferred Bharat Ratna awards on C.N.R. Rao and Sachin Tendulkar, and on Atal Bihari Vajpayee and Madan Mohan Malaviya (posthumously). The Bharat Ratna awards are not given together with the Padma awards. The recipients are awarded through a special ceremony organized at the Rashtrapati Bhavan. In case of Vajpayee, as he was not able to come to the Rashtrapati Bhavan due to his age and ill health, Pranab went to his residence to present the award.

In 2019, along with Pranab, Nanaji Deshmukh and Bhupen Hazarika were posthumously awarded the Bharat

Ratna. In a ceremony held at Rashtrapati Bhavan on 8 August, Pranab and the representatives of the two other recipients were given the awards. The Darbar Hall, where the award ceremony was held, was packed to capacity. Had it not been for the sanctimonious atmosphere of Rashtrapati Bhavan, I could almost feel people shouting 'Dada' as he received the award to a thunderous applause. As then President Ram Nath Kovind handed over the citation and the medal to Pranab, he reportedly told Pranab, 'It's an honour for me to give you the award.'

Pranab being awarded the Bharat Ratna was mired in controversy, which was nothing surprising considering the political climate of the day. Some suggested that it was a 'reward' for his visit to Nagpur for attending the RSS event, while others felt that it was done to spite the Gandhi family. Though senior Congress leaders like Ahmed Patel, Anand Sharma, Bhupinder Singh Hooda, Shashi Tharoor and few others were present at the award function, the absence of the Gandhi family raised many eyebrows. Pranab felt that his award should be seen in the context of the larger recognition of the Congress party's contribution. As told to journalist Sonia Singh, Pranab quoted Rahul Gandhi's congratulatory tweet on announcement of the award, '"The Congress takes great pride in the fact that the immense contribution to public service and nation building of one of our own, has been recognised and honoured." That means a recognition of a Congressman's contribution. I take it in that way.'[143]

---

[143]Singh, Sonia, 'When Narendra Modi Called Pranab Mukherjee to Ask if He Would Accept the Bharat Ratna', *The Print*, 22 May 2019, https://tinyurl.com/28urkxkh. Accessed on 8 November 2023.

LESSONS FOR FUTURE LEADERS

People often ask me about my opinion regarding my father's greatest achievement and contribution. I prefer not to comment on the measures he took while he was in government; the policy decisions and the institutional frameworks that he created in different ministries; the bills he initiated and got enacted in Parliament; and his influence on the thinking of the party and the governments that he worked with. That would perhaps require me to write another book. I believe that Pranab's greatest achievement in his five-decade long public life does not lie in his becoming the president of the country or being awarded the Bharat Ratna. For me, the genuine respect that he had earned from different sections of people, including his political colleagues across the divide, was his greatest achievement and reward. Despite being a lifelong Congressman, being awarded the Bharat Ratna by the BJP government was a manifestation of that.

His greatest contribution was his nonpartisan politics. He would always tell me that politics and governance in a diverse country like India is nothing but management of conflict and balancing of different, often contradictory, interests. For him, that reflected the true ethos of parliamentary democracy. He practised it to the best of his ability by trying to build consensus among different factions and ideologies, and across the political spectrum while he was in government and in Parliament. He put the interests of the nation first, and had the ability to view contentious issues by rising above party politics. Pranab was definitely not the first or the only political leader to do so. He had many illustrious predecessors whose example he could follow. But perhaps, he was one of the last members of, what now seems to be, a lost tribe.

In my opinion, the most apt description of Pranab and his politics has been written by Prof. Amal Kumar Mukhopadhyay, Pranab's old friend and classmate from his college days:

> Politics in parliamentary democracy is essentially a highly civilized and rational affair and, therefore, a politician befitting this system is one whose personality is marked by civility, gentlemanliness and clear and rational thinking, who takes a decision only after coolly and rationally making his choice out of the several options open to him and who never imposes his opinion on others, but instead, listens to all and then only gives his judgement. As we all know, Pranab Mukherjee is a politician of this type... Pranab Mukherjee is a kind of leader who believes in a quiet and gentleman's politics a kind of politics requiring a highly educated mind that excels in humanity, a penchant for serving the people without any ballyhoo or self-interest and a passion for work.[144]

~

My father passed away on 31 August 2020. A few months before his death, during one of our dinner-time conversations, I said to him, 'Baba, God does not fulfil all the wishes of a person. You got everything in life, but did not get what you desired the most—becoming the

---

[144]Ray, Sukhendu Sekhar, *Pranab Mukherjee: The All Season Man*, Deep Prakashan, 2010, pp. 64–66.

prime minister.' Baba was in full agreement. I asked him if he had any regrets. He quoted few lines from a poem by Rabindranath Tagore:

Maajhe majhe bote chhidenchhilo taar
Tai niye ke ba kore hahakar
Shur tobu legechhilo bare-bar
Mone pore tai aaji...
Ki pai ni tari hishaab milate mano mor nahe raaji.

Oft the strings did break
But fret not for that
Remember the melodies that played
On the sum game of life today
Grieve not O soul
For the unattained[145]

Pranab was not a boastful person. He once said to me that he was nothing but a cog in the giant wheel that is constantly moving forward towards nation-building. He was a cog that did its job well and served its purpose. Other than his razor-sharp mind, Pranab had two more qualities that made him what he was: his tolerance and his empathy. His tolerance made him accept the legitimacy of differences of opinion and diverse ideologies in democracy. His empathy enabled him to understand an issue from perspectives other than his own and act towards bridging the gap.

In order to build a truly inclusive society and democratic polity, these are the qualities that future generation of politicians may perhaps learn from Pranab. This is his true legacy.

---

[145]Translated by Sharmila Sinha, writer, storyteller and food connoisseur from Delhi

Index

PRANAB KUMAR MUKHERJEE
FINANCE MINISTER
GOVERNMENT OF INDIA
Published by :
BOMBAY REGIONAL CONGRESS COMMITTEE
Ensa Hutments, Azad Maidan,
Mahapalika Marg, Bombay 400 001.
BUDGET MANUAL